AGENT
ENTREPRENEURS

Every Agent's Guide to
What They Don't Teach You
in Real Estate School

MIKE TURNER

FEVER STREAK PRESS

Fever Streak Press
Agent Entrepreneurs:
Every Agent's Guide to What They Don't Teach You in Real Estate School
Copyright © 2016 Mike Turner

ISBN: 978-0-9913759-6-7

Design by Sarah Tregay, DesignWorks Creative, Inc.
Cover photo by iStock
Author photo by LeAna Earley

AGENT
ENTREPRENEURS

Every Agent's Guide to
What They Don't Teach You
in Real Estate School

CONTENTS

INTRODUCTION

By the age of twenty-five, I'd worked as a commercial fisherman in Alaska, earned a business degree, obtained a captain's license to drive ships, managed building engineers in high-rises in San Francisco, served active duty and reserves as an officer in the US Coast Guard, and worked as a marine logistics operator and location scout on movies and TV shows around the world. I had a wealth of interesting and varied experiences but one big problem: I still had no idea what I wanted to do.

One day I found myself in real estate school with no real intention of becoming a real estate agent. I was focused on being a real estate investor. I'd flipped a house and then signed up for real estate school just to gain access to the MLS so I could work my own deals. I thought maybe I'd learn something valuable in the process. But the more the instructor talked about a career in real estate, the more excited I got about being a real estate agent. I loved the idea that I would be able to make all the decisions about how to run and manage the business; I hadn't had that experience before. The thought of it was intoxicating.

Sitting in a classroom full of prospective agents, I couldn't help but notice how different we all were. We had different backgrounds and different motives for being there. The instructor said to us on the final day that statistically in a room of twenty people, only four or five of us would be left after two years. We couldn't help but look around to our neighbors and wonder who would make it. I didn't yet understand why so few of us would pull through. The job didn't seem that tough. I knew there was a lot of competition out there, but there was a lot of opportunity as well.

I got my license and became one of 4,000 agents working in a community of 400,000 people—of whom I knew only three, and one of them was a real estate agent. I joined a national franchise brokerage, forwent all other job opportunities that lingered from my former life, and focused full-time on my real estate career. My foundation was of optimism and hope. I figured that with my strong work ethic, I could work hard and create a great career and business as an agent.

That was ten years ago.

Today I have my own boutique-style brokerage, located in a hip, downtown office on a busy street corner. I have an amazing group of agents who work alongside me. I've engineered my business so that it allows me to take my family on overseas adventures for two to three months every year. I have done a lot of great things with my real estate business, but the journey has been a brutal one.

My career has been a process of learning things the hard way. Each passing year has brought with it new truths about this industry, and I've often found myself thinking, *I wish I had known this years ago.*

Looking back, I could have saved myself so much hardship, time, money, and stress—not to mention the emotional scar tissue—if I had known then what I know today. Most agents who have been in the business for some time tell similar stories. As real estate agents, there is so much we learn the hard way. Why is that?

I've read dozens of books on real estate and have attended countless trainings and seminars. There is so much bad advice, and there are mixed messages for agents who are trying to figure out this crazy career we signed up for. Why don't they teach in real estate school what you really need to know to be successful?

Why do we have to spend years or even decades in this business doing things the hard way before we discover a better path or a better approach?

Well, here you go.

This book is the culmination of everything I wish I'd learned earlier in my career. I've put it all on the page, with no holds barred, to expose the good, the bad, and the ugly.

Niels Bohr, a Nobel Prize winner for physics, once famously said, "An expert is a person who has found out by his own painful experience all the mistakes that one can make in a very narrow field." And I can honestly say that I've made more mistakes than most.

I know firsthand how incredibly hard this business can be. I've seen so many good agents get chewed up and spit out, broken and demoralized. Many of us encounter the same challenges and setbacks. This book is a guide to help you avoid having to learn everything the hard way and to give you ideas on how to create and sustain the business you've always wanted.

I recommend you read this book all the way through rather than skipping around, even if you're an experienced agent who doesn't feel you need to read parts I and II (which are geared more toward agents at the beginning of their careers). You'll gain insight that may not help you at this time, but it may be something you can pass on to others.

While reading this book, there might be times when your first inclination is to disagree with my advice. During those times, I recommend reflecting on why you feel that way. I say this because I was likely at the same stage and held the same opinions as you at some point in my career. Only later was I able to look back and see my situation from a different perspective. If you get hung up on, or disagree with, some of the advice I give, that's okay—we all have different backgrounds and experiences that have shaped our opinions. But try to keep an open mind. Whether or not you decide to follow my advice is up to you.

However, if you read something that resonates with you and gets you excited, then seize the moment. Put the work in. Take action immediately. It's easy to be distracted from the changes you want to make with your business. Ideas and plans are quickly forgotten if you don't strike while the iron is hot. Business owners who implement change when they see the need are the ones who tend to rise to the top of their fields.

The ultimate benefit of a life in real estate is that you have control over how you run your business. You determine when you want to work, what you want to focus on, and how you will best serve your clients. You control what role your business plays in your community. It's up to you what you do from here. There is no easy way to a successful real estate career, no matter how you define it. However, it doesn't need to be so painful either.

Here are the most important, effective, and impactful lessons and secrets I've learned as a real estate broker over the last decade; I'm passing them on to you.

PART I

This Might Hurt a Little

There are many reasons you might want to think twice about chasing a career in real estate—or about staying in it if you're not having any success or feeling extremely unhappy in it. If you've been in the business for any length of time, this first chapter will make you smile; you know all too well the craziness of this profession. Just about anyone can get a license to practice real estate, but this career is not for everyone.

Often, people seek me out with questions about getting licensed. I don't paint a rosy picture for them. In fact, many of them have decided *not* to pursue a career in real estate after we've talked. My goal was not to talk them out of it but to be completely transparent and honest with them about this business. They deserve to know the ugly side, too.

Whether you're already an agent or investigating a real estate career, here are a few reasons you may want to think twice about becoming—or continuing as—a real estate agent.

CHAPTER 1

What They *Should* Teach on the First Day of Real Estate School

Don't Be a Real Estate Agent If...

1. You Only Want to Work Nine to Five, Monday through Friday.

A lot of agents get their real estate license because of the freedom and flexibility it affords them. No one really tells them what hours they have to work. Naturally, there are people who assume they'll be able to work as an agent while they take care of their kids, maybe choosing to work only a few hours here and there around their family's schedule.

The reality for most agents is this: You can put in a normal day's work, but you often get pressured to work evenings and weekends. And why is that? Because that's when clients are available to look for properties, and they expect you to be available, too. Your clients will want you to be available when everyone else is done with their nine-to-five job. A client might want to spend Saturday afternoon looking at multiple properties, and that might bleed into Sunday.

Once a deal is underway and a client needs assistance, they'll expect to be able to reach you day and night, especially when there are time-sensitive details to be handled. Agents regularly feel like they are "on call" seven days a week—which is why many struggle to ever take a vacation or a day off. In this book, I discuss many ways you can minimize this challenge and better control your time so you can have a life and enjoy more freedom to work when and where you want to, but that is no small feat. Agents often flame out in this business because they underestimate the demand real estate puts on their schedule.

Imagine yourself making plans with your family for the upcoming weekend. On Friday morning, you get a call from a client you've been talking to for months, and they've just decided to fly into town to look at homes. Now you have a decision to make: continue with your family plans, or cancel those and spend the weekend working with your client.

> **CASE IN POINT:** *I remember one time my wife and I were so excited to take our daughters camping for the weekend. We chose the perfect destination, got all packed up, and hit the road. We barely made it into the mountains before I got word of a problem with one of my deals back in the city. I would be able to put out the fire and salvage our trip, but first I needed access to technology.*
>
> *I spent the next two hours running around a tiny mountain town trying to find a fax machine and Internet access. I used a payphone because my cell service was cutting in and out. Meanwhile, my wife and kids were in the car feeling cranky because they wanted to get back on the road.*
>
> *I could tell you many more stories like that. It's frustrating to not be in control of your time and then to see how that impacts your family.*

The longer I've been in this business, the better I've become at controlling my time, so I know you can too. But my point is: If you get into this business, you need to do so with a realistic idea of the demands clients will put on your time.

2.   You're Not Okay with Going Three, Six, Nine, or Even Twelve Months (or More) without Making Any Money.

Every real estate agent's career has peaks and valleys. The most common valley is actually when you begin your real estate career.

Let me give you an example from my office. Heidi is a good agent who works really hard. Her first year as an agent, she worked diligently, took my advice and recommendations, and made a good go of it. She followed a lot of leads that didn't pan out. She started a newsletter that she sent to her sphere of contacts, and she tried new ways to land a listing or close a sale, but those efforts failed to produce a closing.

Six months in, she didn't have a single sale, and she started to stress. I met with her and helped her regroup. I gave her more suggestions, and off she went.

It got to nine months, and she started freaking out. She said she would have to start looking for another job. I told her I understood, but it seemed like she was doing all the right things—if she'd just hang in there, things would work out eventually.

Eleven months and still no paycheck. She had many clients, just nothing materializing yet.

But then she got to month twelve, and she had eight closings in one month. She was a top sales agent in the office that month—but it took her a year to get that ball rolling. Her sales continued, and compared to that first year when she made nothing, her second year was astonishing.

That's a common scenario for any business startup. It takes a while before the income starts rolling in. When you're out there working leads, it's a long process. A lot of clients start talking about buying or selling their home seven or eight months before they act, on average. Owners of higher-end homes start planning one, two, or three years out. So patience is a must. It's difficult to predict how long it's going to be until you get paid. And even when you're established and have some decent years, suddenly you can hit an extremely painful dry spell.

Real estate is also seasonal with built-in cycles. Depending on the climate where you live, your cycles will differ. However, for most agents, their sales cycle cools at the end of summer and gets worse around Thanksgiving. Business stays fairly quiet until the first of the year. You won't get as many paychecks around the holidays when you need them most. So hopefully you have done well enough throughout the year, and you can ramp up again through the spring and into fall. If you can't handle that cycle, it can be tough.

Here is my advice: I encourage you to analyze your business and treat it like a business. A lot of people get their real estate license and don't realize that they are actually purchasing a business. You need to prepare for a real estate business the way you would for any other startup, instead of thinking that once you get your license, success will just happen.

A lot of real estate brokerages provide training, but don't expect them to hand you business—the ones that do provide leads typically provide Internet leads, which naturally take a long time to manifest, and a low percentage actually pan out. It's best to have realistic expectations and prepare accordingly.

3. You're Unable (or Unwilling) to Invest in Your Real Estate Business.

When I took classes to get my real estate license, the instructor had us do a great exercise. He had us budget expenses for the time (a few months at least) during which we would start up our business and have no income. He had us budget for the things we would need to invest in to start up and keep our business going until we had a closing. He had us write down the total amount we thought we'd need to be ready to start our business, and then he asked us to share our number. One person had written $3,500, and another person only $800 because they had other household income they could rely on. Most had figured a couple of grand.

When it got to me, I paused and then told him I thought I had done the assignment wrong. My number was $21,000. It's not that I needed a lot of money to live off of. I was just thinking about all the investments I wanted to make in my business—websites, marketing campaigns, signs, office fees, fixing my car, etc.

You don't need as large of a budget as I had; in fact, you can make it work bare-bones. But do expect that it will take you time to develop a thriving business.

People now congratulate me on having a successful career. Part of the reason I've found success is that from the beginning I treated it as a business. I invested a lot more than most agents invest into their business to reach that success. I was making less money initially because I was reinvesting at a high level, and I still do that because ultimately I'm playing a long game.

Reinvesting in your real estate business feels like gambling in the sense that you're trying to make an educated guess where it's going to give you the best return on investment. That's why you go to a listing and see agents who are taking photos themselves with their phones, and those photos turn out awful. Part of the reason is that they're nervous about investing their money in a professional photographer because they don't know if they're ever going to get that money back.

The agent who does hire the professional photographer is making a calculated investment in hopes that it will all work out. What I've learned is that I'm not only going to invest, I'm going to double down. I'm going for the trifecta because I want to increase the odds that I'm actually going to get that listing to sell, or increase the odds that I'm going to get the home sold faster. That, in turn, means better offers for my client and fewer hours invested to reach that goal.

4. You're Frightened by the Idea of Not Having a Steady Paycheck—*Ever.*

Most real estate agents work solely on commission, and you have to weather periods of unpredictable (and even nonexistent) income. Sure, there are other jobs where you work exclusively on commission—selling cars or furniture or technology. But unlike those jobs, where sales are completed in hours or days, and you see some sort of regular paycheck (even if it's small), a real estate deal might take 45, 60, 90, or even 180 days to close after you make the sale—and you don't get paid until the sale closes. A lot of new agents struggle with that uncertainty. Even wildly successful veteran agents struggle with the fact that they rarely know what they're going to make next month, next quarter, or next year.

In my first office, there was a guy who worked as an assistant to a big-time agent. I worked in the next cubicle, and I was amazed by how poorly this agent was treating his assistant—I mean, it was cringingly bad behavior. I became friends with the assistant, and eventually I asked him, "Why do you subject yourself to that jerk? Why don't you go out on your own?" This guy had his real estate license, but at that point in his life, the thought of not having a steady paycheck was too unsettling for him. He chose to make a lot less money in exchange for predictability.

To his credit, that assistant eventually went to work for a different agent and continued to earn steady pay. Over time, he managed to go out on his own and is now a highly successful real estate agent. His journey was wise. If you can't fathom not having a steady paycheck, be cautious about going into real estate. If you do go into it, consider finding a role where you can earn steady pay until you save enough to go out on your own, even though it'll be a lot less money at first. You'll at least be able to pay your rent or mortgage and cell phone bill.

5. You Can't Handle Working with a Client for Months, Knowing There's a Strong Possibility That All Your Efforts Will Not Produce One Dollar of Income for You.

Here's another reality of being a real estate agent: you might work for months and months on a deal, have something seemingly locked up and done, and have it all fall apart in the end.

My friend Phil, a fellow agent, had this happen to him. He listed this great house—it was priced right, had been professionally photographed, and got a ton of showings. It was built in the 1950s and had some quirks, so it took a little while to get under contract. But Phil did get a buyer. The deal was supposed to close in December. The appraisal was done, inspection was done—but when it came to final underwriting, it turned out one of the buyers had a seasonal job and his income had dropped so much in December that they no longer met the income qualifications.

Because it had taken a while to find the right buyers and they absolutely loved the house, the seller decided to let them rent the home for a couple of months, build up their savings, and try again. It turned out that by doing this, however, a stipulation with FHA guidelines kicked in that requires renters to rent for six months before they can buy the house.

So Phil and his client waited an additional six months. They got to the end again—new inspection done, new appraisal done—and ten days before closing, the couple who was buying the house split up. The deal fell apart, and Phil's seller, after going through nine months of disappointment, decided to take the house off the market. Phil worked on that project for more than nine months and didn't make a dollar.

As a real estate agent, you have to be willing to accept the possibility of things happening outside of your control that will impact how and when you get paid. That's why you work hard to have multiple deals going at one time, because some of them are going to fall through due to forces beyond your control.

6. You Can't Handle High Levels of Drama.

There will be a high level of drama in your real estate business, and you should consider whether you can handle that before you get your license. Clients can be under tremendous stress when buying or selling a house—financial stress, family stress, work stress. Couples divorce. A spouse loses a job. I had a client whose spouse passed away while I was representing them.

Another client had a child commit suicide during the time I was helping them. Emotions run high in this business, and often you are the person your clients lean on.

I've had phone calls from clients at 11 P.M. the night before closing on a property that we've worked on over the past nine months. They are suddenly freaking out because they are now sure that buying the property is a bad idea for them, and they want to back out.

These are big life decisions, and the impact on our clients' lives can be huge. And because we're in so deep with them, we're the ones who often end up counseling them.

Divorce is common in this country, and many divorces involve real estate negotiations. An agent who is not careful can get sucked into the drama. You're trying to help a couple reach an amicable settlement, and the next thing you know, you're being accused of taking his side or her side. That can get ugly.

You might have clients who are scheduled to close on a property they're selling at the same time they close on one they're buying. Then something outside of your control happens, and they're now homeless and scrambling. Even though it's not your fault, they blame you and put all kinds of pressure on you to solve the problem.

Just telling these stories, I can feel my blood pressure rising. This type of drama is really common, especially in residential real estate.

Being an agent is about building a relationship of trust, not just for the duration of one sale but for years to come. I've had times when years go by after a sale, then one of the clients passes away unexpectedly, and the spouse contacts me because they're overwhelmed with financial decisions that may or may not be real estate–related. When that happens, you help them through it because you've built a relationship with them. They've come to you in their time of need, so you help them, no matter how difficult the situation. The job of a real estate agent frequently evolves into something so much more than selling homes. Some days you'll feel more like a guidance counselor or a relationship therapist. Consider whether you're prepared to deal with all the drama before you become a real estate agent.

7.   You're Not a People Person, or Don't Have the Ability to *Pretend* You Are.

Building relationships, being able to communicate, being like-able—these are all important traits in today's real estate market. I say *today's* because, looking back historically, I think agents in the past could be jerks and still remain in business because agents were the gatekeepers to certain information.

These days, information is more available and accessible, and agents who operate without people skills struggle. With information more accessible, the role of the real estate agent has shifted from gatekeeper to problem-solver—a negotiator who finds creative ways to make things happen. Nowadays, much of that role is relationship-based.

I'm a bit of a homebody. I don't go out and meet people very often. That can be detrimental to a real estate agent, because the more people you network with, the more people you attract to your business. When it comes time to find an agent, people turn to someone they know and trust.

Now let's say you're a homebody or a bit of an introvert—can you still make a career of it? Absolutely. I'm in that category, so I work hard at building relationships. I write a lot and host a real estate show on the radio. I communicate in ways that feel genuine to me. To be a people person, you don't have to be out there hitting the networking events and being social. But you do have to find your own way to interact, communicate, and network with people. I hate talking on the phone, but I do it a lot for work. I've accepted that and don't whine about it. However, when I'm not working, I go out of my way to not talk on the phone. I excel when I'm face-to-face with people. Even though I'm quiet and reserved in my personal life, I can talk all day and seem extroverted in front of clients or an audience. You can make this business work for you no matter your personality type, so long as you can bring your A-game when you need it.

Sure, you can do a lot of communicating with people via text and email these days. It seems the younger generations are very comfortable with this form of communicating, which is why they may be surprised by how much face time is involved in real estate. If they are working an open house, an agent could sit there with their eyes glued to their phone, or they could meet and interact with the people walking through the home. If they have talent for starting a conversation with the visitors to the open house, they will pick up a lot more business from the new relationships they form versus the agent who sits at an open house lost in some app on their phone.

You can tailor or steer your business in ways where you focus on your strengths and do less of the things that you find difficult or unenjoyable for you, but it's important to know up front that if you struggle or dislike interacting with people, then you may have a rough road ahead in real estate.

8.   You Are Just Doing It Because It Seems like an Easy Way to Make Money.

The Property Brothers make it look easy on HGTV. That is not the reality of this business. I know it looks easy when you see the ridiculous agents selling mansions on *Million Dollar Listing*. But these shows are produced to make things look easy and fast. Even *House Hunters* is basically a fake show—by the time a camera crew shows up, the clients have already chosen their home. They're basically pretending throughout the show.

You've likely seen a handful of agents who have made a *lot* of money in real estate and thought, *If they can do it, I can too.* I know I thought that before getting my license. However, you should know that getting your license and conducting your business in an ethical manner is the easy part. If you think that business will just naturally flow to you because you're honest, ethical, hardworking, and knowledgeable, you are mistaken. That might be true if there were only a handful of agents in your community, but there are hundreds and often thousands of agents out there who believe they are honest, ethical, hardworking, and knowledgeable. Even if you know you can give the best service in town to customers, they still may never find you or consider using you because they already have a relationship with one of many agents in your market.

What makes it worse is that you are in a negative-reputation industry. A real estate agent is often looked upon the same as a used car salesman or an ambulance-chasing attorney. That is the industry you are walking into. For the good you bring to this industry, there are others bringing the bad. A friend of mine tells a story about the years he was studying to be a doctor— mothers would often push their daughters at him. However, when he started his real estate business, he found the exact opposite reaction. He was suddenly a "low-life salesman." This is the public's predominant view of people in our profession.

Here's another example of how real estate will challenge you. When you're licensed, you hope you'll get some opportunities from the people who know and like you—your friends, family, people from church, your past employers, etc. However, what agents eventually realize is that all their contacts know more than one real estate agent. Most people are even related to at least one agent. There are so many agents that even your best friends may not use you because their niece is now licensed and struggling to get her business going, and they feel obligated to use her.

Even your best past clients offer no guarantee of future business or referrals. Sometimes they get licensed themselves because "you made it look so easy." They didn't see everything you did behind the scenes to make the transaction go so smoothly for them.

Even your own family won't be a reliable source of business. They may expect you to work for them pro bono. They may unknowingly sign up with another agent at an open house or at a builder's spec home, not realizing they're cutting you out of a commission you were banking on.

Here's my point: the sheer number of agents working within the same community as you creates a huge challenge for you to overcome.

9. You Are Not Willing to Keep Learning.

If you are not prepared to be in constant learning mode, then real estate is going to be a constant struggle for you. In today's world, our work environment changes constantly. Every year, the real estate industry undergoes major changes. Technology is transforming how business is conducted and how we communicate, and it has opened up access to information that was previously guarded and controlled by real estate agents. You don't need to be tech savvy to be a real estate agent, but you do need to know how technology is impacting your business and influencing your customers.

Technology may be the biggest cause of the constant changes in our industry, but it's not necessarily the solution. For instance, if technology is changing how your clients shop for homes, you can learn new ways to help your clients where technology falls short. In fact, the more technology takes over different aspects of your business, the more you need to adapt and focus on areas of your business where technology can't solve the problems.

Even if technology wasn't such a dominant force in changing our industry, you would still find that if you make time to keep learning, your business can and will grow much faster and far beyond that of your colleagues.

When I say "keep learning," I don't necessarily mean take more classes or attend more real estate seminars. Learning can simply be taking time to study your marketplace, examining other businesses in and outside of your industry, or reading or listening to books about how to improve your business or life. Taking time to read this book is a perfect example of devoting a piece of your day to the pursuit of learning.

I can personally attest to the fact that just taking some time to grow my knowledge or learn more about other great business leaders has helped me immensely throughout my career. I can attribute specific improvements in my business and in my personal life to reading particular books that really spoke to me.

Taking time for the pursuit of learning is critical for all business owners. The market, the consumers, and the way goods and services are sold are in a state of change. Business owners who commit to paying attention, who can learn from others and are able to adapt the fastest, are the ones likeliest to end up on top.

Don't forget: As a real estate agent, you are running your own business. You may be associated with a specific brokerage, but you alone are responsible for how knowledgeable you are about your industry. One of your main responsibilities within your business is to help people navigate one of the most important financial decisions of their lives. Make sure you're doing your best to be at the top of your game.

10. You Are Not Willing to Lose Money to Do the Right Thing.

On one of my first real estate transactions where I was listing a home, I was ecstatic when I finally got an offer on the home after many months of stress and hard work to get to that point. The offer looked pretty good, and I was excited to share it with my clients. Maybe too excited, because the sellers accepted the offer immediately and had a date set for closing. What I unfortunately discovered a week before closing was that I had missed something very important. Buried in the offer contract in a place I wasn't used to looking was a critical element that effectively would cost the seller $3,500 at closing. Had I noticed this from the beginning, my sellers may have countered the buyer's original offer.

The solution was obvious to me. I needed to sacrifice my commission to the sellers for the mistake. The sellers appreciated my candor and have since sent me a number of referrals over the years. However, I've seen many agents throughout my years in the business who don't admit if they were wrong or messed up. They try to hide their mistake or blame others because they need every dollar of their commission. Or they find themselves in a situation where the best advice for their clients is to back out of a transaction, but since they are so desperate for their commission check, they push too hard on their clients to stay in the contract. It's a fact in our industry that agents become desperate or greedy and often forego doing the right thing by their clients.

> **CASE IN POINT:** *When an agent is interested in coming to work out of my brokerage, I always have "the talk" with them. I tell them that agents at my brokerage must always be willing to lose money to do the right thing. I tell them that mistakes are absolutely forgivable so long as your intentions are good and you do everything in your power to fix the mistake. Often that means they lose money to make things right for their client. This may seem like common sense, but when agents are desperate to get a closing to pay their mortgage or to put food on the table, their good judgment often gets forgotten.*

You can be an unethical agent and still make money—there are a lot of them in this business. If you're willing to be unscrupulous for the money, you may get a short-term win, but you'll ultimately lose the long-term game. This career is about helping people realize their dreams. It's about improving the lives of others. That's what makes it rewarding and fun and enjoyable, because otherwise it's just a lot of work. If you don't feel that satisfaction of doing your job well, it's not worth the money because you won't enjoy the money as much in the end. We all know many unhappy wealthy people. For most real estate agents, their reputation is their most valuable asset—it will pay them dividends well after they retire.

This chapter doesn't come close to warning you about all the hardships of this business, but it does paint a picture of some of the challenges you'll have to overcome. A career in real estate can be hugely rewarding; however, the road can be very bumpy. If this chapter hasn't scared you away from a career in real estate, then read on. The rest of the book is focused on how you can get more enjoyment and higher levels of success with your real estate license, and it begins with charting the right path.

PART II

Charting Your Path and Correcting Course

You've got important decisions to make up front and along the way that will greatly affect the success timeline and enjoyment of your career.

Where you decide to operate your business and how you decide to structure it will drastically shape your business. Making the wrong choice or a bad decision is normal—and common. Having the courage to course correct when necessary is what's rare.

CHAPTER 2

Which Brokerage Is Right for You?

How Do You Choose a Brokerage?

Deciding where you're going to hang your license is a big deal. It will impact not only your success but your long-term happiness with your real estate career. However, even if you do choose well, you may find in time that you grow away from whatever led you to that brokerage. Some brokerages change. Many grow too fast, stop focusing on their agents, lose their culture, or switch leadership. The good news is you don't have to settle. You can change your course.

When considering which brokerage to call home, it's important that you focus on the broker's reputation. There are independent brokerages, and there are franchises. The largest franchises are becoming giant conglomerates—where they used to have 50 to 100 agents, they now have 500 to 1,000+. At the other end of the scale are independent brokerages, many with fewer than twenty agents.

Keep in mind that everybody in the firm where you work will be a reflection of you. This leads to a problem with some of the bigger brokerages. Some of them are so desperate to get their numbers up that they'll hire just about anybody, and then they're extremely reluctant to let anybody go. If they hire some jackass or unethical jerk, and that agent creates a negative experience for clients, it will have an impact on *your* business. Those clients are going to share that experience with their friends and family. When it's time for those friends and family members to seek a real estate agent, they won't necessarily remember the name of the bad agent, but they will remember the bad experience someone had with "Fill-in-the-blank brokerage name." When you do your research, check social media, ask other agents, ask around the community, and avoid those brokerages that have a bad or questionable reputation.

Franchise brokerages are popular choices for agents because they have large national reputation and presence, which is typically a good thing. However, remember that every other franchise owner can have an impact on your business. Let's say you hang your license at a RE/MAX franchise that built a stellar reputation locally, but the RE/MAX office owner in the next county embezzles money or does something shady, and it makes the news. The fallout could affect your business because you're sharing and associated with that same brand name. So even if the predominant reputation of the franchise is good, that could change at anytime.

I was once on a road trip with a friend, and we stopped at a Subway restaurant for a sandwich. Twenty miles down the road, I had to pull over so my friend didn't get sick all over my car. That was fifteen years ago, and he still won't set foot inside a Subway. He still goes out of his way to tell people not to eat there.

Think about the restaurants where you eat. We've all had an awful meal or a bad experience with a restaurant employee. If the experience was bad enough, there's a chance you won't return to that restaurant. If that restaurant is a franchise, you might avoid other restaurants in that chain because your perception is that people who work for that business are jerks or the service is bad.

The same thing happens in real estate. It doesn't matter if it's a franchise or independent, a large or a tiny mom-and-pop brokerage. People will spend a lifetime avoiding a brand name because of one bad experience they had—or even heard about—with an agent representing that brokerage name.

On the other hand, a well-known name and reputation in your community is a great asset for you to align yourself with. But rather than only asking agents their opinion, also ask people in the community about the brokerages you're considering. Make sure you ask a handful of people so you get a well-rounded idea of positive or negative issues impacting the brokerage you're considering.

Be sure to choose a brokerage that is concerned about guarding its reputation. (By the way, they all say they do, but actions speak louder than words.) When you do your research, does it seem like the brokerage is hiring anybody with a pulse? Do they try to close you to join before they know anything about you? If so, they likely don't care much about their reputation and their company culture.

Getting Schooled: What to Watch out for with Education Programs Offered by Brokerages

When you're starting out, you might want to find the brokerage that offers the most education and assistance to new agents. That's a good thing. You have a lot to learn as a new agent. But be aware that some classes offered by brokerages might not be as helpful as others. For example, if they're teaching thirty new agents to go after expired listings and for-sale-by-owners, you're all going to go out and do the same thing within the same community. It's not going to be effective. They're teaching you to follow the herd.

Here are some red flags to look for as you research brokerage education:

Are they pushing to attend an expensive in-house training program?

If so, watch out. Some brokerages will push you into paid in-house education classes because they're a source of income for the brokerage. There are many education opportunities that brokerages, local Realtor® organizations, and MLSs offer for free or almost free. You just need to look, and you'll find them. There's nothing wrong with paying for education that is going to help you build your business. You should invest in your education; just make sure you're not taking it only because everyone else is or because you're being pressured by others. Be selective and seek out education that appears to best fit the subjects and business model you would like to align yourself with.

Be aware of in-house profit centers.

When an agent goes to a new brokerage, she is often shoved into some training programs that up-sell her on things she needs to be successful. In essence, the training provided is really a disguised sales pitch. Agents are told, "You need to do A, B, C, and D to be successful, and you need to buy this and pay for that—and we have all those services available in-house to make it easy." The brokerage might have an in-house marketing department that can create for her an entire brand identity that costs X number of dollars. These can be profit centers for the brokerage, so watch out. In many cases, brokerages are making more money from their education and in-house up-sells than from the agent commissions. That's because they figured out that agents are desperate for answers and will pay heavily for them, whether they're making money in real estate or not. Agents are easily sold in-house trainings and coaching programs that encourage them to keep enrolling in more classes, and the cycle continues.

As an entrepreneur, I see this as genius. As a broker/owner who cares deeply about the livelihood of the agents in my office, I see this as crazy. If all I cared about was making money, I would follow in the footsteps of these brokerages that have created all these in-house profit centers. Don't get me wrong—a brokerage that offers in-house services and education opportunities can be convenient and helpful, but they can also deplete your wallet in a hurry. I've seen agents excel in this environment and others go broke. You'll eventually ask yourself, "Where did all the money go?" For every in-house service the brokerage provides, do your homework and see if there are any less-expensive quality options out there. For example, I've used sites like fiverr.com and upwork.com to hire out for professional logos, flyers, 3 D renderings, and research assistance for a fraction of typical costs. You can find freelance transaction coordinators (TCs) in your town who are far and away better than the TCs provided in-house by most brokerages. The point is: don't assume that in-houses services provided by a brokerage are the best option for you and your business.

Is the education the brokerage provides going to help you establish the real estate career you really envisioned?

If the training they give you makes you feel like a loser—because you didn't have the courage or stomach to make fifty cold calls or knock on doors all day—the problem is not you, it's the training. There are other classes and trainers out there who will teach you strategies that will excite you about going to work each day. This book is full of strategies you can implement into your business that never require you to make a cold call or door knock.

Many brokerages will lure new agents to their offices by offering free classes in using and understanding real estate contracts, using the MLS systems, and many other helpful topics. These are great classes to take, but you should be aware that these classes can be taken in many places; you don't have to learn this through your brokerage. Many Realtor® organizations in your region and local real estate schools will offer these classes for a low cost. All new agents stress about this, not knowing enough when they enter this industry, which is why many brokerages that target new licensees provide this in-house training. Just know that you can get this training in many places, so judge the brokerage on something other than their initial training offerings.

Another common complaint I hear from agents is what happens after they finish their initial training with the brokerage. They tell me they never see the broker or the education staff again. You are often forced to figure things out on your own anyway—so you might as well take charge of your education from the beginning. You can find classes listed through real estate schools, you can search for podcasts or books that cover topics you want to learn more about, you can join online or local groups and organizations that provide a venue for you to ask your questions, and real estate associations have tons of options for you to choose from. Plus, you can and should find your own mentor and figure things out on your own. You don't need to rely solely on your broker—but it sure is nice when they can deliver quality, relevant education and advice to help build your business.

I see brokerages that hound the real estate school, talking about the education programs they provide for new agents. So many programs consist primarily of teaching scripts. You read that correctly—scripts. What to say when calling friends and family, what to say when calling cold leads, sign calls, on listing appointments, etc. The theory is that if you follow these scripts, you'll have a higher likelihood of getting potential clients to take action. That might be the case, *but* the scripts can also lead you to be somebody you're not. The message coming out of your mouth is not authentic and may not resonate with your core beliefs and how you want to do business.

Using scripts can build a negative reputation for you and your company. Do you want to be known as that pushy agent who never gives up? Who doesn't take no for an answer? Who will keep calling until people cave from annoyance? Sure, you might get more closings if you're pushy and don't take no for an answer—but that's not the reputation you want to build your career upon. I can't imagine talking with a friend or acquaintance using a script. Even if you practice them hundreds of times, your contacts may still detect that you're using rehearsed lines. Scripts are well accepted in our industry because so many agents don't know what to say or how to talk to a new prospect, such as an expired listing, a sign call, or a for-sale-by-owner. If you are on a team, the team leader may have you follow a script because she is trying to get her team to do things the way she does. I'm all for you following a plan, but I caution agents who practice scripts. The next time you are being taught scripts, ask yourself: if you were on the other end of the call, would you find it helpful or annoying?

The advice that is commonly preached to agents is that you should be persistent, even if it's annoying, because that is how you win. If you don't win, somebody else will. My opposing advice is to make sure you provide tremendous value to the prospects. Go out of your way to provide more value than your peers. If you are providing more value and assistance than your competitors, you are likely to win the business without having to be pushy or annoying.

Here is an important tip: if you feel like scripts will help you, it's because you either haven't done enough prep work about how you plan to help a buyer or seller, or you don't believe strongly enough in your abilities. See chapter 26 for coming up with a plan to help sellers and buyers, and chapter 8 for building confidence. Once you have a plan to help clients on a high level, possibly on a higher level than anyone else, I bet you'll feel scripts are unnecessary. Scripts are designed to close. If you come in with the right plan, you don't need to close. It will happen naturally. This is why I don't teach scripts in my brokerage but focus instead on encouraging agents to come up with the right plan to help their clients on a high level.

Time in the Business Counts

As an independent broker/owner, I am reluctant to bring on new agents. The main reason is that many people get their real estate license, but most don't make it a year or two. Often this is not from a lack of support but because they discover that real estate is not a good fit for them, and they move on to something else. (They didn't know the hard realities of the business discussed in chapter 1.) New agents, typically in their first year or two, fall prey to "the grass is greener on the other side" syndrome and get lured away easily to other brokerages. I don't fault agents for doing this. It's hard to know if something will get better by moving to another brokerage until they try it. I've lost a handful of new agents to this phenomenon. Most came back when they discovered the grass wasn't greener after all—in fact, it was a bunch of hyped promises not delivered. However, because this is a common situation with new agents, I typically don't bring on newly licensed agents. They must have completed a year or more in the industry somewhere else. Agents in my office feel like family. When they come from some other office, they often appreciate what we offer to them and the culture that we've created in our office.

The only time I consider bringing on newly licensed agents is when they've had past sales experience or owned their own business. In those cases, there's a good chance they'll understand the challenges and realities of this new career better than someone who has had no exposure to sales or running a business. They'll also appreciate the entrepreneurial training and marketing discussions we have within our office, because as a past business owner, they know the information is rare and profitable.

Plus, when you've operated a business or worked strictly for commission, you have a feel for what it will be like to work in real estate. You've already learned that you have to do things in order to make things happen. That you must see tasks all the way through before you get paid, and you're prepared to ride that roller coaster of pain when things fall apart outside your control and you don't get paid for the work you did. Business owners and commissioned salespeople do a lot of work for free—and if you're someone who has been conditioned instead to expect a steady paycheck, it's hard to work for free.

Of course, every once in a while, I'll meet a new agent I just know is going to hit it out of the park. I get the feeling that she's going to work her tail off to make things happen. She'll overcome adversity, won't make excuses or blame others, and will just keep moving forward to find a way to make things work. This is rare, but I'll hire those agents no matter what their background. However, I know I run the risk of losing them to the "grass is greener" syndrome after a year.

Switching Brokerages

When you're a seasoned agent, what's important to you is likely much different than what is important to a new agent. When you've been in business for a while and you decide to find a new brokerage, you're usually moving because there's an issue brewing or you're not happy with the commission split for what you are getting in return, etc.

When you start looking into a new brokerage, make sure you look at the culture of that office. Most agents spend too much time considering location and fee splits and not enough time considering culture. The culture and environment of the brokerage can have a huge impact on whether you'll be able to function well and be happy in that office. If it's a place where you never see the broker but you pay next to nothing in commission splits, that might be the right fit for you. Or maybe you thrive in an environment where you interact with the broker and other agents regularly—you'll want to find an office where you collaborate and then go out and kick ass independently, and come back later to collaborate and celebrate over drinks. Every office will have a different culture and environment. Consider which type of environment allows you to do your best work.

Decide who you want to spend your time with or be associated with. Go to an office meeting and see who is there and how the office functions. You may be acquainted with an agent there, and that's probably why you're checking out that office, but see who else is there, too. You're going to be associated with those people as well.

Be careful of moving just for better commission splits. During the economic downturn, a lot of agents fled to flat-fee brokerages in hopes that paying lower broker fees would translate into higher earnings each month. Many found that was not the case. Others found themselves unhappy in a new environment they didn't research before switching into. My brokerage is not the cheapest in town; however, my goal is to make it the most profitable office in town for the agents. My focus is on the agents, while some brokerages are focused on the volume of agents.

It's common for agents, especially agents within their first few years in business, to leave their brokerage firm for a better split elsewhere, and that's their choice. They view it as a smart business decision, assuming that they will make more take-home money by switching to the better split. But I've witnessed this change not work out for many agents. They gain a better commission split with their new broker but may find they lose a support system they didn't realize was valuable until after it was gone. Crazy things can happen during real estate transactions, and if you don't have a good support system from your broker and fellow agents, you're going to have a harder time putting out fires, keeping deals together, and making the right contacts to help salvage a transaction that's blowing up. You might have five deals pending, but if you're on your own without a support system, you might lose sales that fall apart. In that case, it doesn't matter how good your commission split is—you'll end up making less money because you couldn't close as many deals.

A good broker and agent support system will also help you grow your business and motivate and inspire you. By leaving them, you might find a better split, but in the long term, you may not build your business and bring in as many clients as you could have. It's shortsighted to focus solely on better splits. In other words, a better split may mean more take-home cash, but it also may mean fewer homes sold, so your net income could be less at a brokerage that charges a better split.

On the other hand, I'm constantly hearing from agents who feel like they are overpaying their brokerage for what they get from them. If your brokerage charges you substantially more than what you see other brokerages are charging, but you feel there is little to no support system, no special advantage for you to learn from or leverage your brokerage to help you grow your business, then you may be overpaying for what you are currently getting from your brokerage. Another issue I hear a lot from agents is that they were fine with the split their brokerage charged, but they felt frustrated with all the added fees the brokerage charged them. They felt they were getting nickeled and dimed. Hopefully you find a brokerage that has a solid support system, a stellar reputation, and a fee structure that you feel is fair.

Prior to the housing market crash in 2008, real estate broker-ages were charging *way* more to their agents than they do today. During the housing recession, many flat-fee and lower-cost brokerages began to flourish. This change was also fueled by technology that allowed brokerages to provide more valuable resources and tools for their agents at a lower cost than what was typical in the past. Many brokerages had to lower their fees and commission splits offered to agents to keep agents from moving to the lower-cost options that were available. Now I see better splits available to agents than I ever thought possible when I started my real estate career. However, now that agents are getting better splits, you also see brokerages charging more fees to the agents for services that in the past may have been included. Brokerages are scrambling to make a profit. Small and medium-sized brokerages are really struggling within this new environment to keep their splits attractive in order to lure and keep good agents at their firm. They have to either grow rapidly to stay profitable or change their business model. Many small and medium-sized brokerages have had to sell to a franchise model or close their doors. The new landscape for small independent brokerages is much harder to thrive in in today's market than it was before the market crashed in 2008. Had I known then what I know now about running a brokerage, I might have thought twice about opening mine. On one hand, it gives me the complete freedom to build a company that I've always wanted to build, but on the other hand, the downward pressure on commission splits to remain competitive so I can keep the best and brightest working at my firm has been a much bigger challenge than I ever imagined.

When evaluating brokerages, you must look beyond what they charge for commission. The hard part is that when interviewing other brokerages, you often get their sales pitch about how great they are. The reality is often different. Therefore, this next section will help you identify what to watch for when meeting with other brokerages.

Red Flags to Look for When Interviewing with a New Broker

First of all, are you being recruited? Beware of the full-time recruiter who is trying to tempt you into switching. It's one thing when a friend who knows you and your business style wants to have you work at their brokerage. A recruiter is something else. They're usually full-time employees of a brokerage whose job is to cold call agents like you with compliments. They're going to stroke your ego and make you feel good—but their real job is to hard sell you and get you to move to their office. They're practicing and using scripts in order to have a better chance at closing you. Be aware of that, and ask yourself why that brokerage is trying so hard to recruit. Do they want you, or do they want to get as many agents as possible through the door?

Recruiters will give you a sales pitch and say whatever they can to get you to make a decision that day. Watch out for the hard close. If a broker or recruiter has you in their office and they're incentivizing you to sign with them that day, they're trying to close you before you have the chance to talk with any other brokers. My advice is to walk out of there and give it some thought. You can still go to work for that brokerage after looking around—if they're the best fit for you. But the hard close is the recruiter's way of preying upon your dreams and aspirations, making you promises they might not be able to deliver. Get up and leave, take the time to consider your options, but don't give in to the hard close. They'll still hire you tomorrow or next month if they're really interested in you.

> **CASE IN POINT:** *At my brokerage, I do the opposite. I don't want to hard close anybody into working for my brokerage, because I want them to stay once they're there. I want them to be happy. I won't chase agents or blow up their phones, even if I know they would be a perfect fit in our culture. I won't sell anyone a BS story that we walk on water or they'll double or triple their income if they come to our brokerage, even if I think they could. Hopefully they'll want to come to my brokerage for the right reasons, and it will be their decision, not mine.*
>
> *When I speak with prospective agents, I communicate our strengths. I tell them if I believe they're a good fit within our culture. It's not necessarily top-producing agents who get my attention but rather those whose values are aligned with my core values. A person who is independent yet giving, an agent who is willing to keep learning and to be part of what our brokerage stands for. Ultimately, an agent's moral compass is way more*

important to me than her ability to close homes. You will not hear that a lot in our industry—it's one of the reasons our industry has problems. Real estate is predominantly viewed as a numbers game, when it should be an ethics game. If you're an unethical jerk who closes a ton of homes, I'm not interested in having you in my office. I wish other offices would close their doors to those people as well.

Here's another red flag: when you're interviewing prospective brokerages, are you meeting with the broker or with someone else? If you're not meeting with the broker, then there is a good chance you'll rarely meet or get to learn from him when you work there. Will that broker be able to help you advance your business? From whom will you be getting help and training then? Are those agents experienced in the areas where you need guidance?

Another red flag: watch out for brokerage profit centers. Brokerages need to make money to stay in business; that's a fact. But understand any fees (technology fees, transaction fees, copying fees, etc.) that might be associated with the brokerage. Many of those fees are hidden and not understood by agents until after they've signed with the brokerage. So be sure to ask about any potential fees outside of your commission split.

One of the best things you can do to learn more about this profession and brokerages you are interviewing is offer to buy lunch to a seasoned agent in your marketplace. Ask her what she's doing successfully and how she's doing it. A lot of agents will be forthcoming and open about their tactics and strategies, and they'll give you good advice on what worked and didn't work for them as they built their business. That is going to be far more impactful on your success than any paid training at your office. I call that "leverage." Leverage in this context means "to use something to its maximum advantage." You'll see me use that term throughout this book.

In this particular case, if there are agents you know and respect, then it is wise to leverage that relationship, even if it's only to buy them a beer every once in a while. Establishing mentors and allies for your business is a powerful thing.

Beyond the Features and Benefits

Most agents get caught up in looking at a brokerage's fee splits, features, and benefits. More important than all of those is the reputation of the brokerage and its culture and core beliefs. Does the broker actually give a damn about his or her agents, personally and professionally? Does the brokerage give back as much as it demands? Does the brokerage have a positive impact in the community? Do they care about their reputation? Those are a few of the things an agent should ask himself about each prospective brokerage.

Even if you are a very independent and self-sufficient agent with your own brand, and even if you never go into the brokerage office, the culture and reputation of your brokerage still matter. Like it or not, you are a member of that brokerage. If it doesn't care about its reputation and hires any agent off the street, that could impact your business. On the flipside, if your brokerage is doing amazing things in the community and has a stellar reputation of making a positive impact to your city, that will only help to propel your business.

Consider this: Are there agents or managers in your office whom you hope would *not* say they work with you when they are speaking to people in your sphere or in public? Are there agents in your office whom you'd never let speak to your clients if they offered to help you with something?

The value of having a great culture within the brokerage is harder to define, but it can directly correlate with the amount of enjoyment you have working there.

Consider this: Is your office a revolving door of agents joining and leaving the brokerage? Is it a fun and healthy environment where the people there genuinely like to collaborate with each other? Or is it shark-infested waters where everyone is out for themselves? Even if you rarely see the people in your office, the culture established by the leadership of the brokerage will directly impact your enjoyment working there.

How to Get Hired

Nine out of ten of the brokerages you interview with will likely hire you on the spot, as long as you come across as normal and sane. All brokerages tout that they have a solid screening process, but that is mostly smoke and mirrors. In reality, most brokerages have already decided whether they are going to hire you in the first ten seconds, maybe sooner.

If they don't accept you right away or have a more involved hiring process, it shows they care about their reputation and keeping their existing culture intact. That's a good thing. You may want to pay closer attention to that brokerage.

When you find a brokerage that seems like a perfect fit for you, here's some advice to make yourself a solid candidate:

Find a way to add value to that brokerage or team. What skills can you add to make that brokerage or team more successful? Find a way to prove what you can do for them, even if that means taking classes to acquire skills that are needed at that brokerage. The good news is that skills are easy to pick up, and there is an abundance of free information available today. You just need to apply yourself.

Ask the brokerage or team what you can do to add value to their office. Ask them specifically what skills or experience they're looking for. They'll likely tell you everything you need to know.

Leveraging Your Broker

Some brokerages offer agents a unique opportunity to leverage the reputation of that brokerage. They might have expertise or market dominance in luxury homes, new construction or developments, condo sales or urban housing, or they focus on a certain area of town. A new agent coming in can basically adopt that experience. If a client asks about your experience selling luxury homes, for example, you can discuss what your broker has accomplished and explain that you're mentoring under that broker. It's one way to assure the client they're in good hands.

The big franchise brokerages often tout that they sell more homes than anyone in the state, or they're the largest brokerage in the U.S. Those figures don't carry the clout they used to with consumers. When I got into this business, it mattered to many clients when I said I worked for a particular brokerage. Customers would call the main line and ask to work with someone at that brokerage because they always had. However, with new access to information, buyers today don't care what brokerage you work at; they just want to know whether you can help them or not when they contact you for something. Sellers may be more influenced by flashy facts like a brokerage is the biggest in the state or city, etc., but at the end of the day, the overwhelming majority of sellers pick you as an agent because they know and trust you, or someone has recommended you to them, or your marketing/reputation has led to them interviewing you for their listing.

These days, a broker's local reputation matters most. As I pointed out earlier, it's easy for the reputation of an entire brokerage to be negatively impacted by the carelessness of one unscrupulous agent, even in another county or state. In that case, a large national brokerage could hurt you more than help you. I'm not saying it's a bad thing to work at a large brokerage; I'm saying that the reputation of the brokerage can help as well as hurt your business.

If you don't need to leverage your broker's brand or experience because you already have your own marketing and reputation in place, then look for other ways you can leverage your broker. You might lean on the tools and conveniences your broker offers to make your job easier and more efficient. Your broker might have skills, ideas, and experience you can learn from. Perhaps she's great at marketing or has an extensive list of contacts. Maybe she's willing to mentor you one-on-one and help you build your business.

Make sure you find a broker who will actually help you when asked—not only when you first sign on but throughout your career. A good broker can help you save deals and put challenging ones together. You can't measure how much money that relationship might help you earn (or keep you from losing). That relationship may not be available at an office with a very low commission split by design, or in a big office where there are so many other agents trying to get time with the broker. Therefore, be mindful of what kind of relationship you would like to have with your broker and how you want to leverage your association with your broker.

A Common Mistake

I have a friend who is a hardworking agent at another brokerage. She has cut back to part-time so she can stay home to care for a child. She's expressed interest in moving to my brokerage and leveraging the skills and support I can offer her, but for now she feels it's best to stay at a brokerage that offers her a lower commission split so she earns as much as possible on each sale. I had to bite my tongue recently when she told me that her last five deals had fallen apart and she was frustrated that she couldn't figure out why she was having a spell of bad luck. I wanted to tell her that if she was at my brokerage, she could have leveraged my knowledge and skills as well as those of the office agents, which likely could have saved some of those deals. You don't know what you don't know. I felt deeply for her because her plate is full and she's trying the best she can. She's at a low-cost brokerage because she is part-time and doesn't feel she could fully benefit from paying more in fees at a more hands-on brokerage that offers more support. But I truly believe she is paying a much higher price than she realizes to be at the flat-rate brokerage. I can't help but wonder how many of those deals she lost we could have helped her save.

An experienced broker might know the right lending partner to shore up a transaction, the best negotiation tactic, or the right insight to salvage a deal with an emotional client who is acting irrationally and about to walk away.

CASE IN POINT: *I have an agent in my brokerage who has been there almost from the beginning. He has his own brand and almost never asks for anything. He's very independent and is very successful doing his own thing. When other agents ask him for help, he is always generous. This agent could move to another brokerage where they offer slightly better commission splits, but he stays. And it's not just from loyalty. It's because he still gets value from what we offer as a brokerage. He no longer needs mentoring or one-on-one coaching, but he can still leverage our good reputation in the community. Occasionally he runs ideas by me or leverages someone else's knowledge in the office. He also likes the office environment and culture. Those reasons are all enough to keep him happy and from feeling the need to shop around to other brokerages.*

I have another agent in my office who once owned her own brokerage. She heard me speak at an event and came to talk with me and check out our office. She liked the feel of our brokerage and the fact that we are independent and not a big franchise. Ultimately she liked our culture and environment and decided to join our brokerage. The commission splits were not her main focus. She was looking for an office of people who felt like family, where they looked out for each other and had fun together.

Location Is (Not) Everything

Don't pick a brokerage by location. Many agents make the mistake of picking the brokerage that is closest to their home because that will be the fastest office to get to. It could turn out that the brokerage closest to home is a great one, but I caution you not to select a brokerage until you've investigated others in your area. With today's technology, there is less need to drive to an office to get tasks done. The closest, most convenient agency might be a bad environment that makes you hate your job, when there could be an office five minutes further down the road with the right culture and environment to help you propel your business and make work more enjoyable.

The difficulty of changing your brokerages is different for everyone. However, some brokerages make the process of transferring much easier than others. Just like with anything in your business, you just need to formulate a plan and a deadline and then take the necessary steps. Even though it is often an emotional decision because you have relationships where you are currently working, the decision of if and when you move brokerages is a business decision. Just be sure you are making a change for the right reasons and that you do your homework before you make the move.

CHAPTER 3

Build a Team or Go Solo?

I recently attended a real estate conference and found myself among many successful agents—at least what others would consider "successful." They were team leaders, they had people working below them, and they were closing a high volume of real estate sales. But after a few drinks, they started to open up. Most of them were dreaming of going back to simpler times. Their team, their environment, the overhead and stress they had come to deal with had all taken the fun out of real estate for them. It was no longer what they wanted to do. Some said they felt trapped in their careers but were too scared to change. Others said they planned to go back to just themselves and an assistant, a simpler way to work real estate. They were successful and happy at one time, and then they followed the path that most real estate training leads agents down.

Some agents discover that the path our industry promotes as the way to success—building a team and growing their business in a certain way—is not a good fit for them. I also know other team leaders who are happy with their decision to build a large team, so there is no universal path that works for everyone. As you consider your career goals, be careful to choose wisely. Becoming a mega-agent with a large team of agents below you may not bring you the money or enjoyment in this business, yet this issue is rarely discussed. A simple model may be more profitable and enjoyable to you, so long as it has some sort of support system that you can lean on so you can enjoy time off when you desire to take it.

However, when you start your real estate career, it can often be wise to join an existing agent team.

New Agents: Should You Join a Team?

PROS: You will usually reach your first closing faster. A team will start you off with leads or provide you with a small salary. You should be able to get in front of clients sooner and hopefully not have to wait months for your first closing.

You get the benefit of hands-on mentoring and guidance from your team. Teams are typically structured with leaders and mentors who help you learn at a faster pace than if you were building your business solo.

CONS: If you rely on team members who are struggling them-selves—if their processes and systems are not solid—it might take you longer to make your initial sales. Maybe they treat you poorly or won't mentor you as much as they should. If they put you in a box and only train you in one part of real estate, they're going to limit your possibility for growth in other parts of your business.

You also give up a huge chunk of your commission to the team. This is normal, but for some agents, it's a tough pill to swallow. Yet it still may mean more take-home income than what you would make working solo as a new agent.

The job description you perform on the team may be good for some but not good for you. If they are asking you to cold call all day, move on or don't take the position unless you have a background or an aptitude for telemarketing. If the team asks you to door knock or do other ridiculous tasks, move on. Your team leader should be the primary person generating the leads, while your job is often servicing those leads and following up with them.

CASE IN POINT: *I think a lot of agents make a mistake by not going to a team when they first get into real estate. If you have no entrepreneurial, business, or sales background, you may need to go into a team environment to start out. That's your school. A good team will help you get your business started. If you find the right team, that's a great thing. Just be careful and thoroughly investigate a team before you join them. You can still learn a lot (about what not to do in real estate) from a dysfunctional or poorly run team. Plan to give it a year or two—or stay longer if it's a good team and environment.*

I chose not to join a team when I started. I already had business experience, and I had definite plans in mind for building my real estate business from the get-go. However, I had more expenses and likely made less money in my first year trying to figure out this business than I would have if I'd joined a team.

Experienced Agents: How Do You Scale Your Business?

If you're an experienced agent, you should consider the various ways to scale your business. Do you want to join forces with a partner? Build a team? Hire a buyers' agent? Should you follow the path that your peers in the industry are following?

Here are five common mistakes to avoid as you grow your business:

1. HIRING A BUYERS' AGENT TOO SOON. This is the first hire for many agents. A real estate coach might recommend you do this, or you might find yourself sick of talking to buyers and wanting to focus on listings. The problem with hiring a buyers' agent is that you're agreeing to give away half of your commission to that agent. That's a lot of money (especially once you learn that they do the job less effectively than you do).

Consider the numbers: If your buyers' agent closes on a

$300,000 property, she earns a $9,000 commission and takes a $4,500 split. On the surface, that seems all right; you didn't have to do much work, and you made $4,500. But keep in mind that you have other, more cost-effective options.

If you had an assistant who helped the buyer search for homes online and set up showings (or handled showings if they were licensed), you could have paid the assistant by the hour to handle aspects of the transaction and minimized your time dealing directly with the client. Even if you paid that assistant $20 per hour, they could work on multiple closings and clients throughout the month (not just one) and still be well below the $4,500 cost of using a buyers' agent.

Hiring a buyers' agent is an expensive decision that may be well worth it at some point in the growth of your business, but don't make the mistake of making it your first hire, as there are typically far less expensive options for your business that you should do first.

2. NOT HIRING SOMEONE TO DO THE $10-PER-HOUR WORK. In the book *80/20 Sales and Marketing,* author Perry Marshall asks the reader to consider whether they want to make $10 per hour or $100, $1,000, or $10,000 per hour. It all has to do with picking the right tasks. If an agent does all the $10 work himself, he is actually lowering his income by stifling the growth of his business. He could have hired someone to do the $10- and $100-per-hour tasks, freeing him to focus more of his time on higher-earning tasks. (Specific examples are given in "Alternate Ways to Grow Your Business" later in this chapter. This is explored in even more detail in chapter 12.)

3. HIRING THE WRONG PERSON FOR THE RIGHT REASONS. You might feel obligated to hire a friend or family member who is down on his luck or between jobs. It's a noble gesture, but if they struggle to perform the job you've hired them to do, are you really helping them? Instead, use your connections or resources to help them in some other way.

You want to hire only those who can master certain tasks and add value to your business—it has to be measurable. Find other ways to help your friends or family members besides hiring them into your business when they're not a good fit.

4. HIRING FULL-TIME WHEN YOU ONLY NEED SEASONAL OR PART-TIME HELP. You'll be running around like crazy one day, getting listings and new buyers, busting your tail trying to make it all happen. You'll decide to hire a full-time assistant. Once you get past the learning curve and things finally begin to improve, you may find yourself in a business slump. Now your trained assistant is rapidly depleting your savings. This industry has a weird way of changing your business for you—things slow seasonally, you make investments that don't pan out, money supplies dry up. Soon you have an employee relying on you, and you can't afford to keep him full-time.

Hiring full-time is often not a good business decision for agents. Instead, find alternatives like hiring someone for specific jobs whom you can call upon when needed, or hiring seasonal help. See examples later in this chapter.

5. TRYING TO GROW WITHOUT A PLAN. Some agents are reactionary in scaling their business instead of formulating a plan. They feel like they're in over their head, they drop the ball or feel like they're about to, and they make an impulsive decision to hire someone or to take on a partner without first formulating a growth plan.

If you want to grow your business, either because you want more income or you want more time to enjoy your life, you need a plan. Ask yourself: What kind of real estate business do I want? What does my ideal business look like? Am I being realistic with what I'm envisioning? You might want to speak with people who appear to have achieved the type of business you desire, in order to see if, in fact, what they have is something you crave. You may discover that their business model is not as great as it may seem to an outside observer.

The Downside of Building a Team

Despite industry gurus who push the team model, that business model is not all it's touted to be. Once you're in charge of a team, you're dealing with personality dynamics of new people, turnover, overhead costs, staffing concerns when things speed up or slow down—and you may start to hate real estate, because you no longer have time for the aspects of it you enjoy.

The monthly overhead may impact your ability to relax and enjoy your business. If there are not enough closings coming in, that overhead is scary, and it's always looming. When there's not enough money coming in, you'll have to carry it. If you hire a buyers' agent and there aren't enough leads coming in to support her and her family, that's on you.

Overhead is not necessarily financial. If you, the rainmaker, are not able to bring the business to feed your team, your team will starve. It definitely impacts me when I see my agents struggling, especially ones who are showing up, doing the work, seeking mentors, and taking advice. That stress can outweigh the benefits of having a team.

Many team leaders eventually go back to working solo. They follow the expected path, they build a team and deal with the stress and overhead, and then years down the road they decide they're sick of it. They go back to working solo or with a part-time assistant to help them. Or they semi-retire and start referring out their business and stop selling real estate completely. Even if it feels like it's in your DNA to build a team, it may not be the wisest move for you at this stage of your career, so make sure to investigate other alternatives before going down that path.

Selling your business in the end is a bit of a real estate unicorn. Real estate coaches and gurus who tout the team model will encourage you to build up your business so that you can live an affluent lifestyle, then one day sell off your business and retire. That may have happened to some lucky guy who worked hard and really crushed it, but the reality is that real estate businesses rarely sell. Ninety-nine percent of the time, agents grow a business and then gradually scale it back. Eventually they retire and make some referral income. Not that that's bad. One of the benefits of real estate is that when you work for a number of years and then decide you don't want to work as much, you'll still get calls that you can refer out to agents you trust and make referral income. That's a retirement plan for many real estate agents. Just don't be fooled that one day someone is going to come buy your business from you so you can have your fairy-tale ending.

Alternative Ways to Grow Your Business

Relationships are king in this business. Your goal should be to build and foster relationships. Therefore, what if you built and grew your business around focusing as much time as possible on interacting with your customers and contacts (which is what leads to more business) and hired out specialized contract work to handle the other parts of your business that are taking up your time?

Here are examples of areas where you can hire people for specific contract work:

MARKETING COORDINATOR – Hire someone to handle and coordinate your marketing plan. Have them post listings on Craigslist, design flyers, mail out postcards, post blogs and videos, etc. This is not a full-time job. I recommend you determine a monthly set price based on estimated time and tasks assigned to this contractor.

LISTING COORDINATOR – When you get a new listing, there's a lot to be done: paperwork, scheduling photography, MLS listings, virtual tours, etc. These tasks can be handled by someone you pay $12–$20 per hour as needed instead of hiring a full-time assistant.

TRANSACTION COORDINATOR – TCs can be hired on a per-transaction basis to assist with phone calls, paperwork, document delivery, and other transaction details. They usually get paid at closing, so you avoid any up-front costs.

ERRAND RUNNER – Here's a great job for a family member or a kid in school who has a car and needs extra spending money. Hire them to put up signs, refill flyer boxes, run paperwork, even pick up your kids from school or buy groceries for dinner—whichever tasks are impacting your ability to focus on the high-dollar activities that are going to propel your business.

PART-TIME LICENSED ASSISTANT – Hire a licensed assistant to schedule showings and assist with drafting contracts, addendums, and other paperwork. This is an invaluable service to have someone help with. You have to train them, but that training's worthwhile. Let's say you're out showing a house to a client and they're ready to make an offer. You can call your assistant with the details of the offer and have her type up a draft and send it to you electronically so the client can sign it right there on the spot.

PART-TIME HELPER – This could be someone to help you write personal note cards for your contacts (your "sphere") and help you acquire testimonials from your current clients. For instance, you might desire to write ten or twenty personal note or thank-you cards each week to your clients and new contacts but never meet the goal because you're too distracted by other tasks or embarrassed by your messy handwriting. So you could hire someone with good handwriting to write and send cards for you. All you would have to do is type up what you would want to say to your contacts, and your part-time helper would take care of the rest. They likely can accomplish this valuable task in just a couple hours each week.

OTHER REAL ESTATE AGENTS – In addition to the hired positions, it's important to have real estate agent friends with whom you can exchange favors. Many agents work themselves to death and don't take time off because they feel like they're tied to their business and can't afford to leave town. If they did, they'd be on their phone the whole time and wouldn't enjoy their vacation. Instead of building a team to handle business while you're away—because, let's face it, being responsible for a team doesn't necessarily equal more time off for you—find one or two agents you trust, like, and know, who will handle your clients with the right kind of care, and work out a favor-swapping system. Take them to lunch, give them the rundown of all your clients, prepare them for issues that might come up while you're gone, and then get out of town and have a life. You'll return the favor when they need time away. Building that network of trusted agent allies is a big deal and underutilized in our industry. Even if you don't leave town, you may find that showing homes is not the best use of your time and that you would be far better off paying one of your trusted agent contacts $20-30 per hour to show homes for you.

These examples are just suggestions. You can design your own job descriptions that would be the most impactful to you as your business swells. Hiring out these services costs relatively little, and sometimes they're even free, if you're exchanging or trading services. For example, you might find a way to trade your social media marketer's services for help with their business (by recommending them to your database of agents, etc.). As your business slows down and speeds up, you can ramp up or turn down this assistance.

When hiring these positions, I recommend you hire someone local whenever possible. That way you can meet them in person and discuss their specific job responsibilities. I've hired assistants from all across the globe, and that can work—but my best experiences have always come from hiring someone local whom I can meet and train in person.

It's easier and less expensive to train individuals to master a few specific jobs than to train and pay for a full-time assistant to be a clone of you. It is also easier to find the right contractor to hire if you have a very specific job description. Don't hire someone unless you've mapped out exactly what you want them to do in a step-by-step process. This will help you avoid wasting precious time and money and speed up your contractor so they are adding maximum value with the least amount of cost to you. I recommend any agent try this less expensive approach first before you try growing a big team model. You might find it a perfectly functional and efficient method to scale and grow your business that still allows you to maintain your relationships with your customers.

PART III:

The Agent Entrepreneur

I'm not a businessman; I'm a business, man!
— Jay-Z

Only a small percentage of hopeful, newly licensed real estate agents realize they are opening up their very own business. Fewer still know what it's like to be and work as an entrepreneur. Some find they love it; others never seem to get comfortable with it. Most need some sort of support system (financial and mentoring) to survive the first five years.

The sooner agents adopt the mind-set of a true entrepreneur, the sooner they stop relying on others to solve their problems. They stop blaming the market, their broker, or their lack of education or experience. Rather, they look for solutions, implement, fail, try again, fail, try again, succeed, implement more, fail, try again, succeed, and so on.

You have no boss. You have no one telling you when to wake up to get your work started. There is no set time when you can clock off of work and not worry about it until the next workday. It's always there. There is always more work that could be done. You are a business, not a businessman or businesswoman.

CHAPTER 4

Block out the Shiny Pennies

As soon as you're licensed—and throughout your career—you'll be bombarded by "exciting new opportunities" that promise to help set your business on fire and take your sales to the next level. Every time you open your email, there will be a pitch for the next webinar that will teach you how to get 30 listings in a month. Or a phone call about a sure fire expired listings campaign that guarantees to give you three listings by the end of the week. Or a for-sale-by-owner dominance package that promises to triple your listings. Or a phone call from Zillow or Trulia with new zip codes and a story about agents who made tens of thousands of dollars in your area using their platform. You'll get all kinds of offers from gurus insisting you need to invest in social media campaigns, postcard marketing, done-for-you newsletters, improved websites and search engine optimization, and on and on.

I call these offers "shiny pennies." Some of us are more attracted to them than others. Some agents find themselves jumping from one shiny penny to the next.

The reason shiny pennies continue to exist is because agents have proven themselves easy targets. We sign up for this stuff—we can't help ourselves! We're always looking down the pipeline and trying to figure out where our next paycheck is going to come from. When the future seems uncertain (the market speeds up or slows down, referrals come in at irregular intervals, etc.), we're attracted to the promises of these shiny pennies.

The Problem

The problem with shiny pennies is that most of them don't make you any money, and they distract you from what you should be doing.

Shiny pennies are clever in the way they entrap you to sign up. Maybe you've been to a real estate conference where the presenter is selling a service or product, and by the end of the conference, he has agents signing up in droves. He's artfully led them down a path and leveraged the social proof of others signing up for his product as evidence that you should follow their lead. You've probably seen a webinar that advertises: *900 people have signed up for our webinar—we only have 40 spots left!* The 900 sign-ups are the "social proof" they're using to convince you the webinar is a good idea. If they said nine people had signed up, you wouldn't be convinced.

I don't fault agents for falling into this trap. I've fallen for it numerous times. Even when I know it's a trap, I'll investigate it anyway because I want to know what other agents or gurus are talking about and what new systems they're using. Sometimes I'll investigate and find a small nugget that's useful.

For the longest time, it wasn't just curiosity. I truly hoped to discover that someone had found a magic recipe, because they boasted about having amazing success with whatever system they had going. The problem, I've found, is that the vast majority of these shiny penny opportunities are really C-level ideas, not A- or even B-level ideas. These gurus break sales down to a simple process that must be followed exactly to achieve success, but most of these ideas are rooted in chasing leads: door knocking and cold calling, harassing expired or for-sale-by-owner leads, or annoying friends and family by constantly asking for their business or referrals. I was always hoping they had developed a system that attracted relationships to my business, not leads, where people wanted to be associated with me or my company—not because of a gimmick but because of the way we do business and how we help people. Something unique. Something awesome. But that is not what you'll find when you chase these opportunities, because a done-for-you system (which is what many of these shiny pennies are) is almost never authentic to you, which is why they generate leads and not relationships.

You can make money from shiny penny opportunities the way you can make money selling vacuum cleaners door-to-door. There always seems to be that one guy who makes half a million dollars selling Kirby vacuums. But the thousands upon thousands of other people who try to sell vacuums make close to nothing, and they hate their jobs. I know plenty of people who make very good money selling home security systems door-to-door. If a friend told you that he and others were making $200,000 or more per year and taking months off at a time to go play—"and you could too!"—that offer would be hard to ignore. The dream of financial security and time off to spend with your family would be tempting. Even if the work didn't sound like something you wanted to do, it might sound like something you *should* do. You'd get lured in by the promise. It's the way many real estate coaching programs and products work—they suck you in and sell you a dream.

Too often I see agents sign up for a program and convince themselves that the job of knocking on doors, cold calling, and chasing expired listings, or whatever path the shiny penny is leading them down, is a noble path because ultimately you're helping people sell their homes. The problem is that they begin to hate their job, or it turns them into a type of salesman that they never thought they would be. There will always be someone who loves the shiny penny you are considering, because there will always be someone who enjoys selling vacuum cleaners door-to-door; it resonates with who they are, and therefore they sell a ton of vacuums. But if that shiny penny opportunity, whatever it is, makes you feel like a piece of shit when you wake up in the morning or turns you into a person you're not proud to be anymore, it's the wrong job for you.

Initially the shiny penny opportunities look and sound amazing, but 99 percent of them are C-level ideas that you don't want to make the foundation of your business. What's worse is that if you sign up for these programs and don't follow each step—making cold calls and door knocks, sending emails and posting to social media, etc.—the guru or trainer makes you feel like a loser who doesn't have what it takes to be a great real estate agent. Their advice is to double down on their plan if it's not working for you. Paying for "coaching" isn't a bad thing, but the terms "coach" and "guru" have been bastardized and misused to "sell" products and schemes in all corners of the real estate industry. When anybody can call themselves a coach or guru, what do you expect will happen? (More about this in chapter 14.) This is why I like mentors. A mentor is someone from whom you can learn and get advice, but you are not typically paying them. They are simply sharing their advice because they care about you and others.

A Better Way

There are a lot of A-level ideas that are simple, don't cost a lot of money, and don't require you to pay a guru or a service like Zillow or Realtor.com to provide you a zip code. With these websites, by the way, the reality is that you pay hundreds of dollars a month for leads, and you may not get any. Most of the companies selling you these opportunities will tell you that closing just one home from their system will pay for a whole year of their service. This tactic works great on agents, but the reality is you may be paying for four or five systems that promised to pay for themselves if they produced just one deal a year, so the problem keeps compounding until most agents start wondering where all their money went. Even if the product or service does make you money, it could be distracting you from doing something even more valuable and profitable for your business. The point is: if you have the money to test a shiny penny opportunity, then great—test it. But don't be bullied, pressured, or suckered into it.

CASE IN POINT: *Early in my career, I was at a real estate conference in Las Vegas. I thought most of the presenters were okay, and then I saw one with a totally different message. It resonated with me. I could see why his tactics worked, and he was a good marketer with a new way of marketing I hadn't seen before. I thought,* I know I could use that because I know that would work on me as a consumer. *So I went home and immediately adopted some of those methods, and they started working. I thought,* What else can I learn from this guy? *So I went to a conference that he put on himself, and there was a ton of new information—but, of course, it led down a path that encouraged people to sign up for his coaching program. He brought up agents who said how great their careers were going and how this presenter had changed their lives. One by one, agents in the crowd went to the back of the room and signed up. They had heard the gospel of this trainer, and they were ready. I decided that I would give it a whirl, too.*

I found that some of the strategies were really good. But a lot of them led to making leads and then calling and pounding those leads. There were scripts that told me exactly what to say—and if someone didn't answer, I was supposed to call back at 8:00 or even 8:30 at night. I hated doing that, but indeed the trainer was right—most people will answer the phone if you call them late at night. The more people who answer the phone, the higher your odds of converting those leads into clients. The problem is, it sucked. I hated myself every time I did it. I didn't want to bug people at that time of night. Ninety percent of the time, people were pissed off, just like I would be if someone called me at night. "It's a numbers game," the coach would say, but the longer I did that, the more I realized it's not a numbers game, it's a relationship game.

I told the coach, "I'm not up for this. If this is what I need to do to be successful in real estate, then I don't want that type of success." He suggested I hire a buyers' agent to make those calls for me. But I didn't want to make somebody else call people at night. It's a horrible job. More importantly, I don't want my company being that entity that calls people at night just because statistically it's more effective. I don't want success by a means that compromises my personal code of ethics.

That ended my experience with that coaching program. Of course, I had signed up for a year, so I had to pay for another six months. But I was done with it.

There are lots of ways to make money in real estate, but you need to think carefully about how you go about it. We all want the security that comes with having money, but you don't want to turn yourself into someone who will do anything for money. Too many real estate coaches and gurus and shiny penny opportunities are filled with C-level ideas. There are better ways to make money and build your business. I'll give you many examples and suggestions in this book.

Shiny Products and Gizmos

Beware of convincing yourself that you need to buy special tools and software for your business. It might be a fancy new computer, the latest app, or an expensive email marketing system. I repeatedly fell victim to this because I wanted to find out if there was something new out there that could impact my business. I can tell you that after testing a lot of things, you don't need the fancy gizmos, phones, and computers to do your business. They can help, but the old-school ways work just fine. When I go to a listing appointment, I take a blank notepad. I don't need a fancy presentation. I make notes. I listen. I provide expertise.

That's what people want. They've got questions; answer them. They've got concerns; address them. They need ideas, and they want direction; give it to them.

If you're looking to build your sphere of influence, use that notepad and write down names. Make a note of the last time you talked to someone (see chapter 20). Pick people each week to reach out to. You don't need fancy software to do all that. Don't let the lack of technology hold you back; don't fall victim to the shiny penny idea that you need those things to be successful. That's BS. All you need to do is go out and find a way to help people—not just in real estate but beyond it. That's how you build lasting relationships and a rock-solid real estate business.

Shiny pennies are not going away; there will always be somebody pushing one at you. Just remember that most of them won't do a thing for your business. Real estate is a business of relationships. You don't need fancy gizmos or expensive coaching programs to get there. You can build an amazing career in real estate just by being someone who authentically gives a shit about the people you know and work with. That's what it's mostly about—just care about the people you're dealing with. Look for ways you can help people outside of real estate. Be more than a real estate agent. Be a connector (see chapter 22) and help people build key relationships, or just be there to listen. That's where the real wealth is built.

CHAPTER 5
Learn to Work for Free

Most people who get into real estate come from a job that paid them a steady paycheck. They might get into real estate because they want a career change, or maybe they have kids at home and want to be available for them. The biggest challenge is getting used to not having a steady paycheck.

Very few real estate agents know what they're going to make the next month, and that's a difficult thing to manage when you have bills with deadlines. However, if you can learn to live a lifestyle that can adapt to that uncertainty, the sky's the limit on your income potential since there is no salary cap or glass ceiling to break through. The flipside of your business producing unlimited income is the challenge of getting used to working for free.

When you're building a business, you have to create income—it's not something that's just handed over to you if you work hard. You have to be smart and invest a lot of time working on your business with no guarantee that your efforts will produce a paycheck for you. This is the life of an entrepreneur. You invest your energy into the unknown to create something of value to a market. If it works, the market buys your product or service and there is no limit to what you may earn. If it doesn't work, there is no safety net or minimum wage, at least not in a typical real estate business.

If you study successful entrepreneurs, you will hear them discuss this principle of working for free. Robert Kiyosaki, author of the *Rich Dad, Poor Dad* series, discusses this at length in his books. His "rich dad" understood that you are essentially getting an education by working for free. Even if your ideas and plans don't work, you are learning valuable lessons and positioning yourself to make a lot more money down the road. That was a truth that Kiyosaki's "poor dad" never truly grasped. He paid for a traditional higher education, became a professor, and when that job disappeared, he tried to run a business and give himself a steady paycheck. He never quite got it. His business failed, and he blamed the franchisor for their broken system. He had multiple degrees and was obviously very intelligent, but he was lacking the lessons of what it's like to be an entrepreneur, to work for yourself. If he'd had a stronger grasp of what it's really like to start and run a business, he may have been successful at it.

Part of the reason that book series was so successful is because it highlighted two people who took significantly different paths and had very different mind-sets when it came to money and business. We are taught at an early age and throughout our lives that if we go to school, get good grades, then go on to more school (college), we are setting ourselves up for the best chance at success, to achieve the American Dream. Right?

We've all been taught this. It's true that when you look at what you can typically earn as an employee, you often get paid more if you have more schooling. *But* this does not apply to entrepreneurs. The country was founded by entrepreneurs. A large reason the United States has become such a powerhouse internationally is rooted in the fact that we have allowed more entrepreneurs to dream big and have not held them back. Think about the richest people in America. Most of them are entrepreneurs, business owners who at some point risked it all and created something that changed the world. But when you study these people, you'll find that many of them never attended or completed college. Rather than spending time and money on higher education, they chose instead to invest every penny they had into producing a business or product.

The cool part about being a real estate agent is that it's a fast track to opening up your own business with little investment in time and money to open your doors. The problem is that most people getting their real estate license don't really understand that they are starting their own business or what it means to be a self-employed business owner. They see that selling homes for friends and family doesn't look that hard and even looks fun. At least a million people got their real estate license over the past few decades thinking this. Those who do soon realize that being a business owner is the exact opposite of being an employee; they're the boss, which might sound nice on the surface. But the reality as the boss (business owner) is that anyone can fire you—your clients, your vendors, your leads, even your friends. There is so much personal responsibility. No protection or job security. There is no one to blame other than yourself when you are the boss of your own company. There's just you.

THE TRUTH IS: WORKING FOR FREE = INVESTING YOUR TIME.

Being a prominent business owner in my town, I often have young people ask me for advice on their job search, and I tell them that instead of trying to get hired somewhere, they should pick a business where they'd be excited to work and figure out how they can be an asset to that business. They should tell the business owner why they want to work there and that they're willing to work for free to prove they can be a valuable asset. They should offer to mop floors if they have to, in exchange for getting themselves in the door and being able to learn how that business operates. I tell them to show up every day prepared to learn, adapt, and prove that they can add value to that company.

A lot of people think they can't afford to do that, yet they spend thousands of dollars to go to school. They're essentially working for free then; they just don't realize it. What if you just budgeted for another three to six months of school once you finished school? Instead of spending it on more traditional schooling, you would use it to pay for a cheap apartment and food and other necessities for a few months while you get a hands-on education at a place you want to work. Why not just go to the place you'd like to be employed and work for free there? If they say no, find out what their needs are and go get a skill that meets one of those needs. Then go back. You'll impress them if you keep showing up with a new skill to offer. I wouldn't hire someone who kept coming around just asking for a job, but if they found a way to help my business and showed me that it wouldn't cost me time or money to say yes, I would likely be tempted.

This idea of working for free is a simplified way of saying you have to invest your time with no guarantee of return. However, the better you invest your time and efforts, the higher likelihood of a positive outcome.

As the owner of your real estate business, you have to be better than others, offer more than others, rise above the competition to better the odds, but even then you can still fail. I know it sucks. But that's the blessing and curse of being an entrepreneur.

If you invest time building relationships, educating yourself, providing superior service, and establishing a stellar reputation within your community, you have the highest likelihood of seeing the greatest return of your time, although all these investments take time to materialize into a return.

Not everyone is suited to be an entrepreneur. Some are born with the inherent ability to operate and thrive with the uncertainties and the excitement of being a business owner, while others have to battle it the entire time. But anyone can do it. What helps is just coming to terms with what you signed up for—which is the point of this chapter. When you embrace the work-for-free mentality, you not only open yourself up to unlimited earning potential, but you find it easier to accept the constant roller-coaster ride of your chosen profession as an agent entrepreneur.

CHAPTER 6

Create Your Own Real Estate MBA

Remember that scene in the movie *Good Will Hunting*? A group of guys—kids from the other side of the tracks, so to speak—go to a Harvard bar for drinks. Will (the character played by Matt Damon) and his friend are talking to a girl, until a Harvard guy comes over and starts making Will's friend feel stupid by asking him questions about history and politics he doesn't know the answers to, and he makes profound statements to sound extra smart. Will steps in, and the heated exchange is priceless. Will calls out the Harvard guy on the stuff he's quoting verbatim as plagiarism, because he's making these statements sound like his original ideas. Will can recall not only the book it came from but even the page number. We get a glimpse of how smart Will is. And then he makes the point that the Harvard guy spent $150,000 on his education when he could have spent $1.50 on overdue fines at his local library.

It's a cool scene, and it reminds me of the missed opportunities that exist in libraries and other free resources. The beauty in starting your real estate business is that you can be from humble beginnings with barely a high school diploma, or you can have multiple degrees; when you start a business on your own, you pretty much start from the same spot. The market will treat you the same. Anyone can rise to the top. You can leverage your titles and education to impress clients, but the market doesn't care about your titles and education background if you provide a subpar product or service. You still have to perform well, make solid decisions, and operate in a market where all players have equal opportunity to succeed or fail.

The Truth about Continuing and Higher Education

There's an agent in my office who was studying to get her broker's license. She traveled out of town to attend a three-day class called Broker Management. She was excited to attend and learn what she needed to advance her career—but when she returned and I asked her how it went, she said, "It was awful." She spent lots of money on this class and gave up three days she could have been working, only to sit in a classroom and have a teacher basically read from a textbook. Much of the information was dated and even misguided and inaccurate. It didn't help her at all.

That's similar to the experience many people have getting their real estate agent's license. You might have a dynamic teacher who is good at teaching—but what are they teaching you? Are they the skills that are going to help you operate a business? Because that's what you're becoming: a business owner. Education has become a series of discussions that help you pass a test—yet because of the way it's taught, you don't retain much of what you learned.

This is a big problem in our industry. The education provided to real estate agents is broken. Those who provide continuing education for our industry say it's designed and written to help the consumer, and they restrict some education from being counted toward continuing education (CE) requirements if it doesn't fit inside their box. For example, much of the advice shared in this book would likely not be allowed as CE credit for agents. Why? Good question.

A lot of times, what happens with school is that you get a lot of education, but that education is filtered down through books that have been prescribed for decades. It may or may not be helpful in building a one-person startup business, i.e. your real estate career. In college, two hundred people will sit in a classroom and hear lectures from the same book. Wouldn't it be wiser if two hundred people read different books and then brought that knowledge and those ideas into class? What if they collectively did something great with all that combined knowledge?

The world is not based on the best answer among A, B, C, or D. The world is gray. You have to make independent decisions and have street-smarts. You learn street-smarts by getting out in the world and getting your hands dirty, not by doing well on achievement tests.

You don't have to know it all. You don't need to know everything there is to know about something before you get started. I have friends with minds like engineers who want to get a business degree before thinking about starting a business. They want to prepare to be prepared. They want to get all the certifications and make sure they know everything they'll need to know so they don't make any mistakes. That's completely unnecessary and handicaps their chances to build something great because they overanalyze without moving their idea forward.

DIY Education

You can skip school, but you can't skip education. If you want to succeed in real estate at a high level, you've got to keep learning. Fortunately, you have a choice in how you educate yourself. You can spend thousands of dollars attending workshops and classes and getting certifications—or you can check out free books from your library.

It's difficult to find the right education options within the traditional model. There are few to no education options available to show agents how to run their business as a one-person startup. Agents need a crash course in bootstrapping a business. Even if they're not managing enormous amounts of startup cash, agents need to learn startup principles in order to go out and create momentum and a book of business for themselves.

Does having a traditional MBA help you in real estate? I know many agents who came into the industry with an MBA from a former career. Some have done really well, and some have not. The MBA may have taught them hard work, discipline, and strategies for further learning. But they didn't need an MBA to acquire those skills—they may have possessed them long before enrolling.

A lot of people go to prestigious colleges to get that certification, that stamp of approval, to be able to say they went to this Ivy League school and got an impressive business degree. Often that helps them find employment. But certifications and degrees won't necessarily help you grow a business, at least not a small business. They usually don't teach you how to employ sales and marketing strategies for a one-person startup and discuss the dynamics and challenges of a business you start yourself, but focus instead on how large corporate businesses operate. They might teach you how to write a business plan, but it will be the type of plan used by large companies to present to investors or to a bank when borrowing money. As a real estate agent, you're a bootstrap entrepreneur using your own funds and savings to make your business work. You need a different sort of business plan that is not taught in college and university classrooms.

The good news is that you can acquire the information about just about anything you want to learn through books, podcasts, and online resources. Even the details taught in real estate certification classes can be acquired on your own; you just have to go out and find them. You don't have to actually get the certification. From books, podcasts, and other online resources, you can learn about developing a business plan for your real estate business without going to business school. You can learn how to market sellers' homes better without spending money on some Realtor certification. Just go out and proactively learn it and apply it.

Last month, I listened to an audiobook on negotiating. It contained a wealth of information. I wrote down many notes, not just for myself but to share the points I liked best with the agents in my office. I didn't need to spend $300 on a negotiation class. I've seen that class come through town, and if I wanted to impress my clients with that certification, I could take the class—but the point is, you don't need the class to learn the skills. I listened to the audiobook, and I applied the skills. By the way, the book was free because I got it through my local library.

The only education that most agents get for themselves is whatever class is available for continuing education credits so they can keep their license active, and they do it right before their license expires. I do the same thing—but mostly because I'm avoiding those classes. I'm already busy seeking out my own education.

What do you want to get better at? Marketing? Sales? Social media? Productivity? Organization? Budgeting? Creativity? Negotiating? Leadership? Influencing others? Making connections? These are all important aspects of real estate, and there are so many books and other free sources of information out there on every imaginable topic. Find them, study them, and apply them to your business.

If you want your business to stand out in the crowd, to grow and prosper, then you have to keep learning. Consider these indispensable resources:

BOOKS/AUDIOBOOKS — I'm a huge supporter of local libraries because they deliver free access to so much knowledge. People spend a lot of time reading, but it's fiction—stories they enjoy reading the way they watch a favorite TV show. There are a lot of great books and audiobooks available on building your business, and there are a lot of wise people giving advice on what books to read.

If you haven't been to your local library lately, they're not the same as the one you grew up in ("Shhh!"). Besides books, you can check out e-books for your e-reader and download audio-books as well as check them out on CD. And if you're looking for something specific, they can order it in from another library. You can also visit local and online booksellers. Accessing information has never been easier.

You don't need to read a book cover to cover; just read the parts that interest you and move on. If you don't have time to read, get the audio version—or get them both. It's helpful to buy the book so you can highlight and make notes on the page. Most Kindles and other e-readers let you do this, too. I also recommend keeping a notebook with you so you can write down your takeaways as you read. A friend of mine writes down in his own words the main points of each book to help him retain and refer back to the lessons he wants to apply. I've recently adopted this same practice so that I don't have to re-read or re-listen to a book as often.

PODCASTS - If you haven't discovered podcasts yet, you're missing out. Podcasts are recordings you can listen to on your phone, computer, or tablet. Some of the brightest minds and most successful business people in the world are sharing all of their secrets in podcasts. Search iTunes or look around online—if you dig a little, you'll find podcasts that are absolute gems. You can learn anything from new languages to house repair to business startups from some of the best minds on the planet, either recording themselves or being interviewed, and they're giving information away for free. You can listen to podcasts about real estate, but be careful—there's a lot of questionable information out there about our industry. Just because someone is making loads of money doesn't mean their system is the right fit for you or good for our industry. I recommend you focus instead on finding experts in specific skills you want to learn more about: marketing, sales, management, etc.

That information used to be very exclusive, but now it's free flowing with new content available every day. I wrote this book to save you from a decade of learning hard lessons and speed up your success as a real estate agent. Podcasts help in the same way. Be open to learning about more than real estate—find podcasts on leadership, startups, hobbies, and skills. You can apply all kinds of knowledge to your real estate career.

AGENT MASTERMINDS - Seek out other agents and business owners who have similar mind-sets, goals, and aspirations for their business. Ask to meet once a month for coffee or drinks; discuss what's working, what hardships you face, their outlook for the future, whatever. If it's someone you really admire and they don't have time to meet regularly, they might still agree to meet once. Buy them lunch. Make that connection. If you reach out and ask, you might be surprised by someone's willingness to share.

MENTORS - In addition to fellow agent masterminds who are on a similar career path as you, seek out mentors as well. This might be a successful business owner whom you know personally, or someone you respect but don't know, such as a leader in the entrepreneurial world. You can study them and even reach out to them to see if you can establish a connection. A mentor can really be anybody, such as someone who is highly skilled in an area you want to excel in or somebody who is great at building relationships, if that is important to you. Getting guidance from a mentor you're able to consult with regularly can have a drastic impact on your career. Without mentorship, you're always shooting blind and trying to teach yourself. A mentor can help propel your business forward faster with fewer mistakes.

Get in the Learning Habit

Dedicate at least thirty minutes each day to learning. And yes, do it every day. There are no holidays from learning. You don't take a day off from eating, drinking, and breathing, so don't take a day off from learning.

Watching *House Hunters* or *Flip This House* on HGTV doesn't count. You can learn from entertainment, but I recommend being more strategic with your learning process.

It doesn't matter if you're not an avid reader. You can listen to audiobooks or podcasts in your car, on the way to your next open house, or while waiting to pick up your kids.

Many great entrepreneurs read at least one book a week. It's one reason they're so successful. You don't need to read a book a week, but if you want to perform at a higher level and be able to give solid advice to others, you should absorb advice on a daily basis. It's not only about improving your business but also about personal growth.

You made a huge leap of faith—whether you realize it or not—when you started your new business as a real estate agent. Don't think that you're not in business for yourself because you work at a brokerage. If you've been doing this for any length of time, you know that you're on your own. You make your own decisions; you have your own budget and your own costs. It's up to you to make this business work.

Running, managing, and growing your business is no easy task, which is why so many fail. But when you make a commitment to educate yourself along the way, you learn about the mistakes that others have made and how they corrected course. You can apply these lessons and avoid the same pitfalls. You can fast-track your growth. You don't have to be an agent for ten years and learn all the hard lessons on your own. If you study and apply the lessons of other successful business owners and entrepreneurs, you can get your business up to speed so much faster.

That's how you create your own personal MBA for real estate. Decide what's important for you to learn and dedicate time every day to absorbing that knowledge. I guarantee you'll see results in your business.

CHAPTER 7

Don't Be a Sheep

There is a sense of safety in following others. If things seem to be going well for others—if they're making good money and improving their business—it seems logical to do whatever they're doing, right?

Here's the problem with that plan: When you follow the herd, you have blinders on, and you don't see the dangers ahead. You might be late to the party, and there is no guarantee that what worked for others in the past will still be effective for you. That's why so many people lose in the stock market. Once people see investors making gains in a certain area, they follow the same pattern—but by the time they jump in, they're buying high and selling low.

Society pushes us to conform. When we don't, we're labeled the "black sheep of the family" or a "lone wolf." All because we refuse to follow the same path everyone else is traveling.

America was founded by risk takers and entrepreneurs, people who thought outside the box. Or by people who were escaping the "box" that society told them they belonged in: *You can't have this kind of opportunity because you're poor/female/a different race/not from an Ivy League school, etc.* So they shrugged off society's rules and blazed their own trail.

What happened to that individualism? Why are we so prone to following the herd these days? Part of it stems from the way we were raised within our education system.

HOW WE GOT HERE: *Our current school system was set up in the late 1800s and early 1900s to meet the needs of the industrial economy. Public elementary schools were designed to improve literacy and to provide skilled laborers for the workforce. This was the highest level of education that the vast majority of the population received.*

Secondary education provided more widely applicable skills that could be transferred across different occupations and industries. This supplied the industrial economy with managers and professional leaders. In 1935, only 40 percent of the American population attended high school, but this was higher attendance than in any other nation.

Only 5 percent of Americans attained a higher education by the 1940s. Colleges supplied scientists, engineers, and doctors, which led to the development of technological advancements and the rapid growth of American cities.

Schools were modeled after the factories of the Industrial Revolution, to the point where school bells were used like factory whistles to mark the beginning and end of classes (shifts). The school "assembly line" sorts students by age and puts them through classes where they're taught a specific skill. Students pass tests to see if they meet the standards so they can move further down the line. At the end of this production line, they receive a stamp of approval (a diploma). Schools turned learning into a rote process that was dull and tedious. Nevertheless, by using a "one mold fits all" process, our school system provided education to a large segment of Americans who did not have the resources to attend school otherwise.

The Real Estate Assembly Line

The same thing happens in real estate. There are more than a million real estate agents in the United States. Some brokerages have hundreds of agents operating out of one office—so how do they train, educate, and deploy that sales force into the market when there are so many agents? They use an assembly-line method like those adopted in our school system. And so the cycle continues. Rinse and repeat.

Real estate agents are shoved into the same pasture to feed. They're shown how to use the same methods and tactics that everyone else is using. This is a major problem when it comes to marketing yourself, prospecting for new clients, or building your sphere. If there were only a few agents in a community, they could all go out and use the same method and system for obtaining leads, and it would work fine for all of them. But if brokers or real estate trainers are sending out hundreds of agents into the same community to follow the same system, there will be lots of overlap. The consumer is going to get the same sales pitch from multiple people who are offering basically the same services.

To be fair, agents also love the idea of following a system: *It's easier. Just follow these five steps. Do what I do!* We all want a shortcut to success. Real estate gurus who offer agents easy-sounding shortcuts to success hit the jackpot by getting agents to sign up with them in droves.

Don't get me wrong. It is wise to study successful agents to find clues on how they're succeeding. If they have a unique system that you can adapt to your business, and no one else is doing it in your market, then by all means give it a go.

But here are some examples of the not-so-unique things I see mobs of agents, fresh off their recent brokerage or guru training, being told to go out and do:

Expired Listings - I feel for any seller these days if they decide to take their home off the market. They will get anywhere from ten to thirty agents hounding them with phone calls, packages, and door knocking. *They will get bombarded.*

Agents who chase expired listings are following a system that might have worked for a few agents in the past. Those agents discovered a strategy, designed a unique system, and created something that worked for them at the time. Agents who try to mass-produce that system in a saturated market are going to find that it doesn't work.

FSBOs - For-sale-by-owners can expect calls from dozens of agents who ask to preview their home, claiming that they have a buyer who is looking for a home like theirs. All of these agents, of course, are reading off their newly learned scripts for speaking with FSBOs. The scripts are supposed to get agents in the door, speaking with the seller face-to-face, and converting the seller to a client. Again, this might have been an effective strategy when it was original, but now dozens of agents are contacting FSBO sellers with the exact same script.

CANVASSING NEIGHBORHOODS - When in doubt, agents are encouraged to knock on doors in their neighborhood. Hopefully there aren't other agents who live nearby on the exact same mission. Sure, agents have found success knocking on doors, introducing themselves to their neighbors, and asking if they're interested in listing their home for sale. But what happens when there are multiple agents doing the same thing in your neighborhood? Your effectiveness goes way down. And ask yourself: do you like it when multiple salespeople knock on *your* door?

CHAMBER EVENTS - Some of the common wisdom pushed down onto real estate agents is to join the chamber of commerce and attend their events. Network with chamber members. Too bad so many agents get the exact same advice, because who do you see at chamber events? A bunch of agents. You can still make that time spent at chamber events impactful, but you'd better have a good plan to make yourself stand out. It would be better to find gatherings where there will be few or no real estate agents.

REFERRAL SYSTEMS - Perhaps you've heard an agent say this before: "By the way, I'm never too busy for your referrals." Of course you've heard it—and so has everyone in your sphere.

There are *so many* agents who have adopted this strategy identically, without changing a single word in the script. It worked really well for the agent who invented the system, and it worked well for many agents who followed. But it's become so prevalent—agents sending out postcards, newsletters, and notes, all ending with the line, "By the way, I'm never too busy for your referrals"—that it's become brain-numbing noise to the people in your sphere.

ULTRA-BRANDING - You find this in the large franchise brokerages that have in-house designers/marketing departments. Many of these large brokerages have multiple profit centers built in, and ultra-branding is one of the most common. The brokerage encourages agents to hire in-house designers to create a custom logo and then pay for business cards, signage, and websites all branded with this new image. The in-house marketing team will help promote the agent's business for X number of dollars. Hoards of agents fall for this sales pitch when they can't afford it. They overpay for services that they could have gotten elsewhere for cheaper.

There's nothing wrong with creating your own logo and marketing yourself in a way that differentiates you from other agents. Just make sure that you're differentiating in a way that matters to the consumer. Changing your brand from John Doe Realty to JohnSellsYourCity.com doesn't make a difference to your clients. *You* are the brand. It's you, not your logo—you and the service you provide, and the work you do in the community. When people refer you, they're referring your reputation and service, not the image on your business card.

When you're new to the business, you can leverage an existing brand to help propel or position yourself. You might leverage the brand of your brokerage, because the broker has a reputation or years of experience in a certain market you want to align yourself with. That's an effective use of branding—just watch out for being pushed into ultra-branding yourself. That costs uber-money. Focus instead on developing your business's services so that it stands out from the crowd, which is another form of personal branding that will resonate more with your clients.

Break Away from the Herd

Now that we've covered the risks of becoming a sheep, how do you break away from the pack?

BE ORIGINAL - Do something that is unique to the consumer. Don't focus on being different in the eyes of other agents. Find what makes you stand out as unique and interesting to potential clients. I'm not talking about a fancier business card either. How is your *service* different or unique to clients?

BE FIRST - Do you want to try a new idea or strategy? A system from a new coach or guru? That's fine, as long as you're the first to do it in your market. While we're on the subject, make an effort to be first in all parts of your life. For example, rather than wait to see if the mailman says hello, be first. When you come into the office, say good morning to your fellow agents rather than waiting for them to do it. Get your spouse a gift on Valentine's Day rather than waiting to see what she got you. Once you make a conscious effort to be first in your life, it will become more natural. The opportunities to be first in your real estate business will become obvious. Of course, being first isn't everything. I don't want to be the first one to implement a really bad idea (been there, done that). But being first is a powerful mantra you may want to adopt in your life. If you try it, I guarantee you that others will notice the difference in you.

EMBRACE THE FEAR – Breaking away from the herd is scary. There's safety in numbers. When you go out on your own and try something new or different in your business, there's often no one you can talk to about it. Unless you're in an environment where you can bounce ideas off others before deploying your new plans, you're going it alone. It's not easy, but it's so worth it if you can get past your fears. Start by asking yourself what specifically you're afraid of. If you write a newsletter to your clients, you may fear what others will think of your writing and the quality of your newsletters. I'm going to tell you right now that your first newsletter is not going to be your best. However, if you are authentic, real, honest, humble, and open about your fears, your failures, and your dreams, and you use stories to help illustrate your point, you don't need to be a good writer. Ask yourself, *What's the worst thing that can happen by sending out the newsletter?* Usually it's nothing other than your own hang-ups getting in the way.

If there's something new you're excited about but nervous to try in your business, there's a good chance you're onto something good and on the right path. Embrace it.

SOLVE A PROBLEM – If you're comfortable going rogue from the pack, focus on solving a problem for the consumer. Make sure you're solving a problem that really exists for them. Be a solution.

To get yourself thinking, put yourself in your clients' shoes and finish the following statements the way they might:

When I moved to town, I wish I had known …

I wish someone could help me do …

I can't seem to find any information about …

Check Yourself

Mark Twain once famously said, "Whenever you find yourself on the side of the majority, it is time to pause and reflect." Adopt an alarm system, so to speak, to check yourself occasionally to see if you are following the herd. You can do this by having a consulting meeting with yourself. Look over your business as if you were being paid to do this as a consultant and look for areas to improve. If you find that you are following the same systems as the majority, watch out. The real estate industry is changing fast, and if you're following the same methods and patterns as everybody else—if someone is telling you to keep in line, don't break from the herd, don't be the black sheep—well then, you might not see the cliff that's coming up.

Focus on solving problems for your ideal clients. Study others outside your marketplace—and even outside your industry—for new ideas and be fearless with implementation. Don't get caught up in what agents in the herd think of you. Remember, if you break away from the herd, you will be labeled the black sheep. As long as you are focused on helping the consumer, then you are the one leading them—the other agents just don't know it yet.

CHAPTER 8
The 800-Pound Gorilla of Confidence

Fear of public speaking is common. An audience can easily see when a speaker is nervous—he sweats, he talks fast, he avoids eye contact.

The same thing happens in front of clients and prospects. An agent's nervousness is easy to read. She may think she's acting confident, but that's precisely why she's easy to read—because she's acting and not performing very well.

On the flip side, you can tell when a public speaker is confident and comfortable. It's almost like he has this relaxed swagger. You see this in sports as well. Two boxers face off at the weigh-in. The champion is often calm and collected, because he's been through this before and knows he can compete at the highest level. He doesn't have much to prove because he's already proven it. The challenger is often flashy, provocative, making a big show and talking tough. He might be nervous and overcompensating with this act. It comes off as fake. Humans are inherently intuitive at picking up on signs that someone is nervous, scared, or pretending to be confident. These competitors are often the ones who lose in the first round.

Sometimes it's the champion who makes the noise and fuss. He might be an egomaniac who truly believes he's the best fighter in the world, and he makes a big scene about it. He might be doing this strategically to get under his opponent's skin—but he also may be nervous about this new competitor and trying not to show it. When I see a normally calm and collected champion who acts abnormally wound up at the weigh-in, I instantly think he's masking his nervousness by showboating. I often find that he does not perform as well.

Egomania: The Wrong Kind of Confidence

Someone who brags and dominates conversations about his area of knowledge or expertise is usually trying to cover up his insecurities. Or he's an egomaniac—a person possessed by delusions of personal greatness and who feels a lack of appreciation. Bullying is another way egomaniacs try to demand respect and attention. In some cases, egomaniacs truly believe that they know it all or at least know better than everyone else. Unfortunately, they feel the need to prove this to everyone around them.

In the business world, you'll see this when people leverage their title in a heavy-handed way by tossing it around just to intimidate others. Egomaniacs believe they know better than everyone else and will talk down to people. I know you have experienced this. That type of behavior drives me a bit nutty. Acting superior to someone when it is not necessary or appropriate is a BS move.

We all know people who are egomaniacs. Why do you think they act that way? Are they just bullies, or are they overcompensating for something? Do they naturally think everyone else is an idiot compared to them? It could be.

The reason I struggle so much with egomaniacs is because— regardless of why they act that way—they've closed their minds, they won't listen to ideas from others, and they won't respect alternative viewpoints to see if they can find common ground to move a solution forward. They don't listen.

It's okay if you're the smartest person in the room. It's okay if you know more about real estate than everyone else in the room. But you don't need to pound your chest and mark your territory. It's one thing to show you have confidence; it's another thing entirely to brag and be a jerk about it. If you're ultra-confident and you feel like you're surrounded by people who know less than you do, it doesn't mean you still can't learn something from them. Everyone's viewpoint should be respected. If you're dealing with a new agent on the other end of a transaction, it's easy to get frustrated with her. It's easy to discount or ignore anything that agent says. It may be tempting to bulldoze right over her to get the deal done. However, she may have some knowledge or information that could impact the transaction. If you piss her off, ignore her, or go around her, you may miss something that has huge implications for your client. If you don't care about messing things up for your client because you're so confident you can do it yourself, then you are an egomaniac.

You should never want to stop learning or finding new avenues to doing something better. You might be surprised where (or from whom) you'll get valuable information.

Building the Right Kind of Confidence

So how do you be confident without being cocky? Be internally confident. It's not a contest. It's not about who has the biggest tail feathers. It's an internal belief. You just need to believe in yourself, as challenging as that may feel. Don't worry about what others believe. You don't need to prove to your clients that you know what you're doing; it will be apparent in your body language.

If you feel you are lacking internal confidence, here are four ways to grow your confidence:

1. **FOCUS ON WHAT YOU DO WELL** rather than focusing on what you don't do well. If you feel like your strength is that you can work well with just about anyone, then focus on that quality about yourself to build a connection with your clients so they feel comfortable with you. If your strength is your years

of experience in the business, then think about how you are uniquely positioned to help your clients avoid costly mistakes. If technology or marketing skills are the best assets you bring to your clients, then focus on how those skills will bring them their desired outcome.

2. USE AFFIRMATIONS AND VISUALIZATION TECHNIQUES. This may sound cheesy or lame to you, but there's a reason that peak performers, world-class athletes, and entrepreneurial super-stars implement affirmations and visualization practices into their daily routine. I'm no expert on this subject, so I won't try explaining how and why they work. However, there is a ton of free information on the Internet about how to get started and advice on how best to use these methods to get your desired results in your business and your personal life. I kept hearing and reading about people I admire using these techniques regu-larly, so I Googled the subject and gave them a try. Seriously, if you haven't tried this yet, I challenge you to try affirmations and visualizations for thirty days. You'll be shocked at what happens. I noticed significant changes in my life after just ten days.

3. PRACTICE/IMPROVE. I wish I could tell you some secret that would eliminate your need to practice a skill to get better at it. But the fact still remains that the more you practice something, the more you improve. The more you improve, the more your confidence will grow.

4. DO THE WORK. Often agents are not confident because they didn't prepare enough. If you want to get more confident, really put in the work to be prepared to help your client. It's like kids who have a weekly spelling test. If they put the work in during the week to drill those spelling words, they will welcome the test at the end of the week. Other kids who cram right before the test or blow off studying are likely to feel stressed on test day. In real estate, if you put in the work prior to your appointment, you won't have to *try* to be confident, you will be.

Internal confidence is more apparent than you might think. It can be detected before you even say a word. When you speak, it's often not what you say but how you say it. Think of someone who strikes you as confident—someone in your personal life or workplace, a politician, actor, or athlete. Even when that person is not saying a word, he exudes a confidence that makes you trust and believe him more. You pay attention when he does speak. That's a powerful trait to possess.

When you're a new agent, you're terrified that someone is going to figure out that you don't know what you're doing. Even after you've been doing the job for a decade, you still might feel like they'll discover you're a fake. The solution is to keep gaining experience but also to leverage the experience of others. If necessary, align yourself with someone who has confidence in the areas where you are struggling. Figure out who in your office, brokerage, or industry has a lot of the type of experience you want to leverage. I encourage agents in my office to leverage my experience—the new ones especially. They can talk to their clients about "the broker's" accomplishments, ideology, and home-selling process. It's a "we" not an "I" for them.

CASE IN POINT: *If you're going up against me in a listing appointment, you better have a good game plan, because I'm very confident that I will get it. It's not because I'm better at closing or have a better presentation, it's because I have a lot of confidence in what I do and how I do it. People respond to that. They can tell I'm 100 percent confident in my abilities to get them the most money from their house. It's not a trick, or a bait and switch, or some fancy multilevel marketing trick to get in the front door—I just know I can sell it better than anyone else because I've studied and put the work in. I talk to the sellers about things that no one else talks about. I have a well-thought-out plan for their home and can do some things to help them sell their home that no one else in town can do. I'm also constantly learning new things. I* *watch other agents, and if I see someone doing something that is effective, I figure out how to incorporate it into my next listing. That learning keeps me from being egotistical. I just have a lot of confidence when I walk in the door, because I put in the time and did the homework and research, and I feel confident I can do a great job without being cocky.*

Common Confidence Killers

USING METHODS THAT CONFLICT WITH YOUR PERSONALITY OR DON'T FEEL RIGHT TO YOU - Real estate agents struggle with confidence when they question the methods or the services they're offering. Maybe they're cold calling for-sale-by-owners or cold leads. They struggle on the phone when someone is being difficult, and they crumble because they don't have confidence in what they're doing. Or they're calling expired listings, and they lack confidence because they know they're not the only agent calling. They're not sure that they can list this house any better than the last agent. But the agent is pushing ahead with a script from some guru or trainer, and it's apparent in his voice that he's struggling because he has no confidence in that system.

The solution is for that agent to prospect and conduct his business in ways that make him feel good about what he is doing. Even if it is hard at first, he will ultimately become more confident because he is doing the right things for the right reasons.

Your confidence may waver if you contact other people in a way you wouldn't want to be contacted yourself. That is why it doesn't feel right or natural. The agent is not necessarily shy, but he's using techniques that go against his core character. Or he doesn't have a strong plan for how to actually help the person he's calling.

Stop doing things that conflict with your personality and your sense of right and wrong. If you don't think you can provide better services than the last agent, you need to address that shortcoming. Align yourself with people, methods, and services that you can be proud of, and that will give you the utmost confidence.

DEALING WITH INTIMIDATING CLIENTS - In some cases, an agent struggles with confidence because she's intimidated by a client. I saw this recently with an agent in my office who somehow got in front of an investor client. She had done some things with investments but not a lot. The investor picked up on her lack of confidence, and I think he was testing her. He started talking fast and using big words she didn't understand. Whether he was doing that intentionally or not, she got intimidated and almost lost the client. Fortunately, she came and asked me for help. I have a ton of confidence with investor clients because I've worked a lot with them. I understand them and their goals. And this agent can do the same. If an agent wants to work with investor clients, she just needs to spend some time learning about investment properties—read the books and newspapers that investors read and understand where they're coming from in their investment pursuits.

With difficult clients, you just need to do your homework so you understand them better. Maybe the client is an entertainment professional with an intimidating personality. Or the client makes a ton of money and is looking at really expensive houses, and that's outside your comfort zone. It might be outside your comfort zone because you're unfamiliar with the luxury homes in your area. If you have time to prepare, make sure you go out and see every nice home in the area so you get that confidence. You'll know for yourself which ones are the best deals. You'll know which ones have the right features once you hear what your client is looking for. Don't go in cold. Don't be lazy about it. If it's short notice, then partner with somebody who has that background and understands how to service that type of client, and then shadow them so you gain that same knowledge.

BEING ACROSS THE TABLE FROM A MEGA-AGENT/EGOMANIAC - Agents sometimes lose confidence because of the actions of another agent. You might be on the other side of a transaction with a mega-agent who has been in the business for a long time, and he starts wielding that fact and talking down to you, which starts you second-guessing yourself. It weakens your position in the transaction and with your client. What do you do?

The first thing you do is soften him up. You know what works great on egomaniacs? You play to their ego.

> **CASE IN POINT:** *One of my first jobs was managing people much older than myself. They saw how young I was and either assumed I didn't know what I was doing or that I was some know-it-all brainy kid. Either way, they acted uncomfortable. They weren't egomaniacs, but they were uncomfortable with the position I had.*
>
> *To smooth things over, I first played to their strengths and egos. I asked them each to share with me what they'd learned from their years on the job. I listened and was genuinely impressed with their knowledge and respected their experience. They could see by the questions I asked and how I responded to their advice that I actually cared and wasn't a jerk. I was able to demonstrate that I wasn't incompetent nor would I be needy, and the barriers were removed.*

You want to do that with agents who railroad you or give you a difficult time. Instead of being combative, you need to soften them up. Appease them. Be kind to them. Compliment them. That will get them to like you. Once they like you, you're better set up to gain their respect when you hold your ground and illustrate your competence. Initially when you hold your ground, they might treat you like you don't know what you're doing, or they might get frustrated. But once they've started liking you and you hold your ground, most often they treat you differently.

The same holds true when the roles are reversed. If you're the experienced agent dealing with an incompetent agent who is being difficult on the other side of a deal, you solve the problem the same way. Don't jump down the agent's throat; rather, make an effort to get to know them a bit, give them a couple of genuine compliments. Get on their good side first. Let them know you're not the enemy. Offer to help them in some way to make their job easier (I know this may go against every fiber in your body, but in an effort to get the best outcome for your clients, it's worth it). Their guard will come down, and they'll stop being so defensive. Then you can get something done, potentially learning a lot more about the agent's clients to potentially secure the right deal for your clients.

BEING ASKED A QUESTION YOU DON'T KNOW THE ANSWER TO - If a client asks you something that you don't know the answer to, don't panic. Nobody knows everything. What you don't want to do is stammer and stutter and pretend like you know the answer. When I don't know an answer or understand something, I slow the client down to make sure I fully understand what they're asking me about. I let them know how or who I will contact to resolve that question or find out what they really want to know, which is often something entirely different than what they initially asked. Usually behind the question is a deeper question—the client is trying to solve something. If they ask me what the property taxes were on a house last year, and if I don't have that number in front of me, I can still address part of their question. Based on what they're asking, I can see they have a deeper question about the overall cost of owning that property. I might be able to address that concern by telling them the HOA dues, irrigation costs, and how local property taxes work and how much they can typically expect to pay. Ultimately, that might solve their concerns before I can research their original question.

CASE IN POINT: *I truly believe in myself and that what I can offer the client is something they can't get anywhere else. I've done my homework on my market. I've done my research. I know*

I'm positioned well to help. I care about clients having a positive outcome. I know I'm a rock-solid person for them to hire, and I believe that if they hire someone else, they'll get something less. Sure, I've been in many situations where I felt like I was faking it until I made it. But here is the secret: Everyone feels that at some point. How we handle new and uncomfortable situations is the true test. Once you get used to running on uncomfortable ground, you gain the confidence to run anywhere.

Find Your Gorilla

Before an appointment, before a phone call, before you go into a meeting—how do you get confident? It's perfectly normal to feel nervous. You can't just turn that off, but you can coach yourself out of being nervous. Channel your 800-pound gorilla of confidence. I think of a huge gorilla sitting in the jungle, watching over the band of gorillas she or he is responsible to protect and guide. This gorilla is huge and powerful but stoic, wise, and assured. Ready for any challenge yet peacefully confident. For whatever reason, thinking of that large and peaceful 800-pound gorilla just works for me.

Channel whatever animal or spirit gives you the most confidence. Just make sure you wait until you're off the phone or back in your car before you beat your chest in victory.

CHAPTER 9

You Are More Than Your Label

Have you ever taken a personality test designed to tell you if you'd be good at sales or accounting? One of the most common of these types of tests is the DISC. It's an assessment that terms you a high D, I, S, or C, depending on your personality (you can find detailed explanations and even take the test online).

I was once at a real estate conference where the presenter had everyone—a room full of agents—fill out the DISC test. When we finished, he asked those of us who were high Ds and Is to raise our hands. Forty percent of the agents in the room were Ds, another 40 to 45 percent were Is. The presenter wasn't surprised. He said that high Ds and Is were the personality types that perform best in sales.

I couldn't help but agree with him at the time. Looking around the room, it seemed obvious. But I've learned over time that an assessment is not necessarily a good indicator of performance. How you rate on the DISC might reveal what type of job you're more likely to pursue because of your comfort level, but I think anybody can succeed in real estate no matter how they score on that test.

CASE IN POINT: *When I take the test, my score depends on what mood I'm in that day. Or on the context behind the questions. They give you scenarios like:* What would you do if _____ happened? How would you respond? *You get put in a certain* *box based on your response. For me, there are so many variables that I always get different results depending on my mood or how I interpret and respond to the questions. I also know that at any given time I can put on different hats, depending on the situation or the client, to take on a personality type that is similar to the client or the personality characteristics that are needed in the moment. For example, if I'm in front of a group of people for a presentation, I become very outgoing, much more than I typically am in my personal life.*

Recently I interviewed an agent at my brokerage. She told me she had previously applied for a position as a sales agent with a large homebuilder in town. She was well qualified with many years of sales experience. She had often been the top salesperson in her previous jobs. The homebuilder had her take the DISC assessment, and shortly after that, she found out she didn't get the job. The company was convinced by her results that she would not be strong at sales. They told her instead that she'd do better in a lower-paying customer service job. This company ignored years and years of evidence—her proven sales record—and denied her the sales job based on an assessment. I told the agent that was their loss and that I likely would have failed their test too.

ADD and OCD, Introvert and Extrovert

You've likely heard of ADD and OCD. These are both diagnosable disorders (tons of information is available about them online), but a lot of people joke and casually label themselves as having tendencies toward one or the other of these behavioral conditions.

For example, people with the following characteristics tend to believe they have some ADD issues:

1. They get distracted easily ("Squirrel!"). They can't stay on task and are constantly jumping from one project to another. Maybe at home they have fifteen home-improvement projects started and don't seem to finish any of them.

2. They can't resist shiny pennies. They click on email offerings and deals they don't need. Before they know it, half a day has passed and they've accomplished very little.

3. They're disorganized and messy.

People with the following characteristics tend to believe they have some OCD issues:

1. They hate to deviate from a plan. They struggle with the crazy world of real estate where they can't often stick to a schedule.

2. They're hyper-organized. They need to have their desk just right. Instead of answering important emails, they feel the need to organize and streamline their emails.

3. They're clean freaks. If they're working from home as a real estate agent, they don't accomplish much work because they have to vacuum the floor or clean the toilets one more time.

4. They think obsessively. They focus on one topic and can't move past it until it's resolved.

5. They have compulsive rituals.

Those are a few of the casual ways people diagnose themselves. Whether it's correct to the actual disorder is beside the point. People put themselves in a box and say they behave or act a certain way because of their "disorder." They can't possibly finish that book or complete that training because they have ADD. They can't work from home because their OCD compels them to clean all day.

Another system people use to label themselves is *introvert* or *extrovert*. People who consider themselves introverted might think they'll struggle at being a real estate agent. Introverts may not be as outgoing as extroverts. They might not prefer to talk to people and might prefer to work from home. An extrovert is a "people person" who prefers talking to people and mixing it up. People assume that an extrovert is better suited for success in real estate.

Overcoming Labels

There are all kinds of business books, gurus, and experts who love to talk about all these behaviors, to try to put people in a box so they can better understand themselves and which jobs they would be best at.

Some people find it more difficult than others to complete certain tasks. Their brains don't seem wired for that task. Does that mean they should give up? Should they not become a real estate agent because those tasks are challenging for them? I don't think so. I've seen people of all behavioral and personality types, with all different strengths and weaknesses, be extraordinarily successful in real estate.

Whether you want to work in real estate is up to you—just remember that your behavioral type does not predispose you from being successful. Some people may try to teach and tell you otherwise, but that's all BS.

The key is to find ways to leverage your strengths and to find workarounds for things you struggle with. For example:

NETWORKING - The thought of being thrown into a gathering of strangers and talking about yourself for hours sounds like a shitty way to spend an afternoon to many people. In fact, it's one of the most uncomfortable situations some people can imagine. Networking is essential for real estate agents, so what do you do? Remember that networking is a great way to increase the number of people in your sphere. But networking comes in all different forms. It doesn't mean you have to be in a room full of people. It doesn't mean you need to have meetings with people all week long. There are other ways to build your sphere.

You can connect and communicate with a lot of people through social media. You can create content (a book, for example) about a topic that interests people and build a following from that, and you wouldn't necessarily have to talk to anyone face-to-face; you simply supply them information. You can record your own podcasts or a radio show. That way you're not talking to anyone except yourself, in your room with a microphone, and you can reach a lot of people.

So what do you do about clients? If you struggle with being comfortable around people, you can still acquire clients but find someone else to service them. Align yourself with an agent who is more outgoing than you are and who would enjoy going out with buyers and meeting sellers face-to-face.

HANDWRITING - It's not a disorder, but plenty of people have bad handwriting, poor grammar and spelling, and limited writing skills. They decide their writing is so awful that they never write thank-you cards or note cards to clients, even though that's a valuable thing to do. As I suggest in chapter 3, you can write out your thoughts on a computer and have a willing helper with better handwriting complete them for you once a week.

What about writing in general? I don't consider myself a great writer, but here I am writing this book. I felt compelled to write it, and I didn't want my fears or my concern that I'm a crappy writer to prevent me from writing something I felt was important. That's why I got some help with this book. I got as far as I could and then had someone look it over. Together we revised and edited. Yes, there are other people who could write a book faster than I did, because they may be more talented or educated or skillful at writing—but that doesn't mean I can't do it.

TECHNOLOGY - Some people will tell you that if you're not good with technology, then you shouldn't be in real estate because it's all about technology today. Yes, there is a lot of technology in real estate today, and if you're not paying attention to it, you may be missing the boat in some areas. However, do you know what works really well in today's real estate world? All the same old-school stuff that has always worked. People are using too much technology and neglecting the face-to-face personal communication that was once so common. A lot of consumers appreciate the old-school style. In order not to frustrate clients who are dependent on technology and expect you to connect with them via paperless documents and email and texting, align yourself with an agent who knows how to use technology effectively. Have her focus on the high-tech aspects of the job so you can focus on the aspects you do well.

It doesn't have to be a fifty-fifty partnership. Maybe there's a new agent in your office who is extremely good with technology but doesn't have a lot of business. You can help each other out. She might show you some simple ways to leverage technology that don't require you to become an expert with it.

SPEAKING - I do podcasts and radio, teach trainings, and do videos—I speak in public a lot. But here's a newsflash: I don't consider myself a good speaker at all. I cringe when I listen to my recordings. I'm so critical of the way I sound that it makes me not want to continue doing it.

Knowing you're not a great speaker doesn't have to keep you from speaking. You don't have to be great; you just have to be genuine. It helps if you believe in and care about what you're speaking about. If you're knowledgeable and you're passionate about sharing that knowledge, it doesn't matter that you're not as polished as someone else. You'll improve with practice. In the meantime, if the audience can sense your passion for what you are speaking about, they'll be much more forgiving.

ORGANIZATION - Many agents struggle to be organized. Their desks, their cars, even their houses are a mess. It's not because they like to be messy; it's because their minds are in a constant state of change and refocus. New priorities always pop to the top of the list. They might get started cleaning their desks and find things they should have tackled the previous week, and they'll get to work on those.

You've got to practice organization and cleanliness. If you're unorganized, part of the reason might be because you're committed to so many different tasks. It might help to have a spouse or a fellow agent help you organize. You might hire a transaction coordinator to help with some of the details you normally have a hard time keeping track of. You can create plans and try to organize your day (see chapter 20).

PRODUCTIVITY - Certain personality and behavior types struggle to be productive. They may not struggle to work hard, but they struggle to be productive. They're always bouncing around, and they look back at the end of the day and can't figure out why nothing got finished. They did a few things but not nearly as much as the agents who are structured and focused and create fewer distractions for themselves. Those other agents seem to complete an amazing amount of work in one day.

Even if you're not as organized and productive as others, it doesn't mean you can't be effective at your job. It just means you need to find ways to check yourself and make sure you complete your tasks. For more ideas and suggestions for improving productivity, see chapter 12.

Labels Don't Matter

It doesn't matter if you have OCD, ADD, you're an introvert or an extrovert, or whatever frickin' score you got on the DISC test. None of that matters if you really want something to work. There's always another way. There's more than one workaround.

Leverage your strengths. If you're good at networking, then leverage that. If you're good at networking but suck at technology, then align yourself with somebody who's good at technology so you can go out and network to your heart's content. You don't have to force yourself to do things you're not good at.

I forced myself to finish writing a book. Writing a book is hard, but it was important to me. I also found that I could write faster and do more if I just focused on the content I wanted to cover and then got help from other people to clean it up and fix it. If I went through and tried to fix the grammar and spelling errors myself, not only would it take forever, but the end product would be worse. I had to find people who were more inherently skilled at that type of exercise so I could focus on content.

Don't get wrapped up in assessments and behavioral traits. Sure, some of those are valuable to help you identify why you struggle at some things. But as was the case with the agent in my office who was denied a different job because of her DISC assessment, it just goes to show you that those things are fallible. They might be one tool in the toolbox, but you don't want to let them define you.

Identify your strengths and try to do more of what you're strong at. You might be able to accomplish those things faster than other people. By doing that, you could build a strategic advantage in your marketplace. If you do certain things better than others, find a way to harness that. We don't allow that enough in our society. We try to put everyone in the same box.

If there are certain things you feel you do better than others—or feel like you could do better than others with a little bit of work and training—then focus on those. Leverage those skills. You can be an amazing agent and do awesome work for your community, and do it mostly from home where you don't see that many people. You don't have to be on a bill-board, in the spotlight in front of people all the time—you can be in the shadows but deliver an equal amount of impact, if not more, because of the skills you have learned and honed. You can accomplish more and produce more because you're not as distracted as others.

If you're great at communicating and great with people, then find a way to get in front of more people. You can do it. If you're a people person and you like how it feels to interact with people, then you don't need to spend time on things you're not as talented at. Go out and use the skill set that other people struggle with.

No excuses.

CHAPTER 10

Know When to Sprint

Think of the most famous athletes in sports. Michael Jordan and LeBron James might come to mind for basketball. David Beckham for soccer. Serena Williams for tennis. Jerry Rice for football. These are the players who always seem to get the ball. Why is it that they're able to score so much more frequently? These players have mastered the art of knowing when to sprint. They see things happening before other people do, and they react. They don't rest when others rest. They seize opportunities that are in front of them. These players get tired like any other player. But they see when it's time to sprint, to burst into action, and that's how they end up in the right place at the right time, seemingly at will.

Sprinting, as in bursting at 110 percent of your effort at the right moment, is a skill that has to be practiced. It's a skill that can be learned and adapted to real estate as well. Being a real estate agent is a marathon. It's a hard, hard business. If you don't hone that instinct for knowing when to sprint, this business is going to be that much harsher and pay you so much less.

When Agents Fail to Sprint

Many agents don't recognize opportunity when it's dangling like a carrot in front of them. For example, a long-term lead who has been in an agent's database for a year suddenly shows massive interest and action on the agent's website. However, the agent doesn't react to it because she's busy chasing new leads and doesn't treat it with urgency when she should be sprinting to contact that lead and offer assistance.

Or a deal is about to blow up. Things are falling apart, and the agent doesn't know what to do, so he does nothing and hopes the deal fixes itself. In reality, the agent should be working overtime and sprinting as hard as he can to solve the problem.

Or a client wants to make an immediate offer. The agent is meeting friends for drinks later and doesn't have time to write up the offer. She tells the client they can write up the offer tomorrow morning, but overnight another offer comes in and beats them to it. If the agent had found a way to sprint and get that offer in without hesitation, she would have saved herself weeks or months of work with that client. More importantly, she wouldn't have let down her client.

Or a client pushes an agent out of his knowledge base or comfort zone. Maybe the clients are looking at a farm or ranch, and the agent is unfamiliar with wells, septic tanks, water rights, etc. The lack of knowledge is impeding the deal because the clients are waiting for the agent to find that information so they can decide whether to make an offer. That's when an agent needs to sprint to research those details or get the help he needs before the opportunity passes by.

Or when an agent posts a new listing. A newly listed property gets the most views right after it's posted live on the MLS. It's critical that when an agent lists a property, he makes sure the listing and pictures look as good as they possibly can before it goes live. The house needs to be ready to show, the pictures and presentation need to be perfect. First impressions are everything. Sellers get anxious to have the house listed, and a good agent has to sprint to get all the work done up front so the home makes a strong first impression. Putting the time in, even if it means working late into the evening and getting it right, could mean the difference between the home being on the market one week versus three or more months.

Or when investigating and providing the details the buyer needs to make an offer. A buyer likes a property and needs to know about property taxes, the HOA, CCRs for fencing restrictions, etc. If an agent takes his time gathering the information (when it's the only thing keeping the buyer from making an offer) rather than sprinting, he's impacting his clients. They may lose out on the home to another buyer—and the agent may lose his income for that month.

Or if an agent has short-term notice to pitch a proposal to a builder or developer prospect. The first meeting with a builder or developer is crucial. An agent who knows when to sprint will find a way to show up with a detailed proposal or immediately after the meeting go into overdrive to deliver exactly what the developer is looking for. Instead of putting the work off until the weekend, a sprinting agent will go home, put the kids to bed, and start her second shift. That kind of deal can pay an agent for years and years and totally change the course of her business.

Or an agent learns of a window of opportunity to work with a company relocation department. But they require him to jump through a bunch of hoops that seem ridiculous. Instead of complaining about it and getting to it in a few days when he isn't so busy, he should seize the opportunity immediately. That's how some agents appear to be lucky.

Or with new prospect calls and initial follow-ups. Agents are commonly taught to call new prospects as soon as possible. An agent should strive to follow through with this as often as possible. Yet this rarely happens. Inquiries are often called days later. More importantly, the agent should go out of his way to find out what information the prospects are trying to find and give them the answers they can't find on their own—or before they even ask for it. An agent who sprints to get this information to them will turn that prospect into a client; one who doesn't will lose that prospect to another agent.

Over-Sprinting

The second critical way agents fail to see the significance of sprinting is when they burn out or make mistakes because they try to sprint all the time. For example, an agent might spend more time with a time-wasting client than with a valuable client. He tries to put out the fires the difficult client is causing and unintentionally ignores or drops the ball with the valued client.

Or he forgets important deadlines and responsibilities with current listings and upcoming closings because he's distracted with new leads and prospects. Listings and clients that are about to produce a paycheck should always take priority over prospecting. An agent should do both but have clear priorities. He should sprint to help his client first and then move on to prospecting.

Or he's working hard for work's sake. An agent might be slaying dragons and wearing twenty different hats, either desperate to make a closing or to keep the ball rolling when things are going well. When a task is finished, he finds more things to work on, just to stay busy. He doesn't have a plan or a priority list; he's just reacting. But without those plans and priorities, an agent might work really hard without accomplishing much.

Or he's sprinting all the time and doesn't see opportunities right in front of him. He has tunnel vision, and he's blowing right past opportunities. On the basketball court or the soccer field, a player who sprints all the time tires out and can't make it to the next play when he needs to be in the right spot at the right time.

Or he's not succeeding at anything due to spreading himself too thin with too many endeavors. The work he's completing might be commendable, but it's not as good as it could be because he's spread too thin. If he reduced the number of things he's focused on, he could make the remaining tasks that much better.

Develop Your Timing

How do you get better about knowing when to sprint? You have to learn to pay attention. Watch for it. Know that it's an important aspect of your business. When you're about to clock out for the day and you see that there are two small items you thought you were going to find time to do, it's easy to put those off until the next day. However, depending on how critical those items are, it may be best to sprint for fifteen minutes and get them done—or to take five minutes to plan how you can resolve the items later that night or early the next morning.

Study other people who are good at sprinting. Watch athletes and figure out how they know where to be at the right time. It took them practice, but they also have that "eye of the tiger" mentality where they go for the win. They burst into action; they go all in. They can't go all in all the time. But when they do, they're not saving energy for the next play. They're not saving themselves for later. Pay attention to that. Figure out how to apply that to your business, and you'll get better at it.

The flip side of this is knowing when to sprint for important things in your personal life. You may have reached a point in your career where you're okay if you do less business, or you structure your business so you don't have to return phone calls after 6 P.M. I get this. I've implemented some changes in areas of my life where I don't care if I make less money or if I have to hire someone to cover specific tasks for me. I'm prioritizing my personal time as well as my business time. If you're not making time to enjoy the things you're working so hard for and all the money you're earning, what's it all worth?

When you're starting out in your career and business, you've got to go all in. You make sacrifices, and that's just how it is. Once you have success, then you can reprioritize. That takes skill when you've been so focused on working and building your business. I've talked to very successful mega-agents—the ones other agents look up to and want to be—and after talking to them on a personal level, all I could think was, *Man, I don't want to be him.* They're so deep into the business that it controls them. It owns them. They don't have a life. Their quality of life suffers because their business runs them instead of the other way around or because they're so focused on making more money. I know I don't want that for myself. I want success, but I'm also okay limiting or altering how I do my business so I can also have enjoyment, peace of mind, time with loved ones, and all the stuff that's important to me.

You'll have to judge for yourself what's important to you, but as you progress in your career, you may find that you don't need to sprint as often—or you create a business where others can sprint for you so you can sprint after other pursuits in life. Regardless, whether your goals are higher income or more time with your loved ones, mastering when to sprint will help you reach those goals faster.

CHAPTER 11

Find Your Flock

Simon Sinek said in a famous TED Talk, "People buy what you believe."

We are all unique individuals. Our brains are all wired differently. However, we all have a core instinct to recognize and respond to people with whom we connect and identify. If a politician says something that makes you think, *I like what that person believes,* you are likely to pay more attention to that politician in the future. If that same politician says something that repulses you, it will be difficult for him to regain your trust.

Think about how you feel when you discover a group of people who share your favorite hobby. You're more likely to reach out to that group because you share a sort of kinship with them: *They like what I like. There are people out there who think like I do.*

We are all drawn to people we like and admire. Think about the power of celebrity. I believe the reason society gets so worked up about celebrities is that they have either touched our soul in some performance or because we often know a celebrity's backstory. We know how they got their big break. We've learned what they're passionate about, how they've messed up and then recovered. Because their lives are so public, we get to know them deeply—often more deeply than we know our neighbors and coworkers. Most people don't share those private details with one another. On some level, celebrities have risen above what most other people have accomplished in their field. This intrigues us and compels us to learn even more about them, which is why celebrity news is such big business.

What can we learn from this phenomenon?

As a real estate professional, how much do your friends, friends of friends, vendors, past clients, and current prospects know about your past? About what you have overcome to get where you are today? Do they know what makes you tick? What makes you get out of bed in the morning and work late into the wee hours to help your clients? Do they know why you're passionate about certain hobbies? What makes you smile and why? What mistakes you've made and what you learned from them? What lessons you've learned from your mentors? Do they know what frustrates you and inspires you? Do they know your goals, ambitions, fears, and hopes?

You might know the answers to these questions, but until you share them with the world, people won't truly know you. If you share these pieces of yourself with the world, your flock will find you. Let people into your world, and they will become more loyal listeners and respect you on a deeper level. When you say something that resonates with them, they will keep seeking you out and paying attention to what you say. Be real. Nobody is perfect, which is why people tend to find you more trustworthy when you share your mistakes and struggles. If you share your opinions, don't get too worked up about what others will think of them. Yes, some will disagree with you, but if you explain why you are passionate about a topic, most people will still respect you even if they don't agree with you. They will listen more because you were real and open, which is becoming a rare thing in our society.

Most business owners make the mistake of not letting their customers, partners, vendors, and community know about who they really are. Be an open book and let your flock find you.

CASE IN POINT: *I know a mortgage lender who is an amazing person. She has overcome so many obstacles, not only with her health but with challenges in her family and business as well. She does an astonishing amount of charity work within my community. I don't know how she does it all, but because I know about her history and what she does in the community, I'm ten times more likely to send her my consistent business, even though I know dozens of other great lenders. I'm inspired by her, I'm impressed by her, and I appreciate the work she does in the community.*

Share Your Story

You don't need some kind of Disney story of how you overcame evil and became a hero. But you do need to communicate your values through the stories you tell about yourself.

Let the world know who you are—you're a lot more than a real estate agent.

Everyone likes having a go-to person to recommend to others. If you share these stories about who you are and what you're passionate about with your sphere, they will be proud to have you as their go-to person, and they will share your stories with others.

When I recommend that mortgage lender to my clients, I tell them that she is a great lender, but it's the stories I share with them about her character that always have the biggest impact.

If you are not proud of your business or how you perform your services, then you will struggle to find loyal customers and fans who will refer you. Take a hard look within yourself and see how you feel about the service you offer and how you handle and care for clients. If your business is built on bait-and-switch tactics, that will hurt your ability to get people excited about referring you, even if you're a good agent. If people in your sphere are worried that you'll be annoying, unprofessional, and a flake to their family and friends, they won't give you referrals.

However, if they know that you go out of your way to always

do the right thing, even when it means losing money, and they have a story to tell that illustrates that point, then you are likely to get referrals from them. If your friends also know, on top of that, that you donated money to schools or did something that impacted your community in an awesome way that resonates with them, they may go out and actively try to bring you new business. They're that impressed with you. They think you're an amazing person and want to help you.

Let me tell you a quick story about a friend of mine who built a great real estate business. He started with nothing and grew his business so he was one of the top-selling agents in his brokerage. Eighty percent of his clients were repeat or referrals from his contacts. He had a rock-solid business that he was proud of. From that success, he then began to get recruited by other brokerages. One brokerage in particular offered him enough incentive to switch brokerages.

At the new firm, he was coached or encouraged to build a team to grow his business to new heights. He was excited about the idea and began developing his team model. However, once he built a team, he found that he had to completely change his business tactics in order to sustain his team. He went from having a relationship-focused business with his clients to creating a lead-generating-machine business.

He and his team member agents were given training from the firm on how to be more aggressive sales people in order to convert more leads into clients. They wanted to be successful, so his team worked hard following this advice. His sales increased with the team model, but his repeat and referral business dropped down to 20 percent of his total closings. My friend soon realized that he was stuck in a position he never intended to be in. He had to keep generating more and more leads in order to grow or maintain his business. Generating leads was a challenge that began to get more and more expensive and unpredictable. Finally, he said enough is enough and dismantled the team.

Since his agents were rarely speaking to clients with this team model, he found he didn't have much of a business left when it was all said and done. He had a list of names in a database but few relationships with them. In many ways, he had to start over and rebuild the business he originally created.

In order to reestablish a relationship with the contacts in his database, he started sending them a monthly newsletter that included stories of his family. He wrote a lot about his passion for helping veterans. He was honest about his successes and failures in business. He didn't feel the need to try to sell anything with the newsletter; his goal was purely to reestablish a connection with these names in his database.

The last time I saw my friend, he was back on top. He told me that 80 percent of his business was referrals from his database. He considers his newsletter to be the smartest thing he has done in business. He was shocked at how much it resonated with his clients and how quickly it helped him reestablish a connection with his customers. He told me how much he loves his job again. He was ready to quit real estate after his team disbanded. Now he couldn't be happier.

Finding your flock really means: let them discover the real you. There are hundreds of people out there who share similar passions. Your hobbies and the things that define your character could be totally unrelated to real estate. Be authentic and share the beliefs you're passionate about with as many people as you can. Your flock will find you, and they'll help you build and protect your business.

For ideas on ways to get your stories and opinions heard, see chapters 19 and 22.

CHAPTER 12

The 80/20 Principle for Real Estate

We've all heard of this. It's commonly known as the Pareto principle. It's applied in many ways and seen throughout nature, business, and marketing. Basically, for your business it means that 80 percent of your results come from 20 percent of your efforts.

It might be applied to income as: 80 percent of your income comes from 20 percent of the daily work you do, or from 20 percent of your clients.

In real estate, it might be expressed as: 20 percent of real estate agents close 80 percent of your market's real estate transactions.

Sometimes the split is closer to 90/10 or 95/5 or 70/30. The exact numbers don't really matter. The point is that this ratio is found all throughout your life and work, and if you learn to recognize it, understand it, and leverage it, it can have drastic implications for your business, your life, and your lifestyle.

I was first shown how this principle can be applied to productivity by Tim Ferriss's book, *The 4-Hour Workweek*. In that book, Ferriss discusses how he was doing well in business, making good money, working very hard (sometimes sixteen hours a day), but not feeling happy in it because most of his time was spent dealing with nightmare customers who were causing him to go batty over their petty grievances. After Ferriss rediscovered the 80/20 principle, he decided to redesign his business so that he eliminated the time-intensive tasks that were getting in the way of his happiness. He realized that a small percentage of his customers were causing him the most pain and aggravation—so he eliminated them. He also figured out which clients were making him the most money and which were a joy to work with, and he focused on them more.

Ferriss increased his productivity by focusing on the items he needed to complete each day and applied the 80/20 principle to that list. He asked himself, "If I can only complete one or two of these items today, which ones would they be?" He jokes about it in the book, but sometimes this is a very difficult thing to do. He uses the example of someone holding a gun to your head, forcing you to make that decision. Or if you were going to die of cancer in a short time, what's the most important task you want to accomplish? Ferriss's goal was to reorganize and reprioritize his brain, so he could quickly accomplish the most valuable and impactful tasks, for both his life and his business.

Being productive does not necessarily mean working hard and efficiently. You might work for hours at certain tasks, but the bigger question is: are they the right tasks? Being productive is not only about being efficient, it's also about understanding which tasks to work on and how to prioritize them. Efficiency is only part of the equation.

Productivity is a knife that has to be sharpened. You have to constantly reevaluate what you're doing, because there might be a better way to do things that will produce higher output with less input of time and energy—and less brain damage from banging your head against the wall.

A lot of agents struggle with this concept. They work their tails off and never seem to find the time to accomplish the tasks they know they need to do. Looking at their to-do list with this 80/20 principle might help them.

Busy Does Not Mean Productive

Fighting to stay productive is the curse of most real estate agents, and one of my personal biggest challenges. Once you cross over into working for yourself—an entrepreneur on a quest to be a successful real estate agent—you may find yourself always working. In the wee hours of the morning, you're checking your messages to see if a client has popped up and needs help, or if you need to put out any fires. The demands on your time never stop. If you're focused on improving your business and increasing your income, it's a slippery slope, and you can quickly find yourself never taking time to improve your business, and never taking time for yourself and your family. Changing your business in any way or taking on new initiatives may seem impossible because your time seems already maxed out. It's a daunting feeling to think about taking on anything more. When you become more productive and organized with your time, you gain your time back. You add hours to each day.

> **CASE IN POINT:** *I've read a lot of tactics for time management and tried to implement them in my business. Sometimes I'm good at them. I might set my alarm for an hour earlier than usual so I can knock out a blog post I've been meaning to write. I'll get up and do it. Other mornings I wake up with the same goal, but I make the mistake of glancing at my email. I get distracted by a message that pushes me over to Facebook where I spend even more time looking at pictures or following links to interesting things. Before I know it, the hour is up, and I don't have another hour to devote to writing that blog post. I blew it.*

That's an example of how a lot of real estate agents operate throughout the day. They're reactionary and see little things they need to respond to. They might put in a few minutes of work on something they really need to get done, but then they get distracted. For me, I have a large amount of work I want to get done in a day, and I find that if I'm not planning my day, those goals are never realized. Yet I'm busy all day.

All advice on time management comes back to the same thing: have a list, prioritize it, and get it done. Schedule tasks, set deadlines, meet the deadlines. Stay up late if you have to. I get pissed off when I have to stay up late or wake up early to finish a task, because it means I wasn't organized enough during the day. That motivates me to be ultra-efficient.

A common analogy is to treat your day as though you're about to go on vacation. You know those days when you're just on fire, wrapping things up and meeting deadlines, because you have to. Wouldn't it be nice if you were that efficient all the time?

I've found, as a real estate agent with the earnings from my closings as the only source of income for my family—and with no guarantee when I'll receive my next paycheck—I can keep working and working and never stop. There's always something more I can do, something that will better my odds of getting a closing. It's a cycle that's easy to fall into when you need to have money coming in and you have no idea where it's going to come from. There is always something more or something else that you could work on for your business. It never ends.

I constantly see agents in a cycle where their pipeline is dry and there are no closings in their foreseeable future. So they start drilling down and doing the work to better the odds of generating some new business. Soon they fill up their pipeline— and that's great! But then they stop working on those tasks and focus instead on servicing that pipeline. It takes a lot of time, but they've got some money coming in. Great! But then the pipeline starts to dry up again. And the cycle of panic continues. Highs to lows, all the time.

So how do you stop the cycle of never-ending work? And how do you, at the same time, keep the pipeline full?

➤ Make sure your to-do list has a sense of purpose. It's not just reacting to the things you need to get done that day; it's also including things that will help your business move forward and keep your pipeline full.

➤ Structure your day to always fit in the tasks you need to do in order to have a more consistent income. Think about what's going to help keep potential new closings coming in. This could be interacting with past clients and contacts who often refer you business, or building new relationships with target individuals or audiences who could turn into clients. Prioritize those tasks and strategies at the top of your to-do list each day. They're the fuel for your business. For instance, I work on projects that improve my business or the service I provide to customers early in the morning before my phone starts ringing. I then transition to working on my active clients, prospects, and brokerage duties during the day because I found it was too difficult to work on projects during the day. You may find evenings work well for you instead of morning. Having a quiet time to crank out your work is priceless.

➤ Focus on being organized instead of being reactionary. This is easier said than done for a real estate agent. I wrote earlier about knowing when to sprint, and sometimes you have to sprint and ignore your to-do list. However, this should be the exception, not the rule.

➤ If your to-do list for the day is realistic and not too overly optimistic, you can often complete your to-do list first thing in the morning, which allows you more reactionary time throughout your day. So attack your to-do list at the start of each morning. Your email inbox can wait. If you must check emails in the morning, be ruthless and skim them quickly for anything that is *very* time sensitive. Ninety-nine percent of the items can wait a few hours.

CASE IN POINT: *There is no perfect way to create your to-do list. I change up and test new formats occasionally. What typically works best for me is a handwritten to-do list. Plus I use Google Calendar for scheduling my appointments and meetings. When I write my list, I often use a letter-sized notebook, but I'll draw two vertical and two horizontal lines so that I can organize and prioritize the tasks or projects I want to complete. This is important for me because when I create a list of items, I usually come up with many more items than I can complete that day or even that week. Therefore I put down all the items I want to complete that month on the far right of the page, the most urgent on the far left at the top. I then move items around like checkers so that I can prioritize my schedule for the day. I like using a notebook, because I can reference items from the previous day or week to transfer to the new page.*

It feels good to accomplish all the tasks on your to-do list. It allows you to stop, to go have a life. I know when I am more productive, I feel better about spending time having fun because I feel good about what I accomplished that day. When I don't complete or even do a to-do list for the day, I often feel the opposite. I get more stressed out because I feel like there was more I could have done or there was something I forgot to do. I often end up working long days bouncing from one thing to the next. Therefore, I highly recommend you make time daily to work on productivity.

If you implement these simple strategies, the difference in your income will be staggering. There are a lot of people in this industry who work and work, but their income plateaus or even shrinks. If they'd get organized and productive—not just busy—and focus on the tasks that move their business forward, they would see that hockey-stick-shaped inflection income and projection of growth. It won't happen overnight. This is a long-term, disciplined action that needs to be implemented into a business—but it will have profound effects on your career.

How Much Is Your Time Worth?

Perry Marshall's book *80/20 Sales and Marketing* introduced me to another tool that can be helpful. In one chapter, Marshall breaks down different activities into $10-per-hour tasks, $100-per-hour tasks, $1,000- and even $10,000-per-hour tasks.

Examples of $10-per-hour tasks are cold calling, stuffing envelopes, driving around un-approved buyers, doing traditional open houses, doing traditional social media, running errands, installing real estate signs, chasing cold leads, answering frivolous emails—basically, the tasks real estate agents spend most of their day doing.

Examples of $100-per-hour activities (which will vary from person to person, based on the job you're doing) include solving problems for existing clients, basic customer follow-up, doing social media strategically (rather than haphazardly), monitoring and managing your marketing efforts (rather than just throwing stuff up on a wall and hoping it sticks), prioritizing and planning your day, and delegating $10-per-hour tasks to others. (The last two are potentially $1,000-per-hour activities.)

Examples of $1,000-per-hour activities include delegating $100-per-hour tasks, writing and testing marketing and sales copy (not just implementing marketing you got from someone else but creating your own, testing it, and making it better), building and cultivating sales funnels (platforms that continually make you money or bring in new business), researching new strategies (this type of learning helps you discover the best $10,000-per-hour activities), and implementing the best of the best ideas.

So what activities could possibly be worth $10,000 per hour? Everyone does these activities, from admins to CEOs, even if it's only for a few minutes a day. Maybe you took a phone call from a difficult client and put out a fire, and that kept your deal together. That is an extremely high dollar-per-hour activity.

Other examples of $10,000-per-hour activities include:

SOLVING PROBLEMS THAT OTHERS HAVE FAILED TO SOLVE. If you have that ability—that gift—then focus on solving problems that others have failed to solve, and your income will go up significantly. Succeeding at this will have huge implications for your career.

SCALING YOUR $1,000-PER-HOUR ACTIVITIES. In business, to scale means to multiply. If you figure out a way to accomplish a high-dollar activity, and then you're able to scale it out so that you're able to impact more people, that's a $10,000-per-hour activity.

ESTABLISHING A BUSINESS CULTURE. You wouldn't think so, but if you focus energy on establishing a "business religion," a culture, around an idea or concept, you're building a foundation that will pay dividends for many years into the future. It can create a movement, not just a couple of closings. I'm talking about a shift in long-term value and perception. Any business that has been wildly successful—Apple, for example—first established a business culture that drives people to buy all of their products. Shoppers wait in line outside stores in the cold just to be the first to get their new product.

NEGOTIATING MAJOR DEALS. Major deals have huge implications. When you negotiate for your real estate team or office to land a whole new subdivision that they can then go out and market, that's a $10,000-per-hour activity (at least!).

The 80/20 Principle at Work

I recommend that you look critically at your own business and how you spend your day. Try to identify the $10-per-hour activities in your day. Identify what you believe you should be doing more of. Are they $100-, $1,000-, or $10,000-per-hour activities? Map those out.

When you plan your day, use the 80/20 principle. Try to identify what activities generate the majority of your income and make note of what items are distracting you from doing those activities. Prioritize the items you mapped out on your list. Ask yourself, "If I had to accomplish one or two of these items today, what could I do?" And then do those first. Get up early if you need to. Get the important tasks out of the way. If you decide they're that vital, you'll find a way to do them.

Also, when you're looking at your own business, decide what type of client brings you the most income and satisfaction. It's not always about money. Whom do you enjoy working with most?

Which clients are the most difficult and cause you the most stress and pain? I know you've got them. Is there a way to eliminate dealing with them? Try to identify what areas and what type of clients and tasks cause you the most annoyance and unhappiness. See if you can eliminate them by focusing on other tasks or delegating those tasks that cause you stress.

Use the 80/20 principle to redesign your day—and even your career. As you look forward and visualize the type of business you want to build, how you want to spend your day, and whom you want to work with, focus on those goals to redesign your business. Even if it takes a long time to implement, it's something that you constantly want to reevaluate. Continually reevaluate not just your day and how you spend your time but your strategic plan, broken down into goals that will move you from point A to point B.

CHAPTER 13

Don't Be a Commodity. Be Relevant.

As an agent, are you just there to open doors and put homes in the MLS? Is that what everyone thinks you do? What do you offer today's savvy buyer who watches HGTV and knows how to stage a home and get professional photography? What do you offer buyers who know how to do their own market research and gauge the value of their property? What do you bring to the table? How do you stand out among your peers? What are you doing that's unique? What advantage does someone gain by hiring you over other competent agents?

I don't care how you answer those questions—what matters is that the consumer knows your answers. If you're not communicating your value to your potential prospects, then in their eyes you're just there to open doors and put homes in the MLS. By failing to communicate your value, you're reducing yourself to a mere *commodity,* which makes you replaceable and expensive.

A commodity is a mass-produced, unspecialized product that's bought, sold, or traded on a large scale. Oil, coffee, gold, corn, and grain are examples of commodities. Webster's dictionary further defines a commodity as "a good or service whose wide availability typically leads to smaller profit margins and diminishes the importance of factors (such as brand name) other than price." Meaning that the value you or your company brings to a client is viewed no differently than hundreds of other options your clients have to choose from. So real estate agents who don't bring anything special, unique, or valuable to the consumer run the risk of being viewed as replaceable, unimportant, or a commodity—that is, they hold little to no individual value.

Stay Relevant

Every day, technology moves one step closer to making the job you do seem easy, and to making you seem nearly irrelevant to homebuyers and sellers. There will be a day when a seller can click a button and get a professional photographer to her house, access comps on properties that are selling in her area, get a home stager to drop by, etc. Suddenly, all the tasks that were once complicated will be easily provided. Buyers might be able to wear specialized glasses and literally walk through active listings without being there physically. Technological advances are coming along fast.

So how do you stay relevant? First, make sure you are constantly learning and gaining knowledge that can significantly help your clients. You can achieve this in a number of ways by considering the following questions:

DO YOU STUDY LOCAL HOUSING MARKET STATISTICS? A lot of agents ignore these statistics, even though they're readily available, and agents have no excuse for not knowing these numbers better than their clients do. Study your local housing statistics and share your knowledge with your clients.

IF YOU FOCUS ON AN AREA OF TOWN, HOW WELL DO YOU REALLY KNOW THAT MARKET? WHAT SOLD THIS MONTH AND FOR HOW MUCH? The more in-depth knowledge you can share when you're meeting with a client or a contact face-to-face, the more valuable you become.

IF THE HOMES YOU LIST OFTEN NEED WORK BEFORE THEY SELL, DO YOU KNOW WHERE TO REFER YOUR SELLERS? Do you have a list of contractors you recommend? Have they been vetted? Do they offer good pricing? Can you call in a favor with them? That knowledge and those connections can be of high value to prospective clients. If they know you have that knowledge, they will think of you as a connector, and that carries a lot of value.

WHEN SHOWING BUYERS PROPERTIES, IF YOU CAN'T FIND WHAT THEY'RE LOOKING FOR, CAN IT BE BUILT? WHO DO YOU RECOMMEND AND WHY? Let's say you're looking for six months or more for a client's perfect property, and you're just not finding it. Is it possible that they could buy a lot and build it? Do you know which builders to recommend? This kind of industry information makes a huge impact with your clients.

ARE YOU FINDING INFORMATION FOR THE BUYER THAT THEY CAN'T FIND ON THEIR OWN? MLS information is everywhere now, and there are all kinds of websites where people can tap into resources and get information. What are you able to provide that consumers can't find on their own? Are they finding the properties and doing all the work? If so, you need to find things that you can do for them in addition to that. Otherwise, you're just there to open doors for them—you're a commodity.

How Technology Makes You Seem Irrelevant

To avoid being a commodity, you have to be something better than just "more convenient" to customers. Technology is already solving that problem. Sure, hiring you might save a customer the headache of dealing with a for-sale-by-owner situation, but you need to provide more value than that. Technology is just going to make that process easier and easier for the consumer.

Think about CPAs. Online services and software like TurboTax have made it easy for people to do their own taxes. It might be hundreds of dollars cheaper than having their taxes done by a CPA—and it's convenient. TurboTax is already loaded with information and double-checks to help consumers avoid making the wrong choices, so CPAs really need to be on their A-game and prove they have the in-depth knowledge to be even better than the software and save the consumer even more money.

Don't be lazy. All real estate agents know that technology can't replace the value they bring to a real estate transaction, but consumers are losing sight of this with all the new technologies available to them. Just like tax accountants, technology is forcing real estate agents to change how they illustrate their value to their client.

Get Your Message out There

Once you ensure that your business is different, that it somehow rises above what competitors offer and is sought out by consumers, then the next step to avoid becoming a commodity is to create communication channels to get your message out. Here are some examples of effective tools I've seen agents use as distribution channels to communicate their unique service or message:

PERSONAL NOTE CARDS - Agents send these to people in their sphere with personalized, thoughtful messages. They're not asking anything or soliciting business, just showing that they care about the people they know and with whom they communicate. (More about this in chapter 17.)

E-NEWSLETTERS - Agents email newsletters to their existing contacts list and leads from their marketing every week or biweekly. This can be an effective communication tool *but only if agents take the time to add new and meaningful content.* If the newsletter is generic and never personal, it is just more white noise to your contacts. So make an effort to bring something original and authentic to each newsletter. Examples of what have worked well for other agents are videos or articles with the agent's personal take on what's happening in the marketplace, or information about something in their community from the agent's point of view. It doesn't need to be—nor should it be—just about real estate. Share your stories, your community's stories, life lessons, opinions, and observations. This is what people enjoy reading the most.

PRINT NEWSLETTERS - Print is more effective than email because it gets read more often (instead of being instantly deleted or put in a spam folder). It's true that doing a monthly print newsletter to the people who know, like, and trust you will take more time and cost more money than email newsletters. But when done effectively, a print newsletter can do amazing things for your business. I believe a print newsletter is still one of the most powerful tools agents can use to keep and grow a fan base of loyal customers who send them referrals. I've seen agents do an amazing amount of business when their one marketing cost each month was their monthly newsletter.

As with e-newsletters, print newsletters should not be filled with generic content or clippings found online. They need to be filled with original content about you and things you care about, your opinions, and your take on business. If readers aren't learning about you and your core character, your family, your motivations and hobbies, your business religion and philosophy, then it's just a waste of money. Use them wisely, and newsletters can be awesome for your business. (More about this in chapter 19.)

PODCASTS AND YOUTUBE CHANNELS - These are extraordinarily popular resources for all kinds of information. Agents might use either of these to do a weekly audio or video show of homes that have sold in a neighborhood and new listings that have just hit the market, or to offer a testimonial of a great restaurant they discovered in that neighborhood. Even if they are just a few minutes long, they can show the agent is knowledgeable about an area and knows what's going on there. It establishes him as an authority even if people never watch or listen to the broadcast. I discuss in greater detail how to reach your audience with videos and podcasts in chapter 22.

TARGETED FACEBOOK PAGES AND OTHER SOCIAL MEDIA STRATEGIES - A generic approach often is not effective because you can get lost in a sea of competition and white noise from others; plus, it's expensive to market to everybody. But when an agent targets a specific audience or area of town using social media tools, they can reduce marketing dollars spent and easily become the big fish in a small pond. People who love modern contemporary homes might enjoy your Pinterest page focused exclusively on that style. You might build a Facebook page around a specific area of town and fill it with news, events, and home listings in that neighborhood. Instagram has become hugely popular (and was acquired by Facebook). Snapchat seems to be on the phone of everyone under the age of thirty. Nextdoor is a neighborhood app that helps you connect with people in your neighborhood. Periscope is another platform on which you could do daily or weekly live broadcasts about a topic of interest to your targeted demographic. If you are currently using any of these social media platforms for fun, come up with a list of ten ways (see chapter 16) you could leverage or build an audience for your real estate business using that platform. (See chapter 18 for more social media strategies.)

GOOGLE AND FACEBOOK ADS - If agents have a unique message, they can pay to drive people to their message with Google and Facebook ads. Facebook and Google provide tools to help you narrow your ad to the demographics and locations you want to target. You could be wasting money if you're not driving people to an impactful message that gets them to take action, so make sure your message is authentic, clear, and truly solves a problem for them, or at least targets a specific audience so that you don't go broke in the process.

PHILANTHROPIC INITIATIVES - Business owners are often involved in local charities, homeless shelters, soup kitchens, and organizations like Habitat for Humanity. An agent who organizes and spearheads philanthropic activities and charity events gets recognized as someone who is more than an agent—she's someone who does good work in her community. That's one way to create raging fans. It's not always about being the smartest real estate agent; it's often about being the most impactful one.

To get inspired, look around your community or outside your community for people who are making a difference far beyond what their day job is. I know agents who help organize charities helping kids in low-income communities, raise awareness and donations for specific illnesses, support wounded veterans, support local schools and teachers, and the list goes on and on. Many of the agents who started these focused philanthropic initiatives had no idea their efforts would impact their business, but they soon found that their passion for helping those in need gave them a new sense of purpose and drive, while unexpectedly exploding their network of people who knew them, liked them, and respected them. People want to do business with those who are making a positive impact in their community, and they often go out of their way to refer others. As Winston Churchill once famously said, "We make a living by what we get. We make a life by what we give."

LEVERAGE SOMEONE ELSE'S DISTRIBUTION CHANNEL AND SPHERE - This is an underutilized opportunity. Suppose an agent knows a CPA who has a client list she'd like to work with. Maybe there's something the agent can do to bring the CPA more business. The two might even share each other's articles in their own newsletters. There are many ways to leverage each other's distribution channels. The first step is to identify who has a database with an audience you'd like to tap into and then find a way to add value to the owner of that list. This is a great marketing strategy that will quickly expand your network and sphere but is seldom used by real estate agents.

LEVERAGE SOMEONE ELSE'S CELEBRITY STATUS - Agents who know a local celebrity, professional athlete, politician, artist, or musician can leverage that relationship. People are deeply impacted by celebrity. It gets them to pay attention to the message, so aligning yourself somehow with a celebrity contact can create great momentum in your business (especially if you tie it together with some of the other ideas in this chapter, such as a philanthropic initiative). Look for ways you could help the celebrity. This could be simply helping them get in front of a great cause or giving them a venue to do something fun and cool for their fans.

DIRECT MAIL PIECES - These can be effective because they're not used as much as they used to be. Whether it's a postcard or an entire magazine, a direct mail piece needs to include unique messaging in order to have any impact. Also, it's much better to hit a small list of people multiple times rather than doing one big mailing. For example, if you have a new listing and you typically send out a "just listed" postcard—rather than mailing the postcard once to 500 homes, send 100 postcards five different times to the same list of people. After the "just listed" postcard, you could send one about your unique approach to selling homes and mention another house you recently listed nearby. Follow that by offering a free twenty-page analysis of their home's current value. The fourth postcard could be to alert them that your marketing worked, as you now have an offer on your recent listing. Wrap it up with a testimonial from your current sellers on their experience working with you.

What's Your Message?

Most agents don't put the time or effort into any of these strategies. The ones who do might still fall prey to the biggest mistake

I see agents make with their distribution channels—they don't yet have a unique message to deliver. If you're putting out generic ads that say, "Call Sam for all things real estate" or "Call Sarah: serving buyers, sellers, and investors," that's not unique. If you haven't defined your business culture or business religion, you're in danger of spending a lot of time and money on something that's going to have really poor results.

If you need ideas on how to differentiate your business and make it stand out, I recommend the book *Defeat Mega Agents* by Ryan Fletcher. Fletcher spells out ways to differentiate your business with fourteen principles that will get your ideas flowing. Ryan coined the phrase, "Never speak to anyone until they know you are a someone." That's important because there are hundreds, maybe thousands, of real estate agents in your area, and you have to define what makes you stand out before you can be more than just white noise. What can you bring to the public's attention to heighten their respect for the work you do?

Real estate agents are in a negative-reputation industry. A lot of people have had bad experiences with agents, so if they see you as just a real estate agent and nothing more, you're going to blow a lot of time and money on marketing. Not only that, but you will run the risk of making those in your sphere avoid you. The last thing they want is you pestering them about real estate and referrals if they don't respect what you do. I can't stress this enough—the first thing you need to do is heighten their respect for the work you do. The suggestions in this chapter are just some of many different ways you can accomplish this goal. We all have different passions, strengths, ideas, and ambitions, so put some serious thought into identifying your message.

Agents who continue to ignore the threat of falling into commodity status will soon find themselves wondering why their referral sources are drying up. They might blame other agents, their broker, or entities like Zillow, rather than looking within their own business to solve the true problem.

The steps I recommend above and in the next section of the book can be difficult. They take discipline—to learn your market at a higher level, to write and send out note cards, and to produce newsletters with authentic content. It's very hard initially. But unless you've got some kind of gravy train relationship, like a builder who loves you and keeps sending you work, you need to find unique ways to create impact upon your clients. You want them to respect and appreciate you at a much higher level than they would a typical real estate agent. It's not easy, but it's possible for anyone to do.

This next section, part IV, has more how-to guides and breaks down more specific strategies agents can follow to develop a unique and impactful business.

Declassified: The Tools You Need That Nobody Wants to Share

This next section gets a bit more into the how-to: a reference guide to the indispensable skills needed by real estate agents but skills not readily taught by brokers, trainers, coaches, or schools. Outside of this book, trainings related to these topics are usually tied to sales pitches wanting you to buy new software, how-to guides, or expensive coaching programs. You won't find that here. This is just straight-up advice that I've seen work time and time again. If you are looking for a silver bullet that will solve your problems and make you rich, you won't find it in this book. The best ideas and advice for agents typically involve a lot of work and self-discipline. There is no magic button, but it doesn't mean the steps you need to take are difficult and unpleasant; you might find that you enjoy them immensely.

When reading this section, I hope you'll get excited about implementing something in your business—just watch out for implementing too many ideas at once. I've made that mistake many times. It can slow everything down. Just start mastering the one or two core ideas you like best. Do them well, find a way to be consistent (or delegate them), and then move on to further implementation.

CHAPTER 14

The Low Guru Diet:
Turning Down the Volume

Chapter 4 discussed blocking out shiny pennies. This chapter digs deeper on the issue of the overabundance of bad advice being pushed onto agents every day and what to do about it.

Every day when I open my mailbox, email inbox, and voicemail, I find offers from gurus, trainers, and coaches. *Push your business to a whole new level! Break through your sales plateau! Build better teams! Live the life you always wanted!* There's always someone offering agents some "must have" solution for their business. They all make promises using stats and figures to spin a story into a convincing sales pitch. Look at these figures in a recent *Wall Street Journal* article:

> Keller Williams MAPS Coaching, a division of Austin-based Keller Williams Realty International, which has 107,000 agents, says it currently has 1,605 agents in one-on-one coaching, more than three times the number it had in 2010. *Agents who use coaching earn 315% more gross commission income than Keller Williams agents who don't,* says Dianna Kokoszka, chief executive of the coaching division. *[Emphasis added]*

Coaching companies use stats like these to convince agents they can't afford *not* to get a coach. They make it sound like an agent will be left in the dust, behind more successful agents, if they don't find the means right away to buy into a coaching program. But they're skewing the data. What they *don't* tell you is that the majority of people who buy coaching are established agents who already have a solid book of business; therefore, their gross commissions are already going to be higher than those of agents who are just starting out. These established agents are already earning more *before* they hire a coach, not just *because* they hired a coach. In this case, it's not hard to see how a brokerage would leverage these biased statistics to recruit more agents into their internal coaching program.

Here's the reality: Agents are being bombarded by these offers from all directions—from coaches, gurus, and even their own brokerages—and the ones who feel desperate, the ones who are convinced they won't succeed unless they pay a coach, are signing up in droves. The problem is that most of them can't afford it. They don't have any money, but they sign up anyway. Some of these coaches and gurus now offer "student loan packages," pushing agents who are already in trouble deeper into debt. Ultimately, it's a scam—if they can't close you one way, they'll close you another. Agents sign up, hoping and praying that coaching will help turn their business around, but sometimes they get pushed out of the business because they go broke.

Many of these coaching programs hold agents accountable to making a certain number of cold calls and trying sales tactics they wouldn't normally try. A lot of times it's nothing more than training them to be that asshole salesperson who bugs everyone he knows, on top of cold calling and knocking on doors.

I'll admit, you *can* make money by being pushy and aggressive. You can easily find thousands of agents who sell high volumes of real estate and brag that they're aggressive because that's what works for them. They justify their techniques by saying that they're helping people discover what they really want by pushing them until they say yes.

These agents are often the ones who build big teams, and they push the agents on their teams into that same behavior. They hire coaches who push this mentality (and these sales tactics) further down the ranks. They might become coaches themselves.

I don't mean to pick on agents who run their business this way. Personally, I feel for them, because I know many of them were pushed into this style of real estate by their mentors and coaches. They saw other aggressive agents earning great incomes for their families, and they forced themselves to duplicate those efforts, even when it went against their core character.

That's not the kind of business I want to have. I've proven—and I've seen hundreds of other agents prove it too—that you can accomplish great things in real estate without being a pushy salesperson. I just don't consider that "success"—nor does the public. Agents who practice real estate with aggressive tactics bring a black mark to our profession and don't realize it. Agents who cold call an expired listing eight times until a seller caves to the pressure don't think about the negative image that creates for all Realtors®. Agents who use aggressive sales tactics justify their methods by saying they're acting in the client's best interest and they will tell you that is simply "what works". If they truly cared about and respected their clients, they wouldn't treat them like that because they wouldn't want somebody else blowing up their phone like they do to others. They're so focused on winning or closing prospects that they don't care about how many people they piss off to find their next client. This is a huge reason why the reputation of real estate agents is suffering.

Many of the top agents in our industry thrive on doing whatever is necessary to make more money. They don't care how they go about doing that so long as it's legal. It becomes easier to justify their behavior when they're surrounded by others doing the same things. It's mob mentality. I will likely be criticized by this mob for calling them out. They will likely attack me and this book, because once you convince yourself the tactics you are using to win more clients are a justifiable and even respectable way to do business, you can't help but to defend your position. I get it. I sympathize with these agents, even when they come after me, because I've lived what they are living, I know what they are feeling. Agents get caught up using tactics that go against their core character because they see other agents making money using them. Desperate people do desperate things, and they justify in their minds at the time that it was the right thing to do. At some point, their internal voice that is questioning the methods they're using is silenced or forgotten.

The gurus and coaches know that agents are susceptible to this, that they're desperate and wanting to make something more of their real estate business. So the gurus will never go away—agents are easy targets. The coaches know an agent's job is tough, with a few high moments and a ton of lows. They know agents are all working hard so that one day they won't have to fight and struggle so much, and they'll sign up for anything that promises to give them some certainty. That's why agents get bombarded with offers.

How Gurus and Coaches Leverage Information

Information marketing is big business. Coaching is big business. The gurus know that if they create an informational product, it can be repackaged and resold and twisted and tweaked and then up-sold into coaching. They create entire programs and methods around that one informational product. It's profitable.

> **CASE IN POINT:** *On a strictly business level, it's impressive to see how these entrepreneurs are making money in our industry. I don't have a problem with coaches making money to teach agents how to make more money in real estate, but when their tactics create an army of cold callers, they are not doing our industry any favors.*

There are lots of ways to leverage content through information marketing. I could turn this book you're reading right now into an eight-week boot camp, a monthly hacking real estate coaching program, biannual seminars that up-sell you to additional programs, a getting-started kit to accompany the book, done-for-you implementation software, webinars that sell special reports from case studies—you get the idea. This is why you see your inbox full of what seems like helpful advice, because they give you valuable information in hopes it gets you hooked on signing up for their product or service.

I'm not saying that some of these products or offerings aren't valuable resources for agents, but sometimes agents are so gullible that they sign up for the wrong offers. Or they sign up for coaching programs before they can afford to and before they've learned many other alternatives that I've outlined in this book.

The Guru Trap – Strength in Numbers

The tipping point for many agents who are being lured into a coaching program is when they see how many other agents are doing the same thing. The gurus know that when agents see how many other agents are signing up or using their product or service, it removes the fear for agents. Agents think, *If so many others are doing it, then it's got to be effective or a good program.*

So my warning is this: Just because there is a large number of other agents following a system or coaching program, that doesn't mean it's a good idea for you. If there are other agents in your office involved with it, you can ask them about it—but be careful, as they may be already drinking the Kool-Aid of the guru, or they may be getting a financial incentive to get other people to sign up.

Before you jump into paid programs and coaching, do your homework. Often you can search online for the coach or guru to find some free products and videos of them, or audio courses and other items at a discount. If you do find something and you like the advice she is giving, then just start implementing the parts that resonate with you. If you get stuck on something that seems worthwhile, then consider reaching out to the coach. Don't skip ahead without first mastering the basics. If you pay for coaching before you've mastered the basics, the coach will spend all her time showing you the basics instead of teaching you high-dollar activities. You don't want to hire an expensive coach to teach you to write note cards. You can learn the basics from your broker, other agents, and books.

Before You Hire a Coach or Guru

SEEK OUT THEIR PUBLISHED INFORMATION. Many gurus have written books. Books are hard to write and require a lot of content to produce. You'll end up learning more from a $15 book than you will from attending an expensive conference. Coaches also publish articles, write blogs, and record podcasts and YouTube videos to gain recognition.

Make sure you absorb their free content before you jump into some monthly coaching program. Pay attention, digest it, and implement it.

DO YOUR RESEARCH. This isn't overanalyzing to keep you from pulling the trigger on buying a new program or getting a new coach. It's just protecting yourself. If you're making $100,000, $200,000, $300,000 or more a year in real estate, maybe you can afford to make impulsive purchases. If that's the case, take the time to absorb what you're paying to learn. Some people buy these programs, and then they get a ton of information that overwhelms them, so they don't study it and therefore don't make positive changes in their business. They just hope that their business will turn around. So invest the time into researching and learning what you can, and if you still want more, then consider investing in a program or coaching.

Is Having a Coach or Mentor Really Necessary?

This is a tricky question. First off let's define the difference between a coach and a mentor, or at least how I define them. In the most simplistic form, a coach is paid help and a mentor is free help. A lot of successful agents will tell you they wouldn't be where they are today without the help of their coach or mentor.

Some of the best help I got for my business has been free. Sometimes it was another business owner with whom I'd have drinks and swap stories. Some of the best mentors I've had, I've never met. I've never had a conversation with them. Yet they're my mentors because I read their books, watched their YouTube videos, and listened to their podcasts. I studied them. I learned from them, and they inspired me. They got me to work harder and smarter and more productively.

Many agents will say that having a coach made a huge impact on their business. I've seen that story be true most often with agents who *already* had a high level of success in real estate. They had already built a strong business and then hired a coach to help scale their business or push them to a new level.

More often you hear the opposite story of an agent who was seduced into a coaching program he could barely afford. Or he was encouraged by his brokerage or fellow agents at his office to pay for an in-house program because "all the top agents do it," not disclosing they earned a financial bonus if he signed up.

In the last decade, I've seen the vast majority of agents go broke using a coach, while many others found the tactics taught by coaches to be soul-crushing and ended up miserable even if they were making more money from it. When I've spoken to agents who were happy with their coach, nine out of ten would say the number-one reason they valued their coach was because "they held them accountable."

Accountability. That is the number-one reason many agents pay over $1,000 a month for a coach. Does that mean they can't find other ways—even free ways—to hold themselves accountable?

Here are some alternative (free) ways to hold yourself accountable:

➤ Set goals and write down the dates you want each step completed.

➤ Tell other agents in your office what goals you've set and ask them to hold you accountable to your timeline. Ask them to check in on you and ask you for progress reports.

➤ Ask your broker to check in with you on a weekly or monthly basis on your goals. Any broker or office manager should be happy to help you hold yourself accountable to your goals.

➤ Tell your spouse and family members. Ask them to support you and hold you accountable.

➤ Announce your goals in a social group, on Facebook, or at an office meeting. Tell them when you expect to complete each goal and offer to buy them lunch if you don't meet your timeline. Peer pressure is a powerful thing.

Be Your Own Guru

Have you ever noticed that it's easy to give good advice to others, but somehow with your own life or business, you often don't take your own advice? This comes from being too distracted with life and running a business that we don't see or address the problem; or from not recognizing that we have a lot more answers for our business than we give ourselves credit for.

A good friend of mine shared with me a great way to solve this problem. She has a standing appointment every day at 11 A.M. She pretends she is meeting with an experienced professional (with much more confidence and experience than she has), who values the same things she does, and she has that professional examine specific areas of her business. For example, she will look over her company website with a critical eye like a paid consultant might. She pretends she is that consultant and looks for ways to make the website better, making notes on what a paid consultant would have no problem pointing out as "not working." She told me that, surprisingly, she gets a clear answer or solution every day. It makes her honest about what she knows deep down that she needs to do better. She then implements the changes, which means she is improving her company every day.

The point is you don't always have to pay someone to tell you what you already know, but you do need to find a way to consistently tap into your own knowing, to trust your own advice and make time to implement it.

The noise of the gurus, trainers, coaches, and experts will become significantly quieter by implementing your own advice first. Assess and critique your own business, write down your ideas, set deadlines for implementing your own advice, then get to it. Hold yourself accountable by telling your coworkers, friends, and family your goals and timeline as mentioned above. If you do that, the noise from the gurus is going to get really quiet, because you'll be too busy implementing your own plans and changing your business.

Pretty soon, others might come and ask you to coach or help them. It happens. The point is, if you consistently do your own homework and implement the best of what you learn, in a way you'll become your own guru.

CHAPTER 15

It's Not a Numbers Game

Pros focus on relationships. Amateurs focus on sales.

—*Ryan Fletcher, author of* Defeat Mega-Agents

I've been told repeatedly by teachers, gurus, and respected agents that real estate is a numbers game. In other words, it's a race for leads. And the more leads, the better your odds, because only a small percentage of leads (1 percent is a figure often given) actually make it to closing. "If you upset people on the other end of the line," these experts say, "just brush it off and keep making calls. Behind every no is a yes. Keep pushing."

These experts preach the numbers game when they coach agents to repeatedly contact people in their sphere for business or referrals. In some cases, their friends and family give in—to stop the agent from bugging them. Some of the most popular books for real estate agents preach that you need X number of contacts to sustain X level of business. For example, they say you need a database of contacts in the thousands to become a top producer. However, I've seen agents make a quarter of a million dollars a year with a list of less than 100 contacts with whom they regularly communicate in a non-pushy way.

I understand you have bills to pay and you need to put food on the table. You're determined to succeed because you're a hard worker. But answer this question: Is your goal to pester and annoy enough people until one of them caves in and uses you as an agent or sends you a referral so you'll leave them alone? Is that really how you want to be perceived by the people you're contacting?

Agents have adopted this aggressive behavior because they see that it works. Truthfully, there *is* money to be made in real estate by being aggressive and hammering those online leads, by chasing expired listings and for-sale-by-owners, by pushing your sphere to produce referrals for you. There are so many real estate agents in America that we are tripping over each other at every turn, and so are consumers. Which is why so many agents have adopted this aggressive style—so they can win the client before someone else does.

A Better Way

Agents focus too much on getting leads and not enough on building a community and helping others in ways that make people deeply grateful. If agents focus on the latter, leads come to them.

Before we dive into finding a better way to operate your business, let's first talk about the different types of leads:

REGISTRATION LEADS - These are leads who are forced to register on your website in order to see more information about the properties listed there. The training that comes with this strategy tells agents to call these leads within the first five minutes and read from a script. Yes, this works—I've seen agents eventually make up to ten closings a month when they get proficient at this strategy—but you basically becomes a call center representative. People will be frustrated already because they were forced to hand over their contact information in order to view your listings, so you'll need to handle these leads with care and really try to help them. Hopefully your website is set up to tell you what they were searching for so you can help them with the specific information they're seeking.

EXPIRED AND FSBO LEADS - Coaches and industry gurus tell new agents that their sphere is not very big, so they need to get listings by going after expired listings and for-sale-by-own-ers. Many agents spend hours each day chasing these leads. The problem is that they're competing against an army of other agents who are chasing the same leads. Even if they have a good message and a good offering, it gets lost in a field of white noise with so many other agents competing for that seller's attention.

If you enjoy making cold calls and knocking on doors, if you get used to rejection so it doesn't bother you as much, you *can* make money working these leads—but every market is different. Some markets have very few expired listings and FSBOs. A strategy that might work for some guru in a different state might not work in your market. Even so, agents pour their time into chasing these leads because they don't know what else to do. The gurus and coaches make them feel like they're lazy and unfit to be a real estate agent if they don't commit to making so many cold calls per day.

There are alternative ways to generate leads that are much better for your self-confidence and self-worth. You'll feel better about the business you're doing because you'll be providing a higher level of help to people. They're better for you—but they're difficult. It's not an easier path, but it's a better path. One example is:

PERMISSION-BASED LEADS - These are leads generated by your marketing, where you create an offer of some type and a client reaches out to you to get it. These leads grant you permission to contact them, and they expect to hear from you; therefore, they're much warmer when you reach out to them. This type of marketing is well documented and explained by best-selling author/blogger Seth Godin. This is how he defines permission marketing:

Permission marketing is the privilege (not the right) of delivering anticipated, personal, and relevant messages to people who actu-ally want to get them. It recognizes the new power of the best consumers to ignore marketing. It realizes that treating people with respect is the best way to earn their attention.

Pay attention is a key phrase here, because permission marketers understand that when someone chooses to pay attention they are actually paying you with something precious. And there's no way they can get their attention back if they change their mind. Attention becomes an important asset, something to be valued, not wasted.

Real permission works like this: if you stop showing up, people complain, they ask where you went.

You can see how simple and logical this principle is, but few agents create marketing of this type because it takes more time and skill. I urge you to learn this skill. Following up with leads that contact you and assisting them with their questions is much more fun, and your percentage of leads who become clients is significantly higher than with the strategy of chasing leads that land on your website. It takes time to test different offers and see what works for you—but when you find the right one, you'll be a magnet that attracts new business instead of someone who constantly chases it.

When crafting an offer, think about your target audience. What information do they crave that they can't easily get on their own? How can you solve that problem for them? What do they fear, and how can you help eliminate that threat? Taking time to study your audience to answer these questions directly correlates to the success of your offer. Don't assume their wants, needs, and fears are the same as yours.

CASE IN POINT: *In 2008, after the market crashed, the real estate market got hit with a lot of foreclosures. However, our MLS did not initially disclose if a property was a foreclosure or not, and the agents listing the foreclosures were instructed not to disclose that it was a foreclosure in their MLS listing. Therefore, it was* *often difficult for agents to figure out which homes were foreclosures and even more difficult for consumers. However, I quickly learned that there were only a handful of agents doing foreclosures in our market at the time, and so I would just monitor those agents' listings so I could publish those details to my clients. I didn't realize how popular this tactic was until my inbox was full of new prospects requesting to be on my email list. I was providing a service that virtually no one else was doing, and it was a service that consumers really wanted. This worked very well for me until they changed the MLS to force agents to disclose if a home was a foreclosure or short sale. Then every agent had this information and made my service no longer unique, so I changed my tactics to provide another service that was special and desired by consumers. The offer or service you provide doesn't need to be wildly complicated or elaborate, but it may need to be updated or changed as the marketplace changes and consumers' needs evolve.*

Crafting an offer or a message that gets people to respond is a skill that takes practice and testing. There are many books and resources about this topic that can help you. One of the first books I read that helped me gain this skill was *The Ultimate Sales Letter* by Dan S. Kennedy. He breaks down the strategies used to write sales copy that will get people to respond. Studying marketing will help you learn the psychology of how and why people respond.

Look at your marketplace. What challenges do sellers and buyers face? What things are they not discussing with you that are holding them back? What pain are they enduring by not taking action? What do they crave or desire that you can help them obtain? Are they concerned about not being able to afford their house payment anymore? Have they hired the wrong agent and worry that their home will never sell? Are they in a situation they think a real estate agent *can't* solve? Maybe you can solve it. Maybe you know the right people they can talk to in order to solve their problem. Maybe you've developed a service, unique to you, that can help them.

The greatest benefit to learning how to create offers and messages that lead people to take action is that you can generate permission-based leads at will, turning up or turning down the volume as you like. If you want more leads, you turn up the volume and get your offer out to more people or create a secondary offer. Once you see how this works, it's empowering. You're no longer lost in a sea of uncertainty about how you're going to attract new business.

A simplified version of this is when an agent offers "a free list of foreclosures," "a free list of fixer-upper homes," or "a free copy of my homebuyers' handbook." These were really popular in the early 2000s and were initially quite effective. Searching for accurate information on the Internet was like opening Pandora's box, so an agent who provided reliable information got quite a few leads. These days, technology makes information so prevalent and easy for everyone to access that these strategies are no longer as effective. What you need to do is look at your marketplace and determine what information is still hard for clients to get and then find a way to help them get it. Find ways to hyper-target the information they need in a form that is precisely what they're looking for. Instead of a general list of foreclosures, maybe provide a list of luxury foreclosures in a specific area of town or school district. The quality of leads and volume of responses might both go up, even though you've limited your offering to fewer people.

Research what other agents are doing and offer something of value that's different from what they're offering. Don't just copy what everyone else is doing; come up with your own unique messaging. Look outside of real estate for examples. When you're on Facebook, what ads or messages catch your attention? Why? How do they do it? Some of them pique your curiosity or simply entertain you. Whatever it is, pay attention to what makes you take action, click a link, or subscribe to something. Then use those techniques to make your own messaging work.

SIGN CALL LEADS - The benefit of having active listings is that you get leads or inquiries from buyers. They might call on your for-sale sign or come through an open house you're hosting. These leads can be quite good because they're actively shopping real estate, not just looking at pictures online. If you've done your research on not just your listing but other listings in the neighborhood, and if you know valuable information about the surrounding community and schools, then you stand a high chance of converting those leads into clients.

One of the few occasions for which I recommend you learn some sales scripting is when you're fielding sign calls or greeting people at an open house. So many agents miss out on these types of leads because they don't know what to say other than answering client questions. Practicing on other agents what questions to ask or how to start a conversation (if it doesn't come naturally for you) can be good training for you to build your confidence. Once the conversation is going, however, shut up and listen. The problem with scripting is that it's designed to lead people down a path we want them to go. But if they catch on that your questions and responses are scripted, they'll realize you're not listening to them, that you're just trying to sell them something. They'll want to get away from you. If, however, you listen and provide helpful information, they can see that you truly are trying to help them, not just selling them something. They'll recognize you as someone who has their best interest in mind, and they will want to work with you.

It might already be in your DNA to help people and put their interests first. That's great if you're wired that way. Now make sure you're comfortable conversing with people and letting them know you have their best interest at heart. It's often as simple as asking questions and listening. If you listen and respond knowledgeably, you'll find that people start opening up to you naturally. They are starved to talk to someone with real knowledge who can help them far beyond what they can find out on their own.

Before you end your conversation, think of a way you can help them beyond this initial meeting based on what they've told you. Maybe they've told you that they are trying to stay close to a family member or a school district. Let them know that you will research the information around their target area or the school district and get it to them by a specific day. Ask them the best way to get that information to them. You've shown them that you are about to go out of your way for them, so they are more inclined to provide their contact information to allow you to follow up with them. They've given you permission. This will not work all the time, but if you practice the skill of listening and asking the right questions, you'll find it easier to make more connections with people you come in contact with because you're focused on providing a lot of value to them— more than others are giving them.

REFERRAL LEADS - These will always be the best kind of leads, because in reality they're not leads and they're not prospects— they are ready-to-go clients. Someone else they trust has already convinced them that you're the right person to hire. Your job is to not screw it up.

If you study agents who have been in the business for quite some time, you may notice that the ones who have the most desirable business, who work when they choose to yet seem to always have new listings and clients in their pipeline, are often not the mega-agents who have a team and who work tirelessly each day to keep their machine running. Rather, they're often the solo agents who seem to get referrals handed to them every month from friends and past clients. These agents have created a culture where people are eager to give them referrals. This may have happened because the agent has a good personality, or it might be the result of a well-crafted plan, but it's what happens when agents go out of their way to help others.

Be competent, professional, and someone who will always put the clients' needs first. Once the people in your sphere understand and respect that, they'll be more likely to refer you. If you make the process of referring you fun and enjoyable, and they feel appreciated, they'll refer you even more often. This is common sense, yet a very small percentage of agents operate their business as though they understand the importance of referral leads and dedicate the appropriate amount of time and effort in this area.

The Choice Is Yours – It's Never Too Late to Reboot Your Career

What foundation do you want your business to run on? What type of lead source do you want to have? It seems obvious that most agents would choose to build their business off of referral leads, followed by sign calls and permission-based leads. Yet the majority of agents focus their prospecting time on cold leads from website registrations, expired listings, and FSBOs. That's the same stuff everyone else is doing, and it's shitty work that's not fun. Yes, you can make money chasing down cold leads, but there are so many other ways to make good money in real estate.

Referral leads, sign call leads, and permission-based leads aren't easy. You've got to put the time in and do it right to build up your business. But if you think about that from the beginning, or you're rebooting your career with those types of leads in mind, you will probably find it to be a more fulfilling path with greater long-term results.

I've seen agents who operate big teams disintegrate as soon as their lead flow machine stops because they were operating their real estate business like it was a numbers game.

You don't need a giant number of people in your sphere or hundreds of leads each month to build a solid and profitable real estate business. I know agents who make in excess of $350,000 a year by simply being hyper-focused on their sphere of 150 people and building a cult-like following through monthly newsletters and offering unique services to their clients. They don't have a giant team to pay earnings to, nor do they spend thousands on buying leads each month. So their net income is way higher than an agent who has a team chasing leads each month. Real estate is not a numbers game to an agent like that, and it doesn't need to be one for you either.

CHAPTER 16
Flex Your Idea Muscle

Do you feel stuck in your real estate career? Not sure how to move forward effectively? Are you becoming increasingly unhappy with the business you're in? Have you lost the passion you once had for your business?

If that sounds like you, it's likely that your "idea muscle" has atrophied or never quite developed. It's time to give it some daily exercise.

What is your idea muscle? It's a concept I first heard from author and podcaster James Altucher. At one point in his life, Altucher was feeling so low he was contemplating suicide. He even created lists of different ways to kill himself. The process of making those lists started him on a habit that he credits with not only saving his life but opening up an amazing world of constant opportunities.

The habit that saved his life was flexing his idea muscle every day. Those lists were "idea lists," and he began to write down at least ten ideas every day. His lists could be about anything: ten things to make for dinner, ten different ways to get to work, ten ideas to improve his office space, ten titles of books he would love to write someday, etc.

If you're a real estate agent, you can focus your own lists on real estate: ten ways to get a new listing, ten ways you can help buyers (that you haven't already tried), ten ways to attract relocation buyers, etc. You can make your lists a mix of personal and professional lists. The point is to make a list every day.

Altucher says that the first three ideas come easy and fast, the next couple are much tougher, and the last five will make your brain sweat. The trick is to not get too caught up on listing only good ideas, because 99 percent of them will not be great ideas, and that's okay. The goal is to work out your idea muscle.

Altucher shares a story about an advertising executive who asked everyone on his team to come up with one idea for an important client. He came back thirty minutes later and found that no one had come up with an idea. So he tried a new tactic: he told them he would come back later, and this time he wanted twenty ideas. Sure enough, this time they came up with all twenty. What happens, Altucher says, is that when we focus on finding that one perfect idea, we get stuck. But if we lower the barrier and give ourselves permission to produce bad ideas, we start the process of flexing our idea muscle.

Why Flex Your Idea Muscle?

With any diet and exercise plan, it takes weeks or months before you start to see the benefits of your hard work and diligence. The same goes for your idea muscle. Altucher says that you will need to flex your idea muscle every day for six months to become an "idea machine." Becoming an idea machine will change your life in amazing ways, and it will give you the confidence to find solutions to your problems, and the problems of others, at will. When confronted with obstacles or problems, your idea muscle will naturally kick in and instantly start producing possible solutions.

Imagine how you could help impact friends, clients, and loved ones when they come to you for advice or counsel. Think about how this talent could help salvage real estate deals and open doors to new opportunities. You could help builders find new ways to get more jobs, and help business owners find new ideas to spark more sales. If you share ideas with them and ask nothing in return, what are the chances they'll refer business to you? Chances are extremely high.

Don't forget, however, that most ideas are not great ideas. Great ideas are one in 100, or one in 1,000. You'll get stuck if you try to make all your ideas good. So have fun with the process, and let the bad ideas make you laugh. The point is to exercise that muscle every day. Over time you'll find that your ability to generate ideas is much higher than the ability of others. It will improve your confidence, and other people will notice your ability as well.

Lighting Your Heart on Fire

The added benefit of working out your idea muscle every day is that occasionally you'll come up with an amazing idea that lights your heart on fire with excitement. You'll know deep down that it's an amazing idea.

When that happens, make your next list of ten ideas be about that original idea: ten ways you could implement the idea, ten possible problems with the idea, or ten ways you could enlist help from others to implement the idea. In other words, you want to devote your next idea lists to explore that original idea and see if you still feel it's great. You'll know when you have a potential great idea because it will light a fire in you. It will fill you with the kind of excitement that makes you want to stay up all night working on it. You won't even feel tired because you'll be lit up with drive and anticipation. Note that if it doesn't light a fire in you, then even if it appears to be a good idea, it may not be worth pursuing. Move on.

From personal experience, I can tell you that it doesn't take six months to see results from flexing your idea muscle. The idea for this book came to me within the first couple of weeks of starting this daily ritual. I started by making a list of possible books I could write. The next day, I picked the book idea I was most excited about and made a list of ten possible chapters.

However, once I started, I didn't stop at ten chapters. I realized that there were so many topics and lessons that I could share in order to help real estate agents. This exercise made me realize that there was tremendous value in my experiences and the lessons I had learned. It's what lit my heart on fire and fueled me to wake up two hours earlier each day to work on chapters.

That one idea changed me. That is the power of ideas.

Now imagine what would happen if you gave an idea like that to someone else—if it changed them and lit their heart on fire with excitement. That would be quite the gift. I'm thankful to James Altucher for giving me the idea to do this exercise. It helped change my life. Now I'm sharing it with you—and if you start doing it today, it will change your life, too.

Strengthening your idea muscle may be the best twenty minutes you spend on your real estate business each day. You'll be learning a skill that few people possess or develop.

Don't tell me—and don't tell yourself—that you don't have time to do this. If you feel that way, make your first list on ten ways you waste time each day, or ten ways you could save twenty minutes in your day. Keep a notepad with you specifically for this task. Whether you choose to do it morning or night, don't go to bed until you've finished this task.

I recognize that adding a new daily task to your to-do list may seem overwhelming. From firsthand experience, I can assure you that this one is worth the effort. You'll soon find that you love doing it. It's almost like a game you get to play each day. You'll find yourself incorporating it into your daily life (waiting for takeout, you might write: ten ways this restaurant can improve its menu). Have kids? Why not get in the habit of playing this game. Instead of asking how school was and getting the same bland answer, you could ask them to name the ten best teachers in the school ... the ten meanest kids ... ten things they wish their teacher would teach in class. Ten things they could make for dinner. Ten movies they learned something from. Ten fun family outings that don't cost more than $20. Get them talking and get their brains working. If they struggle to do the game at first, try making a reward if they get to ten. If you somehow give them the gift of a strong idea muscle, I believe it will be a gift that keeps on giving in their lives.

The benefits of flexing your idea muscle as a daily ritual are life changing and will help ensure the success of your real estate business and any other ventures you decide to partake in. It's just that powerful.

CHAPTER 17

Little Cards – Big Power

What's the number-one strategy you can adopt today that's going to have the biggest long-term payoff for your business? You might be surprised because it's so damn easy and inexpensive.

We all get tempted by these different things we're told we need to do in our business—we need to buy the latest Zillow zip code, we need to get a new website, or we need to get the new customer-tracking software. We are not making enough prospecting calls, we are not doing enough for-sale-by-owner campaigns, and we are being bombarded all the time to do more. I have tried what seems like a million different strategies, but going back to basics really works best for most agents. What I am talking about is note cards.

An agent in my office writes ten note cards a week. That's his entire business model, essentially all of his marketing. It costs him maybe five bucks a week.

Every Monday it's on his to-do list to identify ten people to contact that week. Ten is not a very big number; it is totally attainable. This agent had some doubts about the strategy when he started doing it, because it takes some time for it to work. But when you send a personal handwritten note to someone who rarely receives one, they are immeasurably delighted or impressed.

I'm not telling you anything new. We've all heard this—we should write more personal notes. Why don't we do it? What is the problem? The agent in my office has been doing it for two years consistently, and now it's a habit. He's one of the top-selling agents in our office, and that's almost all the marketing he does to generate a healthy living from referrals.

He doesn't have a giant list of contacts. While he started this process, he was also farming his neighborhood, and he was trying some new website designs and online strategies. Fast-forward to today; he's gotten rid of most all that now because making the personal contact with ten people a week has far and away worked the best for him.

Ten a week. That's two a day. He can squeeze that in when-ever. He actually goes to a sports bar and drinks beer while he writes his note cards. He told me this task is kind of a fun and relaxing thing for him. It doesn't have to be a laborious task.

What should you write on these note cards? As I mentioned earlier, *please* don't say, "I am never too busy for your referrals." That is the worst thing to say. Not only are five other agents sending your contact that exact same slogan, but it comes across like you're begging. You don't have to beg for referrals.

A lot of people are intimidated by writing to people they know. They don't want to reach out to them and ask them for their business. It feels slimy. If it doesn't feel right, don't do it! Write something that you feel good about. Share a story about something that's happened in your life, with your family, or whatever. You can check in with them about an experience you shared together, and you can just say something funny about that memory. Ask them how their kids are doing in whatever sport they play. Make notes after you have a conversation with someone, like their kids' or spouse's names and what they are up to, what you have in common, or what they find interesting or fun. Once you have a few notes about someone, you'll find it easier to figure out what to write.

So go against what other people have told you: "Always ask for their referral." I don't agree with that at all. Instead, your goal is to create a reason for them to go out of their way to refer you. If you send a personal note to them and remember their kids' names and ask how they're doing, you may blow them away. Their own family may not even do that. So you come across as someone who listened, cared, and took time from your busy day to reach out to them. That is rare in the world.

Make sure you write it by hand. I know you can get a handwriting font, but I don't recommend it. I have not seen one that looks as nice as a real handwritten note, and it makes it look fake. It would be better to have some pre-printed text followed by a handwritten P.S. or something, rather than using a handwriting font.

I have received letters in the mail, and the handwritten ones are nice. The ones that are from a printer are not as impressive. They're less meaningful. I also think it's important not to brand the heck out of these note cards. I used to do that, but I'm moving away from it. I want to keep my notes simple and basic.

You might even put a joke or something funny inside. You want their getting the card to be fun and enjoyable, so make the note funny, get a funny card, or keep it plain—but don't make it just about you and your business. I get that all the time from lenders. I get these nice note cards that they took the time to write. They're fine, but they would have more success if they sent something even more personal, funny, or memorable.

When do you send them—and to whom? I have agents in my office who feel like they don't know many people. This is something you might need to work on. You have to purposefully focus on building relationships with contacts so you can continue to communicate with them.

Have the mind-set when you meet someone new to send them a personal note. That means listening well enough so you can reference something you discussed, and determining the best way to follow up with them. If you are talking about something that you have more insight about, you could say,

"I'll mail you more details about it. What's a good address for you?" A lot of people don't like to give out their email address because they worry about being spammed, and phone numbers are sometimes too personal. But if you offer them something valuable or interesting to them, they often gladly text you their email address. Plus, it is easy to locate someone's business address.

Once I was on the phone with a childhood friend I had not spoken to in decades. I discovered he was working in a neighboring state as a mortgage broker. I learned later that he happens to be one of the top five mortgage brokers in that state. Before he got off the phone, he said, "Hey, I want to send you something. What's your address?"

A week later, I got a note card from him. It was nice and humorous. I have a suspicion that he does that with everybody. He is successful, and I am guessing that sending personal notes is something he's made a priority in his business.

As a real estate agent, you can get addresses from tax records if you have an idea where someone lives. Or you can look at the MLS and search people by their names. I recommend not just doing this blindly but seeking out people with whom you have some sort of connection. You can surprise them with a personal note because people rarely get them anymore.

Here are some examples of when you could send a personal note, and to whom:

When you're at a friend's house for a barbecue, you meet somebody new, a friend of your friend. You have a nice conversation and you think, *I'd like to follow up with this person.* You can either get their address from the friend so you can send them a personal note, or you can ask the person directly and maybe ask him to lunch or coffee.

In your dealings with clients, you also meet their extended family—their parents, uncles, nieces. If you meet them, send them a note as well. This is also true for your friends.

Lenders, contractors, really anyone you come in contact with through your work is a potential person with whom you could build a stronger relationship. Some of them could be great referral sources for you.

Do you have a great connection with your hair stylist, your doctor? If you find yourself in a great conversation with someone as you go about your life, keep your eyes open for opportunities to build a deeper connection.

Maybe you have a childhood friend and you have a connection with their parents because you were over at their house a lot as kids. Start thinking about this. Dig deeper.

Searching back through Facebook can jog your memory of people to whom you should send a card. This goes for all social media (more about this in chapter 18). Instead of just sending a private message to your friends and contacts, send a personal handwritten note card.

You definitely want to send note cards to people who are giving you referrals. For heaven's sake, if somebody gives you a referral, the least you can do is send them a thank-you card. Make them feel good. Let them know their referral is really important to you.

Is there anybody you shouldn't send a note card to? Not really. This doesn't all have to be about business. However, I would prioritize whom you send cards to and when. You don't have an endless amount of time, so make it a priority to send personal notes to those who are most likely to send you a referral. That being said, remember my friend who is a mortgage broker in another state? The chances of me sending him any business are extremely low. I'm sure my friend knew that, but he took the time to send me a note, and he sends me a funny Christmas card every winter. Even if I'm unable to send him business, he at least strengthened our friendship, which was pretty much nonexistent until he took the initiative. Building and maintaining friendships is another great reason for sending personal notes to people. Many of us are working our tails off so we can afford to spend more time with our family and friends, so take some time to foster and strengthen those friendships. Even if you don't get much time to spend with them, I'm confident you'll feel good about taking that time to let them know you were thinking about them.

Again, this is basic. I'm not telling you anything you haven't heard. But maybe what you haven't heard is how successful and impactful this can be for your business. Don't underestimate the power of sending these handwritten notes. This is a simple thing you can do today. It'll cost you just a few bucks each week.

Finally, I want to talk about why this works. You can be the best real estate agent in the world—you can be the best listing agent, the best buyers' agent, the best real estate broker, whatever. What I have discovered is that even if I'm the best real estate agent in my marketplace and I can prove it, it doesn't necessarily mean I'm going to get more business. It's frustrating, but the fact is that people consistently use—or get a recommendation from—someone they know and trust.

When I get new business from the marketing I send out, it's from people who didn't have a relationship with somebody from whom they could ask for a real estate referral (which is rare). That's why this is important. Almost everybody knows a real estate agent. Make sure you are the one with whom they have the deepest relationship. I can work tirelessly at being the best, but if I don't have the relationships, then my business will be forced to pay big money for new leads. So it's extremely important that you focus on these relationships.

You can go out there and spend thousands upon thousands of dollars marketing to your community, farming, doing all kinds of stuff to get more clients. At the end of the day, that's going to be far less successful and effective than just writing these note cards. So just do it. Trust me on this. I not only have experience doing this myself, but I've watched agents go through my office and try many different things—and this one is a gem that everyone can do.

No more excuses. If your handwriting sucks, get your spouse to do it. Get a kid to do it. Type out a couple of things that you want them to say, and get somebody to write for you if you're embarrassed by your handwriting. Don't let your concern about your bad handwriting be the thing that stops you from doing it.

And don't tell me you are too busy. Like I said about the agent who does the ten personal notes each week, he does it when he is relaxing and drinking beer in his off time, in his lawn chair getting some sun or at his favorite sports bar so he can also watch the game. You are not too busy for this—it's too important. We are in a relationship business. No matter what business you are in, this is something that you should do more of. A simple goal of ten note cards a week is something that we can and should do.

CHAPTER 18

Social Media: Harness That Beast

Social media has been around now for well over a decade. Most real estate agents (let's say 95 percent) are on Facebook, LinkedIn, or some other social media platform. However, a huge number of them rarely touch it, while the rest aren't using it as an effective tool for their real estate business. This chapter is designed to show those of you who use Facebook and other social media platforms how to leverage them to grow your business. If you don't like or want to use social media, you don't have to. Just be aware that social media is the preferred communication option for many young Americans.

Here are three social media strategies you can implement today that can have a profound impact on your real estate business:

1. **START USING THE PRIVATE MESSAGING OPPORTUNITIES WITHIN FACEBOOK THE SAME WAY YOU WOULD SEND HANDWRITTEN NOTE CARDS TO YOUR SPHERE.**

I recommend sending out at least ten handwritten personal note cards a week, so I also recommend sending out ten personal private messages on Facebook. Write the same type of message you would write in a personal note card. This is not a time to sell—this is a time to connect with friends and acquaintances, to build relationships. If you don't have many friends on Facebook, that's okay. Take the time to go through your friends' lists of friends and find the mutual acquaintances you haven't yet connected with through Facebook. Obviously, you'll want to focus this effort on building more local relationships. However, don't ignore your friends or clients who have moved away. I still get referrals from friends who live in other states. They either still know someone local or often know someone moving to the area where I work.

Spend time each week private messaging somebody, asking them about their family, reliving a funny moment with them, or discussing something they posted on Facebook that was entertaining or moving. Use those things as your opportunity to engage with people and let them know you're out there. Invite them to coffee. Start building stronger relationships.

The point is, so many of us are not using this powerful tool that's right at our fingertips. The benefit of using private messaging is that those messages cut through the clutter and noise and jump right up on the screen of someone's phone just like a text would, and they're also copied to the recipient's email inbox. Facebook does a great job of making sure those messages get read, and often it will tell you if they've been read. This is a great opportunity to build personal relationships.

2. SHARE MINI-MOMENTS.

Some real estate agents do a good job of posting pictures of their client at the closing table or in front of their house with a sold sign, letting their friends (and friends of friends) know that they're out there helping people. That's good! Here's how you can expand that strategy and create more moments with clients on social media:

You have first-time homebuyers preapproved and scheduled to look at houses. You drive to the first house, and you can sense their excitement as you're walking to the front door. Capture that moment by taking a selfie, with them in the background walking to the front door, and post it on Facebook saying, "Here are Rob and Susan looking at their first house! They're super excited about buying a home." It's that simple.

There are so many of those moments inside your business that you can capture if you just slow down and think about them. It's a muscle you have to train. Suppose you're going out to celebrate because you got a home under contract, or you are in the backyard with clients and you see an awesome swimming pool that looks like fun. Capture these mini-moments and share them on Facebook, and your sphere and their friends will see you out with clients, being a real estate agent, having fun and helping people. That will do wonders for bringing you potential referrals.

3. DON'T OVER-POST.

Many people tie in other social media like Twitter, Pinterest, and Instagram, and those automatically feed into their Facebook. That's okay as long as you monitor how much you're sending to your friends. Make sure you don't over-post business news to your personal Facebook. Some agents have a personal page and a business page. Depending on how often you post to Facebook, you might not need a business page.

Personally, I like when clients know about me, my kids, my family, and my hobbies. The more your clients know about you personally, the more invested they are in your family and career—and the more likely they are to refer business to you. Let them into your world; that's how you build relationships. However, if you are posting all your real estate listings, market updates, and articles about real estate to Facebook, those should probably stay on your business page.

You can leverage your business Facebook in an entirely different way than you leverage your personal page. Keep your personal page more about you, your family, your interests, etc., but occasionally post those mini-moments you have as a real estate agent. I don't recommend trying to sell anything on your personal page. Use your business page to promote and advertise real estate listings, testimonials, mini-moments, and all the cool things happening with your business. However, don't be upset if your friends don't like or follow your business page. Your business page is not that interesting to your friends and contacts—however, it is of interest to anyone looking for a real estate agent or interested in one of your listings. It's basically your online resume.

If you do feel the need to post real estate listings and news to your personal page, I recommend you use a newsletter strategy. Create an electronic newsletter elsewhere with all your listings and real estate news and add a short link to it on your personal Facebook page or whatever social media you're using. That way, you can keep those friends who are interested informed without over-posting business information, which can be annoying to them or come across as too salesy. Try reserving mentions of your business on your personal page to those mini-moments where you engage people, create relationships, and help people achieve their dreams. That's Facebook gold.

4. USE HUMOR OR ENTERTAINMENT.

If you want your friends and contacts to go out of their way to look at your posts, I recommend finding ways to make them laugh or smile. We humans like to be entertained. This doesn't necessarily mean you should post jokes or cute cat videos from YouTube. But look for opportunities to send something funny. It could be a funny or silly video of you. If you find yourself laughing during your day, what caused it? Can you share it? Or did you see something amazing or silly at a home you previewed today? Maybe that would be a fun post to share. Just try to turn your brain on to look for those moments and opportunities. They happen all the time, but you have to program yourself to try to capture and post them. Again, this isn't for everyone—but for those of you using social media, this could help you build a stronger and more interactive following.

5. LEVERAGE A PLATFORM OTHER THAN FACEBOOK.

Facebook is a great platform because so many people use it. However, if you want to grow a new following and expand your sphere, I recommend you pick one of these other platforms so that you stand out better and reach new audiences:

INSTAGRAM is now owned by Facebook and has the attention of so many consumers. It is a picture-based platform, and people love pictures. As a real estate agent, don't just post listings. That's lame. Instead, create an Instagram account around a theme. Pick a theme that you know will attract an audience. For example, if you really like mid-century modern homes, you could create an Instagram account all about mid-century modern homes in your community. Chances are, if you like those types of homes, others do too. Or maybe you do photography as a hobby; you could create an Instagram account with cool pictures of your city. Remember, it doesn't have to be about real estate—your goal is to build relationships first.

PERISCOPE is owned by Twitter. This platform is based on live broadcasts. It alerts people who are following you and people nearby that you are doing a live broadcast. If people miss the live version, they can only view the replay for the next twenty-four hours. After that, it's gone for good. Because the broadcasts disappear, people feel compelled to watch them. They don't have a chance to see it later, so they make a point to watch it that day. It's rather genius on a social level. You can also save each video to your phone if you want to save it for other uses.

Don't know what to broadcast? Why not do a daily or weekly broadcast on what came on the market in your neighborhood this week, or what sold and for how much? Or something completely unrelated to real estate, such as shoes. If you love shoes, you likely have a lot to say and share about shoes. I recommend giving it a local twist, such as advice on where to get good local deals and where you found your favorite pair of heels or boots. Your weekly broadcast can be about anything, the themes you and other local residents care about. As long as you're truly passionate about the topic, it can work; if you come across as fake or disingenuous, don't expect a lot of followers. It takes time and diligence to create a following, so don't give up too soon. You need to give it three to six months minimum to see it get some traction.

SNAPCHAT is a texting platform that is similar to Periscope in that the text will disappear in twenty-four hours, so your friends and followers have a limited time to see it, which again compels them to read what you posted. Snapchat does some cool things for your pictures and short videos, such as allowing you to do text overlays. You can easily write fun messages over the pictures or videos, which gives you a great opportunity to add humor or entertainment to your posts. Snapchat can search your current contacts on your phone to see if any of them are currently using Snapchat—so if you have a ton of contacts on your phone, it could be easy for you to get your account rolling quickly. Again, come up with a theme or fun idea around which to base your posts. Even though your post will only be live for twenty-four hours, you can save the photo to your phone and upload it to Facebook, Twitter, and Instagram if you want to get more mileage out of your efforts.

YOUTUBE is owned by Google. Everybody knows about YouTube; I don't need to explain what it is. I will say that many entrepreneurs have catapulted their careers with YouTube. So how do you leverage YouTube for your business?

Let me start by saying what *doesn't* work well: doing a video that is too long, that is a basic market update, or merely turns your listing slideshow into a movie. If you expect hundreds or thousands of people to look at this, you'll be disappointed. If you're putting these types of videos inside a newsletter that has other content, you get a few more views. But consumers and your contacts don't really want to watch those types of videos.

What do they want to watch? Have you tried searching the name of your city on YouTube? You might see a video produced by the visitors' bureau or chamber of commerce. However, you may also see some random person who has made a video highlighting something cool in your town. Often these videos have thousands of views. Why? Because people will search for information on a city, and often the YouTube video will appear as a source of information. It happens organically. So let's say you just moved to town and know very few people, but you have your real estate license. You could start to post weekly videos about your favorite discoveries in your new city—a great restaurant experience, or someone you met while getting your hair done. Share knowledge about traffic bottlenecks that happen at key times each day or the procedure for dropping your kids off at school. If it's useful information to you, it's likely useful to other people. You could end each video with a sign-off letting them know you're a real estate agent and something you can do for them (not what they can do for you). If you do four or five videos, don't expect any results. If you do forty or fifty two-minute videos over three to six months, then you'll have truly done something unique and memorable. You'll likely show up in search results when somebody searches for information about your city.

The cost of doing this is zero dollars. If you don't know YouTube, watch a couple of how-to videos on YouTube. It's simple, and you can record your videos with your smartphone or with your built-in webcam on your computer. They don't need to be high quality; just have fun with them. Don't take yourself too seriously. It's okay to be silly or your normal self. Be personable and don't force it. They won't be perfect, but that's what makes them authentic and real. If you need help editing the video, you can find people on Fiverr.com and other sites who will help you for less than ten dollars.

TWITTER - If you already use Twitter and like it, these ideas might help you. If you don't use Twitter or hate it, then don't bother. There is so much data and so many feeds being pushed through Twitter that it shouldn't be used the same way as the other social media platforms. I haven't used Twitter very much, but I've found it useful to read firsthand accounts of breaking news from people who are on the scene. You just search a hashtag (#) to get other perspectives and details not being reported by the news companies.

In real estate, you can post listing links and include a #yourcity or #yourneighborhood hashtag, but if you've tried this, you likely haven't had much luck. Where I have seen agents use Twitter successfully is when they find popular hashtags in their community and either join into the conversation or create a theme that will create a large following of local people. For example, let's say one of your kids plays soccer. Because of this, you're knowledgeable about the different leagues and tournaments, and you have opinions and stories to share about the local soccer scene. You could regularly post scores and tournament information on Twitter and become the go-to soccer source for the local community. (This idea of being the local soccer go-to person would work on all the social media platforms discussed in this chapter.) They will also learn more about you the longer they follow you. This gives you opportunities to develop more relationships.

There are more social media platforms than the ones I've mentioned here, such as Pinterest and LinkedIn. By the time you read this, there may be others capturing the attention of your community. You can easily find resources and how-to guides that will show you the best ways to post on these platforms and build your audience. If you decide to create a social media plan to grow your business, I recommend you pick one or two of them and try to hit it out of the park rather than doing all of them poorly.

Agents, this is a game changer. One of the best parts about social media is that it's free. You can build an audience and grow your business for zero dollars invested. For the platforms you choose, invest time to really master them. Buy a couple of books or read through the many blogs out there sharing information about the platforms. To get the best results, you need to learn more than 95 percent of the other users. But that's easy. If you study it for thirty minutes every day for a month, you'll be in that top 5 percent even though you started at ground zero.

Put the time in, and you will see a significant impact on your business in the next six months. Get started, stick with it, and it will happen.

CHAPTER 19

Stories Trump Recipes

I get at least five emails a day from mortgage lenders who send me their mortgage market updates. These are mass-produced emails that all look alike and say the same thing. They contain nothing authentic or personally revealing about the lender. They're an annoying waste of my time. I'm still waiting for one of them to seize the opportunity and send me something that I'll actually care about. Even if I don't give them my business, that would at least make me respect them for making an effort to be authentic.

It reminds me of some of the worthless stuff that real estate agents send out to their contacts. They might pay for a subscription service that sends out postcards with recipes printed on them. Or a premade newsletter with content that is actually manufactured by a national subscription service.

Some will argue that sending something is better than doing nothing. That might be true, so long as the person receiving the information is not already being bombarded by similar marketing material from other real estate agents. But they likely are. Most people know more than one real estate agent.

What if another agent was sending your friend a monthly letter that shared stories about how she saved her clients money by going the extra mile? Or about how she used her deep knowledge and industry contacts to help avoid a disastrous situation for a client? Maybe she shares funny stories about things her kids do and how that reminds her of something that happens in real estate. Or she shares the amazing stories of people who are helped out by a local charity where she volunteers.

Can you see how much less impactful recipe cards would seem compared to the newsletters full of authentic content being produced by the other agent? Consider how that makes the recipe sender look. The recipient doesn't even have to read the newsletter; he can tell the difference in effort just by looking at it. Think about how the recipe sender will be perceived: lazy and inauthentic. At the very least, the recipient is going to have a higher level of respect for the agent who sent that newsletter.

Your goal should be to rise above the white noise that people have learned to ignore. Think about the mail you receive at home. Most of it goes straight into the trash. If somebody sends you a personal note card, that gets your attention. Anything that is authentic and unique earns respect.

Send What You're Passionate About

How do you determine what to send? First of all, if you're passionate about cooking and love to talk about food, it's okay to send recipes. But also send the story behind the recipes—who they were passed down from, what memories they evoke for you, etc. What happened the first time you made the recipe? Did you mess it up? Impress or bewilder your guests? Make them gag?

Talk about shopping if that's what you love. Or fitness. Anything you're passionate about. It doesn't have to be about real estate.

Humans are wired to love stories. Becoming a storyteller for your audience is something we're all capable of doing. We do it all the time without thinking about it: "You won't believe what just happened!" or "I was showing homes, and this funny thing happened." It's part of our DNA to convey our experiences as stories. However, we don't always have our audience in the car with us, so it's a good idea to record those stories on a phone, or write them down, or snap a picture as something happens so we remember to write about it later.

Are you doing something fun and unusual this weekend? Make sure you take pictures so you can add them to the story when you write about your experience later.

Some agents are diligent about sending personal note cards to their contacts. Others find sending note cards an extremely difficult task and therefore don't do it consistently. If this describes you, then writing one newsletter a month might be a perfect solution for you. It might take you eight hours each month to write it, edit it, and put it into a nice document, but the time commitment might not be that different from someone who is writing individual personalized note cards all the time (two hours a week). And instead of sending out to just one person, you're sending out to many.

Your newsletter doesn't have to be fancy. In fact, the more un-fancy it is, the more authentic it may seem to your contacts. Microsoft Word, Google Docs, and other word processors have newsletter templates. Just plug your stories into one of them, and you're done. Your efforts will improve over time, so don't worry about making it perfect. It will even be fun to look back years later and see how far your design and writing skills have come. That only makes you seem genuine to your contacts.

Make the focus of your newsletter about sharing stories— not about real estate facts and not about your listings. It would be better to tell an interesting story about how you got a new listing or about something crazy that happened to one of your listings and how you fixed it. Tell the story of a house or the clients who are selling it. That would show that you care about people, and that elicits trust from the people who are reading your stories.

If you get stuck or don't know what to write about, then write about something you care about—your hobbies, your family, whatever comes to you. Make it authentic and not a business tool. Show your personality. Don't worry about pleasing everybody—write from the heart about things you're passionate about. Use humor and be vulnerable.

If you struggle with writing or don't think you're a good writer, try recording stories into your smartphone and then transcribing them. You can even pay someone to transcribe your recordings for you. Just do something. But don't let your opinion of your writing skills stop you. Write something down, even if your first attempt is more time-consuming and painful than you thought it would be. Keep at it and keep practicing, spend time on it each week, and pretty soon it will get easier and you'll find you can accomplish a lot more in the same amount of time. Writing will become a manageable task that you might even grow to enjoy.

Your contacts don't want to get more junk mail. If you send them something that is generic, they'll view it as generic. If you send them something that is personal and original, it doesn't matter if they read it or throw it away—they will respect you for sending something authentic. If you do that consistently, over time that respect will grow to admiration. That is when you will begin to see a significant impact in your business.

CHAPTER 20

Get Your Sh*t Together

Picture an agent who gets up in the morning and makes a plan for her day. She has things she wants to accomplish. She starts off organized and ready to go. Then, while she's dropping her kids off at school, she gets a text from a client asking if she will contact his neighbor about listing their home. She scribbles their information on the back of a Starbuck's receipt. On her way to the office, she gets a phone call from a listing client who has questions about home sales in her neighborhood. The agent makes a note to call her client later with that information. When she gets to the office, another agent asks her opinion on the pricing of one of his listings. Before she helps him, she checks her email and finds something that's flaring up with a pending transaction. The title company needs certain documents; the lender says the buyer is not giving them all their financials, so closing might be delayed. A couple of hours pass while she deals with these unexpected tasks, and she needs to run to make a lunch appointment with a past client. During lunch, she gets a message from someone requesting information through her website. She makes a mental note to call them later because after lunch she needs to finish dealing with the messages she got that morning. She gets back to her office, sits down at her desk, and gets a call from someone who wants to see her listing located across town. They play phone tag for a couple of calls, and she leaves to go open the house for this prospect. On the way home, she stops at the grocery store to pick up dinner, and she notices on her phone all the messages she missed throughout the day. They're coming at her from text, phone, email, and Facebook private messaging.

Even though that agent started her day with a well-intentioned plan, she looks back and says, "Jeez, what did I actually get done?" There's a good chance that she dropped the ball on one or more of the messages that came in that day. They were unexpected, and they reached her while she was busy doing other things. That's often the life of a real estate agent.

How do you keep track of it all? How do you avoid missing out on a lead or forgetting to complete an important task requested by a client? Often these items are not on your daily agenda but pop up unexpectedly. That's why a lot of agents don't even have a daily agenda, because their day is always so fluid and constantly changing. So you need to have a plan. If you don't have a plan for the things you need to accomplish that day, you'll spend the day reacting to things and will actually get very little done. You need to plan for the unexpected and find an effective way to keep track of things. You're going to get messages and tasks thrown at you from all different angles at inconvenient times, so you need to have a system in place to channel that back into your organized plan. Those messages and phone calls need to be channeled to one location that can be reviewed and referenced at any time, even if that's a notebook that you keep with you at all times. That way you can contact them later that evening or the next morning. You don't have to use technology to be organized, but you do need a plan to keep track of everything that gets thrown at you.

Keep Your Contacts Current

One of the biggest mistakes you can make as a real estate agent is to not put a new contact into your database so that you can follow up with them at a later date. You meet somebody either through your job or in your personal life, and you form a great connection with that person. Even if it's not for real estate purposes, they're a connection you want to keep and follow up with. But somehow you don't get their information into your database. So a week later when you're looking at people to follow up with, they're not in there, and they are no longer on your mind. Make sure to capture that opportunity to build your sphere while it's in front of you.

CASE IN POINT: *I've made this mistake so many times over the years. Eventually I may have corrected it when I crossed paths with that person again, but I'm still shocked when I see that someone I've known for years is not in my database. It's a shame, because had they been in there I might have been able to foster that relationship deeper, which could have led to more referrals or connections from their own sphere.*

There are dozens of kinds of customer relationship management software (often called CRMs) for agents to choose from to keep track of their contacts, tasks, and follow-up assignments.

I've used many CRMs over the course of my career, and I can tell you that they all have pros and cons. More importantly, they're only as good as your ability and willingness to keep them updated. There are all kinds of fancy ones that claim to make your life easy, but that's not going to happen unless you keep monitoring, feeding, and maintaining your CRM database, adding new people, changing and updating information—all of it takes time. Your results will only be as good as the time and energy you put into making your CRM a valuable resource for your business.

A word of caution: some CRMs have a fifteen- or thirty-day free trial period. If you don't cancel in that window, you get locked in for six months or a year. They don't let you cancel until you've paid your full term. I had this problem with Top Producer—it took me over thirty days to figure out that their software was not a good fit for me, but by then I was stuck, a fact that they buried in their fine print. Their customer service and sales tactics were so despicable that I've decided to call them out in this book. They suck.

Of course, you don't even need fancy software to keep track of your contacts and tasks. I've seen many agents do it using free email software like Gmail and Google Calendar or Outlook to store their contacts and follow-up information. There is certainly nothing wrong with using a combination of writing things down and using electronic to-do lists either. You can enter your contacts in an Excel spreadsheet and write down the last time you followed up with each one. You can even write everything down in your notebook, especially when you're starting out and you don't have a big contact list. You don't need fancy software, but you do need to track whom you communicate with so you know the last time you followed up with them. This helps you make an organized effort to develop important relationships. And when new things pop up throughout the day, you have a place to throw those tasks so you can remember to do them later. If you just try to go off memory and follow up with them when you're done, like many agents do, things will fall through the cracks or you waste a lot of time trying to find where you scribbled down a note or put a contact's phone number.

The point is that it doesn't matter how you organize your contacts and manage your to-do lists and tasks. I'm not going to tell you which software out there is the best, because that could change tomorrow. I just want you to avoid making the monumental mistake of *not* making it a priority in your business to manage your leads and contacts. It's of the utmost importance. Your list of contacts is the lifeblood of your business. Treat it that way.

CHAPTER 21

He Said, She Said: Testimonials

Another colossal mistake I've made over the years in real estate is not consistently obtaining testimonials from my fans and clients. Agents often don't get testimonials from clients because either they forget to ask for them or they are too uncomfortable to ask for them. Regardless of the reason, you need to have a system in place so that you don't miss these opportunities.

I've known a handful of agents who had stacks of testimonials from their clients. Hundreds. Imagine having a folder you brought with you to a listing appointment that had 100 testimonials with pictures that sellers can leaf through while you're at the home with them. That is powerful positioning. Imagine if your website had 100 or more testimonials that buyers and sellers could scroll through before they gave you a call to set up an appointment. Having social proof that you are a great real estate agent makes your job of acquiring new clients easy. So make it a priority.

When and How to Ask for Testimonials

Your success in acquiring great testimonials is often tied to your timing for asking for them. Keep your eyes open to when your clients are feeling particularly happy about something you did for them. Let them know then how important testimonials and referrals are to your business. Sometimes I'll use the analogy of online shopping. I ask them if they ever read the reviews before buying something online. Most everyone looks at reviews before buying, and the reviews often impact their decision to buy the product or service, which helps me articulate the reason why testimonials are so important in my business.

Some agents wait until the closing, but then something crazy happens at closing and you don't get the opportunity you were hoping for or you just forget with everything going on. I've also had clients promise that they would email me one, but they never did. They get busy moving and readjusting to their new home with a million things on their mind. So waiting until the last moment is typically not the best way to ask for a testimonial.

Make It Fun and Easy

Make the process of them providing a testimonial easy. Give them a few options. If you can get a picture or even a video of your clients to include with the testimonial, that's as powerful as having ten written testimonials without pictures. If your clients are uncomfortable about having their picture taken, you can take it from a distance or have them supply you with a picture they do like. Often your clients have a Facebook account, so you could use their avatar or another picture they recently posted to Facebook.

You can do something funny or silly with your testimonials, which often makes the experience more memorable for your clients to participate. Creative testimonials are more enjoyable for your prospects to read or watch.

When You Have a Tough Transaction

Sometimes closings are stressful. Sometimes your listing takes longer to sell and you get less money than everyone was hoping for. Asking for testimonials during those situations may not seem appropriate. However, they could be good opportunities to get feedback from your clients. If they are not happy with something, learning more about the cause of their frustrations will only help you do your job better the next time. Therefore, if you know or have a hunch that your clients are less than super ecstatic about the service you provided, then you or your broker could reach out to them for specific feedback. It could be a simple questionnaire to rate agent performance on different areas such as marketing, communications, knowledge, professionalism, etc. It can ask the clients to describe the most frustrating part (and the best part) about working with you. The questionnaire should also include an option for the seller to include a testimonial.

Letting the client know that you are asking them these questions so that performance and service can improve helps even frustrated clients feel comfortable sharing their honest feedback. You might discover they were super impressed by you but frustrated with your lender referral or some other aspect of the transaction. Sometimes it's the clients that you are the most worried about who give the best testimonials and the most referrals.

CASE IN POINT: *I was working with a client for months, trying to find them a home. They were tough clients because the husband and wife were constantly not agreeing with each other on what house they wanted. Even after we got a home under contract, I was right in the middle of many disagreements between the couple. At some point during the transaction, I let them know I would love to get a testimonial from them. They told me they weren't ready to give one yet. This, of course, surprised and concerned me. I worried that I asked them too soon, or that they weren't happy with the service I was giving them. I didn't sleep well for a couple of days from stewing on the situation. Then one morning I checked my inbox and saw an email from my clients. They gave me an amazing testimonial and sent me a referral. It was a good reminder that if you go out of your way to provide a lot of value to your client, you don't need to be shy about asking for a small favor in return.*

Leveraging Testimonials

Regardless of what type of client you are working with and how the transaction goes, you will get testimonials from your clients if you make it your mission to.

So what do you do with these testimonials? Here is a list of ways to make the most of the testimonials you get:

1. **WEBSITE:** The most obvious place to put them is on your website. Anyone researching you will find them there. If you have dozens of them, it will have a significant impact on the customer. If you don't have a picture to include with the testimonial, you could put a picture of the home.

2. **PRINTED BOOKLET:** Create a binder or a booklet of your testimonials that you can take on listing appointments. You don't even need to talk about it; just set it out on the table while you're discussing a plan for their listing.

3. **SOCIAL MEDIA:** You can post testimonials on your social media accounts. I always recommend that if you do this you tag the client who wrote the testimonial and you write a testimonial back to your client below. For example, if your client says that you are an amazing real estate agent and that... you can post below their testimonial how great your client was to work with, something about how hard they worked to get the home ready, etc. When you publicly give testimonials back to your customers, it shows everyone that you have raving fans and you care and appreciate your clients—thereby turning one testimonial into the power of many.

4. **BLOGS AND NEWSLETTERS:** Just like with social media, you can and should include your latest testimonials in your blogs and newsletters. Don't forget to include the testimonial back to your clients, maybe even some backstory of how it went selling or finding them a home. Your clients like to see their names in print, and it will help you give context to what your clients said about you.

5. **MARKETING MATERIALS:** Including testimonials on marketing materials you are sending out to prospects helps give you social proof that you are helping and getting the job done for your customers. Therefore, add your best ones to your marketing materials. If you want to take it a step further, you can really impress the neighbors of the home you just sold by scrapping the "just sold" postcard and instead sending them a letter that includes the testimonial from your seller clients, plus the backstory and your testimonial back to your clients. Nobody is sending them anything like that. Include your business card, because they'll likely hang on to it.

If you are not making it a point to obtain testimonials from your clients, you are making a huge mistake. Follow the ideas in this chapter to start acquiring them. Make the process fun and easy for your clients. Publish the testimonials and your testimonials back to your customers, and enjoy the huge impact you see in your business.

CHAPTER 22

Be "The Connector"

As a real estate agent, you are uniquely positioned to help people far beyond real estate matters. Over time you will acquire all kinds of contacts—plumbers, landscapers, painters, doctors, lawyers, restaurant owners, bankers, hairdressers, dentists, builders, investors, photographers, key employees at businesses all over town. They might be people you've helped in some way with a listing, or they might be former clients or family members of past clients. The longer you're in business, the more people you end up knowing.

Other agents may not be as connected as you are. Therefore, why not leverage your knowledge bank of contacts to forge deeper relationships by helping people connect with each other? What if you tell your clients to contact you before having work done on their house because you know many great contractors? Or let them know that if they need a referral outside of real estate—for an accountant, auto mechanic, caterer, etc.—to contact you, because you make it part of your job to know the right people to recommend.

You become The Connector. Think of yourself as the superhero who helps people find the help they need within their community. Let all your clients and the people in your sphere know to contact you for trusted recommendations. They don't have to be related to real estate.

Your contacts will soon learn to rely on you any time they

need a recommendation. You become a trusted resource for them, and your business contacts will love you because you're referring business to them. They're more likely to return the favor and refer their clients to you. The cycle continues until you have one heck of a great referral source for your business. At the same time, you get to help people in multiple ways.

> **CASE IN POINT:** *There is an agent in my office I would describe as a connector. I hear her frequently tell her clients to call her anytime they need a recommendation for something. She tells them that she has been doing this for a long time and has learned through her clients' experiences (and her own) whom to call when somebody needs help with something. A few times, she has emailed out to agents in the office to see if they have recommendations on a particular type of contractor. The other day, she asked if anybody had a go-to drywall contractor. Sure enough, she got two recommendations from agents and was able to share that information with her client. She is The Connector. If she doesn't have a connection, she knows where to get it.*
>
> *She doesn't need to spend money on marketing her business; she doesn't make cold calls or chase leads of any kind. She just focuses on helping connect people, and as a result, she has a very enviable business. As a trusted resource, she has referral clients coming in every month.*

Protect Your Superhero Status

Are there any downsides to becoming The Connector?

Yes. What if you refer someone to a contractor who does crappy work or causes some sort of problem? It happens. Your contact could blame you for referring them to this nightmare.

Here are ways to prevent problems from arising and to protect you from the negative effects if they do:

First, speak with the contractor or service provider before

you send them referrals. Let them know that you tell your contacts to call you immediately if they ever have a problem with someone you refer them to, so you can help them resolve it. You effectively put the contractor on notice that if you send them business, you expect them to give your contact the red-carpet treatment—and that if there's a problem, you likely won't send them any more business. By having that conversation with them up front, you help ensure that your contact will receive excellent service. If there is an issue, the contractor will be more likely to handle it himself, even if that means losing money on the job because they want to do the right thing by you.

Second, if you are referring somebody new whom you've never used before but came recommended by another agent, tell your contact, "I've never personally used XYZ contractor, but they come highly recommended by an agent in my office who said nothing but great things." If there is a problem, you've at least positioned yourself so it won't bite you. Even still, before you make the referral, you should do the first step—call and speak to the contractor and let them know your expectations. Let them know it's important to you that your clients are well taken care of and that you do send out a lot of referrals.

Wielding Your Superpower for Good

Let's take being The Connector one step further:

What if every week (or every day) you posted a short video on YouTube or Facebook about a business, restaurant, hair salon, or shop you recommend (and why) in your target community? Share your in-depth knowledge of the local community and end each video by saying that if the viewer ever needs a recommendation on something in your community, you're the person who can help them. Let them know how to contact you at your real estate office. The fact that you're a real estate agent is minimized but still communicated.

After you post a video about a business, send the business

owners a link. Thank them for the great service, product, meal, or whatever, and let them know you look forward to visiting their business again—and let them know they're free to share the video if they would like to. They'll appreciate what you've done for them and probably will share the video on their own Facebook page with their own audience and customers, people who are likely beyond your own personal sphere. Now you're being exposed to new audiences.

If you keep doing this, over time you'll find that anyone who searches online for recommendations on places to eat, where to get their hair cut, which chiropractor to visit, someone to landscape their yard, or whatever will find your videos listed prominently in their search engine. This builds your credibility as an authority figure and someone in the know within your community. Whom do you think they'll call when they need a real estate agent? On top of that, imagine the referral business you'll get from those local businesses.

This strategy costs no money. It could take less than an hour of your day. It would help a lot of people and certainly could help propel your business to new heights.

Doesn't that sound better than making cold calls on expired listings or paying huge amounts of money to Zillow or Realtor.com to help you get buyer leads? Then stop reading and go record your first video now. Start with your favorite restaurant in town. Tell people why you love going there and list your favorite items on the menu.

Just start. Be The Connector.

CHAPTER 23

Fighting Fires without Getting Burned

How good are you at putting out "fires"? Why does that matter?

Real estate agents fail to realize how important this skill is. They often focus on how many people they have in their sphere, how many leads they have in their pipeline, and the broker fees they'll have to pay as the best means of assuring a good income for the year. In actuality, they need to make sure they are honing their firefighting skills. Agents often don't realize how much they struggle with putting out fires. They believe deals fall apart outside their control. These agents will make far less money because they close fewer deals. Many transactions could be saved if an agent developed solid firefighting skills.

Firefighting is one of my strongest skills as a real estate agent. Agents who are skilled firefighters bring in more money and need to work with fewer clients. It's an extraordinarily important skill to learn and master.

Here are some examples of firefighting:

BUYER - I had buyers who were purchasing a short sale that took about nine months to process. The home was a great opportunity at far below market value. This couple had to jump through hoops to get through the short sale process, but they exercised extraordinary patience. And then, at 10 P.M. the night before closing, the wife called and said her husband didn't want to buy the property anymore. He wanted to give up their earnest money and walk away.

I got him on the phone, and together we talked it out. He had convinced himself that this short sale was a crazy idea and a bad decision. He doubted the value, condition, and location of the house. He didn't care about the money he would lose; he just wanted to walk away.

I listened. I empathized with his concerns. I didn't try to talk him out of walking away; I just wanted to hear his concerns. Then I walked him through the process of walking away, if that's what he was set on doing. I wanted him to know how that decision would impact him. I explained that the odds of finding a similar deal were slim, since the market had changed significantly in the last six months. I told him a story about a client I had helped recently who was looking for a similar property. Over the course of an hour or more on the phone, I led him to see that this short sale was a fortunate opportunity, and he started to come around. Because I took the time to talk with him supportively and explain his options, his sense of panic and buyer's remorse subsided.

That deal would have blown up on many inexperienced agents. It's okay to walk away, if it's truly in the client's best interest. In this case, I knew that if they closed on the house and decided they didn't want it, we could turn around and sell it, and they wouldn't lose money.

To this day, that couple thanks me for putting out that fire. Emotions almost got the better of them, and they're glad that I took the time to help them.

SELLER - Sellers are proud of their homes. They put their heart and soul into fixing up their home, and then they list it and show it. People seem to like it, and sellers get excited because they hear an offer is coming in—and when it does, the offer is insultingly low to the sellers. This is common in real estate. Most sellers will be pissed, and their reaction will be: *Screw these buyers; I'm not even going to respond to their piece-of-shit offer.* In most cases, the situation blows up, and the buyers move on.

This happened to me with sellers who had a unique home in a unique location. I knew it was going to take a unique buyer to see its full potential. When a lowball offer came in, I took the time to find out more about the buyers. I could tell they were a perfect fit for this house, but for whatever reason, they sent over a crappy offer.

I did a couple of things to fight the fire. First, I agreed with the sellers that the offer was extremely disappointing. Then we talked about buyer behavior. Every buyer on the planet wants a great deal, and sometimes they let that desire cloud their decision making. They don't realize when they write a low offer how much that is going to upset (and insult) sellers who take pride in their home. In the buyers' mind, it's a business transaction, and they expect the seller to counter if they don't accept the offer.

I told my sellers that I had met the buyers and I thought they were a great fit for this house. They likely didn't realize the error they made, and they would possibly pay a higher price that the sellers would accept. I asked them to contemplate that while I phoned the buyers' agent to see what was up with the crappy offer.

The agent was embarrassed and apologetic. He explained that the buyers really wanted the house, but they got talking to a friend who gave them advice on how to negotiate. The agent begged me to please get the sellers to send a counteroffer. I wasn't sure they would, and he wasn't sure he could convince the buyers to send a higher offer. This is where a deal usually falls apart.

I went back to the sellers and explained that the buyers got some bad advice from a friend, and they were hoping the sellers would counter. The sellers, of course, were indignant and wanted to counter at full price, even though days before they would have been flexible with what they thought was a respectful offer. I asked them to think it over.

Meanwhile, I went back to the buyers' agent and let him know that we were moving forward with showing the house to other buyers. But I kept a dialogue open. We kept talking and hashing it out. The buyers—who had originally offered $100,000 less than asking price—eventually came up to within $10,000 of what the sellers were asking. We ended up working out a deal. Open communication and keeping everyone calm saved a deal that almost blew up on day one.

DIFFICULT AGENT - One of the most frustrating situations for an agent is with a difficult agent on the other side of a transaction. Recently, an agent in my office called me and admitted she lost her cool with another agent. She felt she was doing all the work, and the other agent was doing nothing on the other end—and when she did, she ended up messing things up. The listing agent wasn't communicating with her seller, so the seller began contacting my agent directly for information. At first my agent told the seller that he would have to ask his questions through his agent, but then he shared that he had been trying but hadn't been able to speak to his agent in over a week. So my agent began helping the seller get the information he was asking for. Eventually the other agent re-entered the picture and blew up at my agent for communicating directly with her client, accusing her of overstepping ethical boundaries, which was the match that set my agent ablaze with frustration. Meanwhile, their buyers and sellers were fine but at risk of having the real estate agents blow up a deal because they couldn't sort out their differences. Luckily my agent came to me for advice, which lead to me to stepping in to handle communications with the other agent to calm things down enough to get a date set for closing. Unfortunately, these type of stories happen all too often, and it's the clients who often lose out. Having the firefighting skills to defuse a situation with another agent so that it doesn't impact your client is a critical skill to master.

BAD APPRAISAL - Bad appraisals happen all the time, and they blow up deals. When an appraisal comes in too low, it takes a savvy agent to calm a seller who is freaking out and pissed off—or to manage the expectations of a buyer who now thinks a house is worth thousands less than the original offer. These situations are a recipe for disaster, and only an agent who knows what to say to each party will be able to move it forward and find a solution. The better you get at that, the more deals you'll be able to save. So many deals end abruptly with a bad appraisal.

Part of your job is also understanding how the appraiser does his job, what rules he has to follow, and where the gray areas are. The last thing you want to do when an appraiser tells you that they're having a hard time coming up with a value to support the purchase offer is to say something that will piss off the appraiser. For an appraiser to dig deeper, to look at your other sources of information for the appraisal and then make the case to support that new information, he or she will have to put a *lot* of extra time into their appraisal. Appraisers are paid at a fixed rate, so don't piss them off and blow your opportunity to get them to take another look at the valuation. They don't get paid extra to spend more time on their evaluation, but they often will if you show them respect and know how to help them.

If you're lucky enough to have an appraiser who notifies the parties that the appraisal appears to be less than the offer price, usually they give agents involved a chance to send any additional information that would help substantiate the offer price. You may have knowledge of other comparable home sales the appraiser may not have seen. You may have extra information about the comparables used in the appraisal, especially if you have seen that home and the appraiser has not. The more you know about the appraiser's situation and limitations, the better you'll be able to put out the fire of a low appraisal.

Practice Your Fire Drills

So how do you become a better firefighter? First of all, practice. Experience helps. Get in there and really work with people. The main thing is, when things get heated and emotional, stay calm and keep your cool. That's not an easy thing to do, and some might find it comes more naturally than others. You might already know you have a short fuse, and you'll need to check yourself and audit your behavior. Know your triggers. One of mine, for example, is when somebody uses their title or status to do something shady, something in their own best interest instead of their client's best interest or what is most ethical, given the situation. It happens all too often in our industry, and it drives me insane. I see agents use their standing in the community or their years in the industry to talk down to fellow agents and take advantage of them in ways that make me want to blow my top.

I helped one of my agents through a situation where she was representing a seller, and the buyers tried to weasel out of the transaction and also demanded their earnest money back. This was a day before closing, and the seller had already made the repairs the buyer had requested, which far exceeded the value of the earnest money. But the buyers wanted out, and they found some technicality that was really gray and weak within the contract to use as a reason to back out of the transaction and ask for their deposit back. I assured my agent she was in the right—the buyers were backing out of their own choice. The right thing to do was to let the sellers keep the earnest money because they had done everything the buyers requested.

The broker on the other side of the transaction held a prominent position in the real estate community. When I phoned to discuss the transaction with her, she started talking down to me and insisting it was black and white in favor of the buyer. She belittled my viewpoint, and that got under my skin. I found out that the buyer was a client who did a lot of business with the broker, and that was why she was behaving unethically (she didn't want to lose their gravy train client). She was trying to keep her clients happy, even though they were doing something shady. The harder she pushed her point, the more pissed I got, and I totally lost my cool. As soon as I hung up, I regretted that I hadn't handled it well. I didn't help the situation move forward because I let my emotions get the best of me. It's really important to stay calm and keep your cool when you're in these types of situations.

Things go south in a hurry when you lose your cool, and it's hard to recover and regain your ground. Often it may be best if your broker or another agent steps in temporarily. As a broker, I try to coach my agents to never let things get to this point, but it can still happen. Sometimes it's necessary to get someone new involved, even if you maintained your professionalism but the other agent is acting inappropriately. Part of your job is to know when you need help and when you need to step aside.

When everyone else freaks out, you need to do the opposite. Your calmness will help everyone feel calm. When things get heated, it's up to you to maintain a calm, steady voice. Acknowledge feelings and agree that measures need to be taken. Listen. Empathize with their frustration. If you start arguing against someone who is combative, you will only heat things up further. Show that you understand how they feel and then calmly suggest alternatives.

Another way to hone your firefighting skills without having to handle a real-life scenario is to learn about other agents' fires and how they handled them. Listen for agents talking about some nightmare situation they recently experienced with a client or their listing. (This is a favorite subject for many agents to talk about.) As you hear them share their story, pay attention to how they handled it. Do you think they handled it well or not? What could the agent have done differently? If the deal failed and you don't have any ideas of how it could have been saved, then talk to your broker or other knowledgeable agents in your office about the story to see if they have any wisdom you can learn about that type of fire. Learning this firefighting skill will save you weeks of time and save you thousands from having fewer failed transactions.

Know More Ways to Put out Fires

In addition to practicing, you also need to be skilled at coming up with solutions. When a situation develops, I turn on my idea machine (see chapter 16). Sure, some of these ideas won't work, but often you'll develop an idea that works for everyone involved. When there's a problem with lending, I'll rapid-fire some possible solutions to the lender. He usually tells me that won't work because of reason X, and the next idea won't work because of reason Y, but often I get to one that makes him say, "You know, that might be a good workaround." I don't give up easily, nor should you. Think outside the box. Be creative. Once you figure out a way to put out a fire, you can implement that solution on future deals before a fire starts.

For instance, I've had lots of fires due to delayed closings. They start this domino effect that creates multiple fires in multiple places. Having gone through this many times, I know to implement protection plans for my sellers or my buyers (whomever I'm representing) at the beginning or in the middle of the transaction. That way, if the closing gets delayed for any reason, my clients won't suffer. For example, I often negotiate for the sellers to be able to stay in the home for at least a week after closing, even if they have to pay rent for that week. I don't want them to go through the trouble and cost of moving their stuff before closing, and then have the deal blow up at the last minute due to the buyer's loan not closing. I want my clients to have the cash in hand before they move out of the house. I help sell the idea to the buyers by throwing in a carpet cleaning or something of value to them. I work hard to get a plan in place to avoid the potential fire from ever igniting.

Firefighters in Action

If you find yourself engulfed in fire, here's a breakdown of how you might handle it:

EXAMPLE #1: I'll use the delayed closing example. The home is not going to close on the date it was expected to. Your buyers are freaking out and angry. Their boxes are packed, and they've arranged a moving company. They have no place to live. The lender says she sent in the underwriting and doesn't know why it's not back yet. The sellers panic and think the deal is never going to close, and they want to put the house back on the market. Everyone is freaking out. What do you say to put out the fire?

TO THE SELLERS: Listen to their frustrations. Agree with them. Offer suggestions. Maybe you can get a fee for every day the closing goes over, to help offset their expenses, carrying costs, etc. Let them know you spoke to the buyers' agent and they're equally as frustrated. They don't know why the lender's not done—they got them all the paperwork and were told it would be ready on time.

TO THE LENDER: Be firm with the lender and let them know the deal is blowing up because whatever systems they had in place didn't work. The lending should have been finished on time. Let them know the buyer is now going to be charged for going late and will likely be staying in a hotel on top of that, because of the lender's processes. If they make excuses and try to shift blame, be firm with them. Push them to pay the buyers' fees to keep this deal alive.

If you can bring that together, now you have a fee for the sellers that calms them down. You can avoid having to charge it to the buyers, which may have blown them up because they're already facing unexpected expenses. The lender steps up, and you put out the fire.

If the lender doesn't step up, get more creative. What can you offer the buyers and sellers to calm their fears and lower their stress? You can use part of your commission to reimburse something to smooth things over, but before you go to that option, make sure you haven't overlooked a better solution that doesn't make you the sacrificial lamb. I use that option a lot because I would rather make less and have the property close on time than start over.

EXAMPLE #2: During an inspection, mold is found in the attic, and the sellers have no money to fix it. If you tell the buyers they'll have to buy it as-is and fix it themselves, the deal will likely blow up. They are either going to freak out because they're buying a house with mold, or their lender won't allow the loan to close if there is a mold problem reported in the home. What do you do to put out the fire?

TO THE BUYERS: Acknowledge their concern but stress that mold is a common problem that can be fixed. Once the mold issue is resolved, you can get third-party testing to verify that the home is safe. Let them know you want to find a way to cover the repair without the buyers incurring any additional cost.

TO THE LISTING AGENT: Let them know that the buyers are still interested but want a solution that won't add additional cost. Suggest deducting repair costs from the price of the home, since the sellers don't have the money to make repairs up front. Then let them know there's a strong possibility the lender won't let the buyers close on the home without having this mold issue resolved. You have an idea how to make this happen even though they don't have the money to do it themselves. They just need to allow the contractors access to their home prior to closing.

TO THE CONTRACTOR: Find a mold remediation contractor. Explain the situation. Ask if they'd be willing to do the work now and be paid at closing. If they want to haggle and insist for half up front, remind them that they often wait thirty days for an invoice to be paid by another contractor, or even two months to be paid by an insurance company. They're used to that type of waiting. If the house doesn't close for some reason, they can place a lien against it, and remind them that's something they do anytime a homeowner doesn't pay. Handle any objections they throw your way. If needed, you can have the buyers' earnest money released to the contractor. Finally, offer a favor in exchange for a favor. If they wait to be paid at closing, offer to spread the word to other agents about the great service they gave in order to save your deal. Give them a shout-out or free advertising in your newsletter. Get creative. Hand over their invoice to the escrow company to make sure it's paid at closing. It's not a perfect solution, but the fire may be put out so the home can close.

Fight a fire with solutions. The better you get at coming up with alternative options or workarounds, the more deals you will save. This has a *huge* impact on an agent's annual income. Agents could save so many of the deals that blow up on them, if only they were more experienced firefighters.

Lean on agents in your office or your broker if you are struggling to come up with solutions or workarounds. The odds are they may have faced a similar situation and learned something valuable they can share with you.

Warnings for Firefighters

WARNING: How good of a firefighter is your broker? Brokers can sometimes be too strict, almost like an attorney who thinks too rigidly or narrow-mindedly, and they can blow up deals for you unnecessarily. Sometimes to get a deal done you've got to get creative and think outside the box. Even if your broker is a good firefighter, how accessible is he? This may be a difficult issue if you work in a large office, because these situations are often time sensitive, and the broker may be hard to reach on short notice. Do you have a collaborative environment in your office? Deals can be saved when you draw on the expertise of fellow agents. Forget commission splits and other things agents focus on too much—it's the number of deals saved that brings in the most money to your business.

WARNING: Some deals may not be in the best interest of your client and shouldn't be saved. Remember whom you're fighting for. Sure, you want to save any deal you can to earn your commission, but not at the expense of your client. Sometimes the best solution to a problem is to let the client walk away or get them out of the transaction. It's going to be painful, especially if you spent months and invested hours and hours trying to make that deal work. If your client wants it desperately and it's the best fit for them, then fight like hell. But if something major comes up and they're unsure what to do, your experience might tell you that it's in their best interest to move on. Help them move out of that transaction and resume their search. Always do the right thing and recommend the path you think is best for your client.

WARNING: Commissions are a tool in your toolbox. They're a resource you can use to save deals. Don't go to this toolbox unless you've exhausted everything else, but your 3 percent commission can be leveraged to solve a problem. Sometimes agents go there too quickly—and good for them; they're trying to do the right thing, and they're willing to sacrifice their commission to move a deal forward. But if you're not willing to tap into your commission, even when it means you blow up an amazing opportunity for your clients because you're too focused on your paycheck, you're not going to be hired at my office. I believe in doing the right thing at all costs. That doesn't mean you have to be a martyr and constantly give up your commission to make a deal go through. If that keeps happening, it means you're not getting creative, not coming up with enough solutions. Your commission is a last resort you can tap after exhausting other options. You can get the agent on the other side to split the cost to solve a problem—or lean on them to take ownership if they caused the problem.

If you do dig into your commission to solve a problem, make sure your client fully understands what you are doing. Sometimes they're not very appreciative. Sometimes they expect you to do it. When you do it voluntarily, they sometimes don't appreciate it, in part because you failed to communicate what you're actually doing for them. You'll learn to get better at communicating to clients that you're giving up part of your commission to solve a problem so they can have a successful closing. Ideally, you'll get them to agree to return the gesture somehow. Let them know exactly what hoops you are jumping through to get the deal closed for them. This opens the door for you to let your client know how they could help you. This could be a video testimonial or posting an endorsement on social media. Let them know their referrals will help you recoup some of the commission you gave up. People are willing to help if you present your request the right way, frame it in the right context, help them understand what you gave up to help them, and make it clear how they can help you. Done the right way, they'll feel indebted to you and happy to help.

WARNING: Always do the right thing. Sometimes the solutions that you or others come up with to solve a problem might put your license or your reputation in jeopardy if they come unraveled on you. Consider this scenario: buyers want to get into a house before closing because their previous home has sold and they have no place to live. The sellers say no, but they've already moved out. So the listing agent says maybe they can get in a little early, they'll just bend the rules. Agents get put in a situation where they try to help somebody but at the risk of putting their clients or their license in jeopardy.

Similar things happened during the real estate crash, and it's the reason people went to jail for mortgage fraud. Lenders and agents pushed loans through to help people get into a house they wanted, when in the end it was something they couldn't afford. Lenders massaged numbers for their own benefit, to earn a commission check, or to help out the people who were sitting in front of them trying to get into a house.

Whatever the motive, make sure the solutions you find to help people don't compromise the business and the reputation you've worked so hard to build.

CHAPTER 24

Buyers: The Art of Showing Homes

The most basic piece of advice you'll hear from real estate professionals about showing homes is that you should only show homes to qualified buyers. Yet the vast majority of real estate agents don't follow their own advice. They end up showing homes to unqualified buyers.

They do this for a handful of reasons. The most common reason is because they're so excited about having a new client, a new lead, a new prospect—and they throw caution to the wind and hope it works out for the best. They don't want to create any restrictions or hoops for the buyers to jump through that might make them hire someone else as their real estate agent.

Another common reason is because the buyers might have come from a referral, especially a trusted referral source, so the agent gives the buyers the benefit of the doubt because of who referred them. Maybe it's a parent referring a child, and they say the son or daughter is in "good shape" to buy.

Maybe it's the buyers themselves telling the agent how financially sound they are and how it's going to be "no problem" for them to get financing. They're sure their credit scores are amazing, and they have a bunch of money to put down.

Whatever the reason, it might give the agent the confidence to start showing clients houses before they have a prequalification letter.

Get Them Prequalified—Period

Let's say you're that agent, and your buyer doesn't have a prequalification. What should you do? To avoid further pain down the road, you want to make the first meeting simple. Limit the meeting so that you're not showing a bunch of houses, maybe just one or two—or even better, hold the meeting at your office. During that first meeting, you want to articulate why it's important for the buyer to get prequalified. A lot of buyers don't know what it means to get prequalified. They might say they've talked to someone at their bank, but that doesn't mean they've started the process. Make sure they understand why it's so important and get a firm commitment from them that they'll get prequalified before they ask to see more homes.

Novice homebuyers are usually eager to listen to anything you say, and they'll do it. More experienced buyers tend to drag their feet because they've been through the process before and don't anticipate having issues getting financing. Articulate to them that it's not *your* requirement—many sellers require you, as the agent, to show evidence that the buyer is prequalified or otherwise able to purchase a property like theirs. You see this more often with higher-end or luxury homes where the seller requires an agent to provide a prequalification letter or proof of funds from the buyer before showing the home. But I can tell you that *all* sellers would prefer to have only prequalified buyers viewing their house. So it's important to stress to buyers that this could be a requirement—and even if it's not a requirement on the home they want to see, their perfect home could be bought out from under them if someone who is prequalified makes an offer when they are still scrambling to get theirs.

Ideally you'll assign your buyers to a lender you recommend and know. The prequalification letter is fairly easy and fast to get. I typically call the lender to get details on their opinion about how solid the buyer's chances are and what price range they should be shopping in. That will give you an idea of how much time to invest with these buyers and which price range you should be shopping in at that particular moment. If there is some uncertainty they might have some issues getting financing, then it might be worth slowing things down until you can get that uncertainty cleared up.

Showing a Home

So what happens when you actually get to the house and you're showing the home? My advice is to avoid being that stereotypical real estate agent you see in movies—the one who is overexcited about the home and oversells it to the buyer. You really don't need to "sell" the home. Don't let your excitement lead you to showcase "all the wonderful things that are so amazing" about the house. If you come across to the buyers as fake or trying too hard to sell them on that home, they're going to stop trusting the information you give them. All they'll see is an agent who is trying too hard to sell them a home and who doesn't have their best interest at heart. When you finish showing them that house, they might be "thankful for all the information you got on it," but they probably won't ask you to show them more homes. You've crossed the barrier between being a trusted resource and a salesy real estate agent.

Instead, pay attention to the type of buyers they are. Engage them in conversation, and it doesn't necessarily need to be about the house. If you can get good at polite, fun conversation, your buyers will loosen up and let you know more about their situation and what type of home they're looking for. When they come in, at first they're often guarded. But if you get them talking, they'll start expressing more about their situation. Once they do that, pay attention to what type of buyers they are and what information they're interested in, so you can tailor the discussion you have with them to items they're concerned about. Some buyers want to be shown around the house and have things pointed out to them. Others want time to discover for themselves.

Sometimes the items that buyers are most interested in have nothing to do with the house. Their questions might concern the lot or the property, or the neighborhood and school district. The clients might be ho-hum about the house, but once they hear about the schools or specific amenities in the neighborhood, that ho-hum house becomes something they can work with. It's important that you know those facts about the house and the area. The more you know, the more homes you're going to sell.

Navigating Objections

You also want to help buyers understand simple and complex objections. For example, if they're really hung up on wall paint, it's your job to illustrate how easy that is to fix. You may have used a paint contractor with a previous client and already have a basic idea how much it will cost to have the interior of the house painted. You might say, "To have the interior painted will cost around $2,000. We can include in our offer to ask the sellers to pay for that before you move into the house." Ask if the house becomes more workable to the buyers once that matter is dealt with, to get their minds past that objection. That simple objection might be blocking their ability to see the true benefit of that house and how it might be a good fit for them. All they see is a house that feels dark because of the paint, and you can illustrate how simple it is to improve by changing the paint color.

A more complex objection might be that the roof looks old, and buyers worry about the cost of replacing such a major issue. Offer ideas to get them looking beyond the roof. I would say that I know a roofer who will do an inspection and tell us if the roof needs to be replaced or estimate its remaining lifespan. If it does need to be replaced, we'll ask the seller to take care of it as part of the offer. It's a quick process to see if the sellers are willing to cooperate—and if they aren't, we move on to another house. But if the buyer likes the house except for the condition of the roof, then we can tailor our offer to mitigate the issue.

A lot of times, agents either don't speak up when buyers share concerns about a house, or they talk too much and don't listen to the buyers' concerns. They don't truly address those concerns, offer workarounds, or allow buyers time to process certain information. It's an agent's job to pay attention to how the buyer reacts to certain houses, and know to move on if a home is not the right fit.

When Buyers Like the First Home You Show Them

Sometimes a buyer will be pleasantly surprised by how much they like the first house you show them. They start talking to themselves about where Johnny's or Suzie's bedroom is going to be. They wonder if there will be room for dinner parties on the patio. They'll start envisioning themselves in the house. You might be thinking, *We have a slew of houses to see, but this might be easier than I thought.* Even the buyers are thinking this might be the one, but you have ten homes on your list to show them. Buyers most often want to check off all the boxes, so you leave that house feeling pretty good about it and head to the next one.

The next house may not be as good as the first, but it has a couple of features that beat the first house. They might say, "We don't like the layout much, but this kitchen is gorgeous." The third house may not be quite as good a fit for them as the first house because it doesn't have as many bedrooms as they need, but it's a wonderful location and the house has a good warm feeling.

Be cautious about showing too many homes. What happens is that you keep looking at homes, and each one could have a single feature they like better than the first house they liked. When you finish looking at homes, they are overwhelmed. They look back on the first one and say, "I'm not sure what it is, but I don't think that one's the right fit for us anymore. I think we just need to keep looking." They look at more and more houses, and it all becomes muddled. They might have looked at three or four houses that could have worked for them—they were really excited when they were in those houses—and if any of them were the only house they looked at, they might have been sure enough to move forward with an offer. But they looked at so many that they all blend together, and the buyers can't make a decision.

Part of your job as a real estate agent is to prevent them from getting too confused. Help them stay focused on what it is they really want to get from their purchase. I recommend that you take a break after you've seen a few homes that fit the buyers' needs. If they really like a house but you have others on your schedule, take a break as soon as you can. Schedule a lunch or bathroom break and go over the notes of things the buyers really liked about the first house. Focus on the things they liked and disliked about the second house, and the third. Based on that conversation, see if there are any homes they can take off the list. Illustrate why some of the houses should be ruled out. And then extend that to the homes you still have scheduled to look at. If you ruled out the second home because of a lack of bathrooms or patio, you might skip showing them the next house on your list because it has the same shortcomings. Tell them it would be better to focus on the remaining homes that will be the best fit first, and then go back and review the ones they liked best. That way you can hone in on which houses are truly at the top of their list and rule out the rest.

Most times, buyers will be amenable to that plan. If you go through the process of showing ten homes, and they liked the first one best, there's a chance their enthusiasm will fade and they'll rule it out by the end of the day. However, if you go back to it at the end of the day, they might fall in love with it again. Or if you get a sense throughout the day of what details they're responding to the most in each home, and maybe you know of a specific property in the stack that will be the best fit for them, consider moving that house to the last showing of the day. Some homebuyers are pretty easygoing and can picture themselves in many different houses, but if they see the best one at the end, after they've seen a bunch that were close but not perfect, that one will rise to the top of the list, and they'll likely move forward with an offer. Even if they have simple objections to the house, they'll have seen enough others to know that one best suits their needs.

When Buyers Don't Like Any Homes You Show Them

If the buyers don't seem to like anything, try to identify their triggers. What is causing them to say "Nope!" and move on? Is it something controllable? The more time you take to understand them and their objections, the less time you'll ultimately spend driving all over town showing them houses. Really, you should be saving them time. You should be helping them find the best houses faster. That's not taking a shortcut; it's doing your job. It's worth the investment of time to really understand your buyers so you can hone in on what properties will and won't work for them. Sure, they're going to ask to see homes that you already know are not going to work for them, and you'll oblige them so they can understand the process better. Afterwards you can say, "I have another home that I'd really like you to see, because based on what we've seen I think you're going to like it—and if you don't, it will help me understand more about what homes might work best for you."

The better I understand my clients, the more I can help them. As I get to know my clients, I learn what they respond to. I can often find their ideal home by digging deeper and previewing more homes. If I find or recommend a home not on their list and get them to look at it, often they say, "Wow! Thank you!" And they think I'm amazing. I get all kinds of referrals from them because I helped them find something they weren't able to find on their own, and they see and appreciate the value my service brought to them.

Showing homes to buyers is not as simple as showing up and opening the door. If you're just opening doors, you're not adding value to the potential buyers. Make yourself more resourceful. Pay attention and listen. Help them discover information they can't discover on their own, such as details from the MLS data sheet that may not be readily available to the buyer, or details you're aware of about the community. Help them learn about other properties they might have overlooked. There are a lot of great homes out there that aren't listed well, so people reject them based on the online marketing of the home. That's a shame—but *you* know it's an awesome location, you've previewed the house or showed it to another buyer, and you can tell the buyers, "I looked at this house. The pictures suck, but you really need to give it a look for yourselves." Most times, the buyers will take your advice. You might find a house that's now a great deal because the agent did such a poor job marketing it. It's seen a few price drops, and now it's a great price for your clients.

Using Buyers' Agents and Showing Agents

If other agents are out showing homes to your client, be sure they understand the concepts discussed in this chapter. They might all seem like common sense, but I've seen agents frustrate buyers because they are not listening, which causes undue stress and adds time to the process of buying a home.

When *Not* to Show a Home

There are indeed times when you should not show a home.

It's tempting when somebody is standing in front of a house looking at your real estate sign and phoning you to show it. You can say yes, but before you confirm a time with them, ask enough questions to make yourself comfortable. Not only do you want to protect your safety, but you want to make sure you're not wasting your time—or the seller's. So when they call you and say, "I want to see this property as soon as possible," say,

"Absolutely"—then ask about their situation, their financials, whether they're working with an agent, whatever you need to ask to make yourself feel comfortable before showing the home.

Safety First

Safety is a topic that could fill an entire chapter. At the very least, use common sense. Take more caution than you would normally take for yourself. Everyone has a different threshold for feeling safe, and you know your threshold. Take extra precautions so you won't have any problems.

Be wary of showing vacant homes, and avoid situations like a foreclosure home in a questionable area at the wrong time of day or night. Again, use common sense and an abundance of caution, and don't put yourself in a compromising situation. Trouble can find you even in a good neighborhood. Many of the female agents in my office will not show the basement of a home if they're showing a home to a man. They point out where it is and tell them they're welcome to check it out—but they don't lead the way down there. Especially in a vacant house. Again, it's about knowing your comfort zone and taking extra precautions. You can say your broker requires you to operate that way, if needed.

> **Case in Point:** *I once previewed a foreclosure home in a very high-end neighborhood, and as I was walking through the house with the power off, I couldn't see where I was going. I tried using my old cell phone as a light, and I got myself trapped inside a room I couldn't find my way out of. It was pitch black. I couldn't get cell reception, and I thought I was stuck there. I thought I was going to have to break through a wall to get out or even risk being stuck for days because I didn't tell anybody where I was going. It was scary. So take extra precautions, tell somebody where you're going and what you're doing, take a flashlight—whatever you need to do to feel safe.*

Narrow the List

Another mistake agents make is they show fifteen, twenty, or thirty homes in a day. They show all kinds of properties to a buyer. That is a colossal waste of time. When I see an agent show a client twenty or thirty homes in a day, it proves to me they didn't ask enough questions or learn enough from their client.

If you have a client who insists on seeing that many homes, you don't have to agree to it to prove you're a good agent. Rather, schedule a batch of them first and try to pick ones that are significantly different from the others. During that first outing, you can often identify what criterion is a no-go for your clients. Use that information to narrow down the list the client has given you. You can narrow the list further and add to it once you better understand their needs. For example, if the clients decide they don't prefer homes with the master bedroom upstairs, there are likely five to ten other homes you can cross off the list. As that happens, call ahead to the properties and cancel the showings. If you're in a home and they rule it out for some reason, don't linger there. Get them on to the next place. If you don't manage that, some buyers will take forever at each property.

Stick to the List

Another scenario where you shouldn't show a home is when you're at a showing and the clients ask about a home across the street. There's a real estate sign out front, and they want to go see the house. For whatever reason, that home is not on your to-show list. There's likely a good reason for that: it could be out of their price range, or not available, or pending.

Many times I'll see agents force that showing because they want to accommodate their clients. They'll look it up on their phone, and even if they see a sale is pending, they'll still show it. That's okay if you make sure you contact the listing agent and let them know that you would like to show their listing, because many agents don't. They see a lockbox, knock on the door, and go in. Put yourself in the shoes of the listing agent: You have a pending property, you're getting ready to close, and suddenly you get a showing alert on your pending listing. That causes all kinds of alarms, so don't do it unless you get permission to show that home. If your clients insist on seeing it, go grab coffee and see if you can arrange to show it. Don't just randomly show something you haven't done your due diligence on, because you could create a firestorm of issues.

Never Show a Home until It's Ready

Excluding foreclosures and other distressed properties, if the home doesn't show its best, it's rarely worth having a buyer see it. In most cases, I've found it's a mistake to show a home when it's not spruced up, clean, with the lights on, etc., because even if the buyers are interested, the offer they write will not be as strong as it could have been. Therefore, the odds of getting to an agreeable price with the seller are low. It's frustrating when buyers look at the right home for them but they don't pull the trigger because they are too distracted by the state of the home.

Let's say buyers have a short window of availability, and they tell you at the last minute there's a home they'd like to see before they leave town. You call the seller to schedule a showing, and they say they've got something torn up or the house is a mess and it doesn't show well right now. There's not enough time for the seller to get the house ready to meet the buyer's window.

Agents often go ahead and allow the showing and warn their client the house doesn't look great. Even when the buyers say they understand and they appreciate the opportunity to see the home, it's almost always an unwise decision to show that house. If you show a buyer a house that is not show-ready and not in its best condition, it could backfire on you.

It's really important that you understand this point: Buyers have so little imagination (even though they think they have an open mind), and they end up responding emotionally when they're in a house. If the house is not clean and doesn't show well, or it's dark and the blinds are shut, that will have an impact on them. It won't feel like a place they are excited about living in.

Buyers often decide if they like a house within moments of walking in. It's rare that a buyer will look past a house that smells or doesn't show well. They won't have a positive emotional experience with that house and will move on. If they had seen it in its best condition, they might have fallen in love with it. There are exceptions to this rule, such as if you anticipate there will be multiple offers on the home, you better get the buyer over to the home as soon as possible.

It's important to everyone—agents, sellers, and buyers—to see the house in its best condition so the process can work the way it's meant to. If you, as the agent, get people into the right home that meets their criteria and price point, you hope that they don't get distracted by people's dirty laundry. You hope they see that the home is really a great option for them and take action. As a listing agent, you work your tail off getting the house ready and marketing it well. You hope that marketing produces a buyer. But if they show up and the house doesn't show its greatest, you'll be frustrated because that buyer could have been the one that house was meant for, and you blew it by rushing the showing.

If either you or the house or the seller is not ready, then don't show it. You may not be ready because you don't know enough about your client, and the seller might not be ready because the house doesn't show well. Your job as an agent is to show buyers not only the right houses but the right houses at the right time.

Ultimately your job is to use your skills and resources to reduce the time it takes for buyers to find the home they want. It's your job to make the process easier for them, to help them avoid costly mistakes or setbacks. Saving the buyers time will save you time as well.

CHAPTER 25

Lenders: The Hard Truth

Working with the wrong lender can double, triple, or even quadruple the level of stress in every one of your transactions and have devastating impacts on what you make in a given year. Identifying good lending partners for your business is crucial. So how do you know when you're working with the right lender?

> **CASE IN POINT:** *One of the first lenders I ever worked with was new to the business, like me, and was a funny, friendly, seemingly hardworking guy. I figured, why not use him? What I didn't know then was that he was disorganized, sloppy, and a little arrogant. He made mistakes—and he ended up screwing up the deal I was working on. Luckily, a different lender stepped in and saved the day. But because the original lender was a friend, I gave him a second, third, and fourth chance and had a similar experience each time. I started to think this was just the normal process, until I had an experience with an awesome lender who was really dependable and knew the lending business inside out. It was a night-and-day experience.*

When a lender is new to the business, or is a veteran who doesn't evolve with changes in the industry, or switches banks where different systems are in place—all these scenarios can cause problems. Agents underestimate the importance of having a solid lending partner.

Experience matters. A seasoned lender usually has better firefighting skills. They're better able to think outside the box and find solutions when there's a problem. If they've been in the business a while, it means they've seen a lot and overcome a lot to stay in business.

It also matters how many deals they close each month. Are they closing one or two a month? Eight to ten? Twenty to forty? Personally, I'm only concerned if a lender closes just a few deals each month—which may seem backwards to you, since a lender who is doing two deals a month will have more time and availability to give you and your client superior service. The problem is that these lenders likely don't move enough business across their desk to help them understand the issues that arise with loans. A seasoned lender will have intimate knowledge of what their underwriter is thinking and potentially going to ask for, so they can pre-plan and pre-engineer the loan to go as smoothly as possible.

On the flip side, if the mortgage broker is doing a lot of business, I don't worry about it unless I see them start to drop the ball and delay getting back to me and my clients in a timely matter. Mortgage professionals who have good internal systems can handle a much greater volume of business. It's the mortgage people who are trying to do it all themselves without systems in place who tend to find they can't maintain their desired level of service on a consistent basis.

You may have a great lender, but your client will often ask to use their local bank. A lot of banks don't close many residential home mortgages. They might have an attractive rate, but they don't process many home loans. Plan for the worst. If your client's loan gets denied there, you want to be ready with other lenders. I work with lenders who work exclusively with home loans—that's their business, that's what they do, they're experts at it. I want them to have that wide knowledge base of all the products that are available to my clients, to know how to quickly move things forward.

How Does Your Lender Communicate with Your Clients and with You?

Are they personal or impersonal? Some lenders want to communicate strictly through email and text, while some want to do everything face-to-face. It's important to find a lender who will match their communication to the preferences of the client—and to you. Maybe you like to be texted or blind-copied on emails, while your client prefers phone calls. Have that conversation with your lender and pay attention to how they communicate with your client. Some lenders may be good at what they do but are not good communicators, and that can cause undue stress and aggravation.

Some lenders go too fast, make mistakes, over-promise, and under-deliver. Other lenders go too slow; it feels like they take forever. Be aware of your lender's speed.

How well does your lender prep your clients initially for the lending process? The better the lender communicates to the borrower what to expect through each step, what will be asked of them and when, and what frustrations they might encounter, the easier the process will feel to the client. The lender should also work to understand the client's schedule and needs and ask what's important to them. Some lenders will brush through that process, and others will pay close attention. So you want to watch that with the lenders you work with and see who preps your clients well for the process.

CASE IN POINT: *The biggest issue I have with mortgage lenders in general is that they have a bad habit of telling me what I want to hear instead of what I need to hear. They tell me the best-case scenario all the time. But then that doesn't happen. In reality, they're sugarcoating the situation, and that causes many more headaches and frustrations later on when I'm scrambling to save a deal. Lenders wait way too long to tell me the bad news, and that pisses me off because it shortens the time I have to fix the problem. You want to have that conversation with your lender ahead of time so that it doesn't happen to you or your clients.*

How Would You Rate Your Lender's Ability to Coach Clients so They Can Get Approved?

There are a handful of lenders out there who are particularly good about coaching clients who need help improving their situation before they qualify for a home loan. The consumer might be waiting for a stable job situation or saving a down payment. They might need to improve their credit score. Whatever the situation, it's a lender's job to walk consumers through the steps and get them ready to qualify. Often it's the real estate agent who ends up doing the heavy lifting, but a good lender will take that burden off your shoulders and help your client get in a position where they can purchase a home.

Some lenders have good intentions initially but don't follow up. Other lenders stay on top of it with regular phone calls to check on a client's progress. If you find one of those lenders, it makes a huge difference in how many deals you're able to put together.

Ask the lender how they intend to follow up with that client. Do they have a system in place, or do they seem like they're winging it? Some lenders will only focus on getting a client's credit repaired without coaching them on other financial habits that will hold them back from getting financing in the future. Check in with the clients you have referred to the lender and ask the lender about your clients. This will help you track how accountable your lender is with people you refer to them. The best lenders will alert you on the status of the prospects you have sent to them on a regular basis.

Does Your Lender Finish Early or Last Minute?

This drives me nuts. I get an offer and get the property under contract. I send the paperwork to the lender, and he gets working on it. He asks for the buyer's financials, W2s, and bank statements. The house passes inspection, and the appraisal gets ordered and delivered. I check in with the lender. All is well and looking good; there should be smooth sailing to closing. We're a week out from closing, and I check in with the lender, who tells me he should have the docs out on Thursday. But we're supposed to close Friday. "Yep," the lender tells me, "we're right on time."

That's not on time to me. This infuriates me. The lender had a month to six weeks to work on this, so why is he finishing the day before closing? When you cut a deal that close, seconds count. What if my client or the seller isn't available to sign papers at the last minute? Or one of a million other things happens outside our control? Then that property's not closing on time.

I like lenders who get the file done at least a week before closing. That should be their goal. If the closing date is set for September 1, the lender's goal to have that file ready should be August 24. You can schedule signings accordingly, and you have flexibility in case something goes wrong (or if both parties want to close early). It takes the stress out of closing.

One caveat: I know lenders who pride themselves on going really fast, but their deals blow up because they're going too fast. They make mistakes or they miss something important. They didn't check the file well enough, and the deal blows up, wasting weeks. So speed isn't necessarily what I'm looking for. It's scheduling their tasks so they can actually close one week before the contract deadline. If you're a lender and reading this, please take note. Your agents will love you so much more if you do this.

How Organized Does Your Lender Appear to You and Your Clients?

Does your lender always seem to be behind the eight ball? Are you more aware of what's happening with the files than he seems to be? Does he seem disorganized and unaware? A lot of lenders seem unorganized. Hopefully they have some internal systems in place to help them, but it's important that you recognize and address that behavior if it's affecting your deal. Some of your clients are going to get really frustrated if the lender comes back to them ten or fifteen times throughout the month asking for one more thing. The client will want to know why the lender didn't ask for everything at one time, a month ago. The lender might try to blame it on an underwriter who is asking for additional information, but that just shows me that the lender doesn't know his underwriter very well, and he doesn't understand his own internal loan process well enough. The lender should anticipate what the underwriter will ask for and collect it from the client up front. He should help the client prepare and have their information ready instead of sending them running back throughout the month for one more piece of information.

Odds are that you know lots of lenders, and some of them are going to be really great people and even good friends. They stop by your office and do nice things for you. You want to do business with them. But if you ever struggle to get a deal done with them and they're not finding ways to help you fix it, they're not a good fit for your business. Maybe the lending institution where they're working is the problem, so you may have to have a hard talk with them about that if you want to continue using them. For example, your lender may have been wonderful to work with, but his company was bought and the internal processes with the new company are different. Every loan you do with them feels like you're having teeth pulled. So you can have a great lender relationship, but if they work at the wrong lending company, you may have to look elsewhere until they solve those internal issues.

How Creative Is Your Lender with Solving Problems and Putting out Fires?

Just as your ability to put out fires impacts the number of closings you'll have this year, the same thing goes with the lender you're working with. There are always fires, always things that seem to flare up. The *wrong* lending partner will say and think: *We've exhausted all possible solutions, and I'm sorry, but we can no longer provide financing to your client.*

The right lending partner will say and think: *...But I know someone who can solve this for you.* Or: *...But I have an idea how to solve this for you.* The right lender will look for solutions outside the box that get your client's financing back inside the box. Fires flare up, and the clever lenders are good at solving them.

Does Your Lender Blame Himself and His Company When There's a Problem, or Does He Blame Everybody Else?

Does your lender hold himself accountable? Does he offer to make a situation right? When there's a problem, does he offer to pay for closing extensions, reduce his lender fee, or even release the entire file and appraisal to a competing lender who can finish the file? He should, because it's the right thing to do.

You'll get resistance from lenders who don't think the delay is their fault. Here are some examples:

The buyer took forever to get me X, Y, and Z documents, so the loan isn't ready on time. It's the buyer's fault. I say BS to that. The lender could have informed the agent weeks before that he was having difficulty acquiring information from the buyer, so the agent could have helped communicate the urgency to the buyer. The agent would have known beforehand that there was a looming problem and could have started asking for extensions early on or whatever was needed instead of having the sale blow up at the last minute. Asking for extensions from the seller is much easier when an agent asks weeks before closing. Asking right before closing is likely to add costs and stress to all parties involved and possibly blow up the whole transaction.

The loan docs are still in underwriting. They were supposed to be out yesterday; there is nothing I can do. Delayed docs create a domino effect of issues. A lender uses this excuse if she feels the delay is not her fault—but it is her fault. She knew for the last month or six weeks what the deadline was, and if she didn't hit it, she needs to own up to it. It's the lender's problem, and she needs to figure out a way to make it right.

By that point, what's done is done, but she could have gotten the papers to the underwriter sooner, especially if there was a backlog. Now she can get a company executive involved to speed up the process. She can help soften the burden of the delay by paying the seller a daily fee until the problem is resolved. Will the buyer or seller be temporarily homeless, need a hotel, or be delayed from closing on another property now? Will either party be charged extra fees and expenses because of the delay? The lender needs to step up and cover those expenses if she's the one who caused the problem. If the lender doesn't end up making any money on the transaction because of this, I say good for them. Doing the right thing often means you don't make money or even lose money, but that's the price of a good lesson learned. The pain and cost of that transaction will hopefully help her put steps in place in her business so that she doesn't have this happen a second time. Unfortunately, what I see happen all too often is that the lender doesn't take responsibility, and it's the real estate agent who sacrifices his commission to help save the deal. If this happens to you, I'm proud of you for going out of your way to help your client. But going forward, definitely change whom you recommend for lenders.

The buyers didn't disclose that they had a short sale three years ago, so now we can't do the loan. I hear this excuse from lenders a lot: the buyers had a foreclosure or short sale they didn't disclose, so now the lender can't give them the loan. This is a BS answer, because it means the lender was lazy when he took the initial application. He should have asked for complete information on the application and worked ahead of time to really vet the buyer and discover up front if there was anything the underwriter or the lending institution was going to have a problem with. The lender would have seen on the client's credit report if there was a foreclosure or bankruptcy—if they checked. They could have told the buyer right away that they were going to have problems getting a loan and saved everyone the time, expense, and paperwork involved in viewing multiple properties and making an offer. As an agent, you don't have the luxury of wasting a full month showing properties to a buyer who can't buy, all because the lender was too lazy to determine if they were actually qualified.

How Easy or Hard Does the Lender Make the Application Process for the Client?

When you initially work with a client, they may not even know if they want to work with you. You might be showing them a house from a sign call or a website. They're still getting to know you, but you introduce them to a lender. Suddenly the process turns into a pain in the ass for them to find out if they can get financing. It might be due to the lender's frustrating process. You can lose clients that way.

A lender should guide clients in the right way and make the process as smooth as possible for the way that specific client likes to do business. Some buyers prefer to fill out a mortgage application in person with the lender or over the phone, while others want to do it online. Instead of spending hours filling out a complicated application, some buyers might prefer to answer a few questions via email and let the lender fill out the majority of the application for them. It's important for a lender to recognize which process will make each individual buyer happiest when applying for a mortgage. Sometimes what's convenient for the buyer is not convenient for the lender, but that's the price of business.

Some lenders are trying to be so streamlined that they force everyone through a one-size-fits-all process. That's a sure way to lose clients. If the application is a pain in the ass to finish, people will stop and move on to another lender. Someone else will pick them up and help them later with a process that appears easier to them.

Has Your Lender Helped Any Clients Who Weren't Able to Get Financing from Other Lenders?

Some lenders I work with are specifically on my go-to list because I've brought them a borrower who was unable to get financing elsewhere, and they got it done. They got it done because their company has more programs, or that lender was smarter at figuring out how to fix and tweak things. Each mortgage banker offers common loans, but they might have their own internal loan overlays that make it potentially more complicated. Or they might have narrower product offerings than a company that looks and acts similar but has more products. So how big is your lender's box of options for the consumer you send over there?

I'm not talking about scraping together loans for borrowers who can't afford to buy a home. I'm talking about buyers like us—strong buyers, self-employed, who make good money but are sometimes outside the box. I can afford my mortgage, but I'm not a W2 salaried employee, so it's a pain in the butt to get financing. Half your town might be self-employed. So what are your lenders doing to serve that demographic? What about a buyer who doesn't work but has money in the bank, a pension, or a trust fund? They have a solid credit score, but you'll be shocked how hard it is for those people to get financing.

I know certain lenders who love those types of borrowers, who treat them like the good borrower they are, and make the process easy for them. They get it done.

Has Your Lender Ever Brought You Any Business? Has She Helped You Grow Your Business in Any Way?

Your lender might be your friend. She might take you to lunch every once in a while. But is she reciprocating the business relationship you have? If not, it's probably not because she doesn't have the opportunity—it's because she has twenty other agents just like you.

Some lenders will go out of their way to help you grow your business. They'll find or create a way to help you get more leads. They'll go out of their way to invest in this partnership with you, so that you can both improve your business.

I don't need a lot. I don't necessarily need a lender to throw me new clients. My first priority is that they get the lending job done and make it a smooth process. But I might be sending that lender a ton of business. If someone was sending me a ton of business, I know I'd be treating them right. I'd be finding ways to reciprocate—finding ways to help them with their endeavors and goals, because they're helping me with mine. A good lender will think like that and work at solving that riddle to support you. That's a good relationship to have.

CHAPTER 26
Listing Appointments: Stop Talking, Start Listening

I see agents experience more anxiety over an upcoming listing appointment than anything else. Some agents get nervous because they're new and inexperienced. At the same time, I see very experienced agents get nervous when they see they're competing against other agents for the listing. Agents tend to get anxious for listing appointments unless the appointment is with a friend or from a referral, or they're following a process, procedure, method, or system that gives them confidence.

Nerves are normal, and it's not necessarily a bad thing to be nervous. It's not like you can turn off that part of your brain. However, it's important to understand why you're nervous. Most times, people get nervous because they're unprepared.

A lot of agents will learn some fancy listing presentation from either their brokerage or some guru or somebody who sells "millions of homes" and has a fancy listing presentation. Some agents will go in with their tablets and their fancy technology to show prospective clients what they can do.

All of those things might impress sellers. But I would say, more than anything, sellers don't pick you as their agent because of the listing presentation you give. They pick you because of *you*.

Be Unique
First off, stop looking at it as a presentation. That means you're trying to prove something. Hopefully you've already proven

237

your value before you even got there—the best-case scenario is that they already know you as a trusted resource and advisor before they call you. That way you're not competing; you're just going in there and getting to work.

Establishing yourself as an authority prior to showing up at their home is a huge advantage—which is why I show up ready to work on getting their home sold, rather than proving to them why they should pick me to have them sell their home. But when that's not the case, when you haven't been able to establish yourself as an authority, just note that all the fancy presentations in the world won't hold up to their impression of *you*. You need to establish your confidence and ability to net the seller the most money when the home sells.

Some agents will try to get more listings by coming up with special promotions where clients get a certain percentage off of commissions or some other gimmick. I've found from experience that gimmicks are gimmicks. A lot of times when I offered them, I didn't need them and therefore took less of a commission because of some gimmick that was supposed to get me more listings. Or people didn't care about them. Ultimately, they care more about picking the right person to sell their house.

A lot of times, agents will go into a listing appointment with the same messaging as other agents. They say the exact same things. They offer the sellers the same type of information. It's very difficult for the client to decide, so they might pick an agent who tells them their house is worth the most. Or they'll pick the agent who charges the smallest commission. The real problem is that all the agents gave the same pitch and made it very difficult for the client to choose.

As an agent, you want to develop a method to build up your confidence and the client's. There are a number of ways to do this. First, when you go into somebody's house, make sure you pay attention. Listen to them. Find out if they've ever sold a home before and how it went. Have they previously listed this home, and how did that experience go? You need to get details about what went wrong. Maybe they felt the first agent wasn't the right fit. Or the agent did something that they found annoying or troublesome. Pay attention.

Take Notes

You also want to ask plenty of questions about the house. If it was listed before, you need to figure out why it didn't sell. It might become obvious once you walk through the house. If you want that house to sell quickly, you need to pay attention and take notes. Make a list of things the seller needs to improve or change before listing the home. Make notes of what kind of photos you'll need and what kind of help you think the sellers will need to get the house sold this time.

If you're going into a listing appointment and you know you're not competing against other agents, my advice is that you take those notes and then go get started. Schedule the next thing that needs to happen right there in front of the clients. Move it forward. Don't focus too much on the paperwork, even though that needs to happen. Focus first on getting the process started rather than trying to close them on choosing you as their agent. They'll get excited because they can see the process starting. Sometimes sellers choose the agent who takes the most action to help them get their home sold.

If you are competing against other agents, then it's all the more important that you bring something to the table that the sellers are not hearing from anybody else. It's critical that you offer something different—for example, your ability to listen, understand, and address their biggest concerns. If you can do that, it might get you the listing.

Maybe you can share with them specific market insights that are meaningful to the sellers—not just generic charts but information that shows them that you have a richer understanding of the market than the other agents do.

Maybe you have a unique way of conducting your business that resonates with the sellers. Or you have a method or a unique approach to selling real estate that gives the sellers confidence in their decision to pick you. Do you have proof to back up claims that your system gets sellers more money for their homes? Find a way to articulate that, and the sellers will feel assured and excited about the expectations they have going forward.

You might be the most confident—and least arrogant—agent they meet with. A lot of agents appear to be confident when they're not, so they come across as being arrogant. Confidence comes from having a rich understanding of not only the job that needs to get done, but understanding the needs of your clients and possessing the ability to address those needs. It doesn't come from being blinded by arrogance and telling yourself, "I've done this longer or sold more than other agents in this neighborhood, so I'm the best," as that often develops into agents who stop listening to their clients (see chapter 8). If you have testimonials from other sellers, those do wonders for letting sellers know how great you are without you having to toot your own horn. (For more about collecting testimonials, see chapter 21.)

Be confident in your process because you do it better than anyone else. You've mastered it, and it's tried, trusted, and true. You can show them that, and if they have questions or concerns, you can bend that process here or there—but ultimately you may not take the listing because they're resistant to following your advice. For example, you may know they'll net $10,000 to $50,000 more when they sell their house if they follow your advice. Part of the problem is your ability to communicate the importance of following the steps you're advising (that's not their fault—it's yours). But you can decline to take the listing of someone who doesn't trust your method or advice, and that's okay. You may not be the right fit for them. You may want to focus on working with sellers who will work with you to maximize the selling price of their home.

The more ways you can help a seller beyond what is typical, the greater the odds you'll win more listings. Maybe you can solve a problem for the seller that the other agents can't—or won't. The sellers might have a big problem they're trying to figure out. If you can help them solve that problem, then it becomes very clear whom they should choose as their listing agent.

With listing appointments, I usually counsel agents not to overthink their approach. They need to be as prepared as possible but don't need a fancy presentation to get the listing. I've seen agents win hundreds of listings with just a notepad and a pen. A fancy presentation is not a requirement. If you have it in your box of tricks, great. If that's what gives you confidence, fine. Just remember, it's not a one-sided presentation—it's a consultation. It's a chance for you to learn more about your clients and their home and to let them learn more about you. If you make it a sales presentation, you won't get the same results as an agent who actually listens and counsels the sellers and has the best approach to selling the home. See chapter 27 on the Listing Triangle™ for details about developing a great plan for selling your listings.

Secret to Selling: The Listing Triangle™

You have a listing that won't sell. You reach out to your broker, fellow agents, coaches, and gurus, and what do they tell you? It's overpriced. *Drop the price. Price is everything.*

Sound familiar? It's likely that you've given that same advice to somebody who asked you about their listing that wouldn't sell. It's an easy answer: *Drop the price.* Even if agents resist that advice, because the listing seems to be priced in line with similar properties selling in that area, the response always seems to be: *No, if it's been on the market for months and it's not selling, it's got to be the price.*

On the whole, it's a mistake to assume that the listing is all about price. It's true; if you drop the price on a listing, someone will eventually buy it. But that's not what the seller hired you to do. They hired you to sell it for the highest price possible.

Some agents convince themselves that it's their job to make the seller "accept reality" and lower the price to a point where the agent thinks it will draw an offer—as though everything depends on price. The agent's advice could potentially cost the seller tens of thousands of dollars. It could also cost the agent months of unnecessary headaches as he continues to drop the price and wait for an offer. It might even cost him the listing.

WHY DO AGENTS LOSE LISTINGS? – A listing is lost when a home doesn't sell after months on the market. The sellers may feel that another agent could do a better job—or they might convince themselves that the home will never sell and take it off the market. In either case, it's an awful situation for the agent who has put a lot of effort and money into the listing with no return. No matter what the agent says or does, the sellers' perception is that they may need a different agent or they may need to cancel the listing.

There are things you can do as a listing agent to help your clients and prevent those issues from ever arising. If you follow the principles I present in this chapter, those problems should never be an issue for you with future listings.

WHAT GOES WRONG WITH A LISTING? – You get a listing, you work your butt off, you do everything you can think to do—list it on the MLS, get nice photos, host open houses often—but the property won't sell. Your clients won't drop their price any further. You blame the sellers for not lowering the price.

In fact, most real estate books, trainings, and gurus will teach agents how to avoid this outcome by learning the skilled art of getting the seller to lower their price. Some agents do this before they even take the listing—they get the seller to pre-agree to lower their price after so many days. I'm not arguing with that strategy. It could be an important aspect to selling the home. But there is always something else an agent can do to alter a listing besides dropping the price that could better the odds of that home selling. It might need both a lower price and changes in visibility and presentation. There's always more that can be done to make that property more appealing. It doesn't take long to spot it once you get good at looking for it.

When agents focus solely on price and use the skills they learned from their broker or trainer to basically beat up sellers to get them to lower their price, they're perpetuating the bad reputation that real estate agents have earned. How many sellers have you personally heard saying, "My last agent was only focused on dropping the price"? That's how people feel when that's the only solution an agent brings to the table once they do the work up front. Clients aren't sure what their agent does after a property is listed. They're not sure what options they have other than dropping the price. So if an agent gets aggressive about it because he wants it to sell before he loses the listing, that's how our industry gets a bad reputation for using slick, car salesman tactics to get sellers to lower their listing price. (Note: I know some very decent and ethical car salesmen, but you get my point.)

There are two other important strategies agents should focus on before reducing price.

Where agents drop the ball is by not focusing on the visibility of the listing and the presentation of the home. Price, visibility, and presentation are *equally* important—which is why I call this the *Listing Triangle*™.

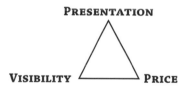

You need to become not just proficient but truly a master of each corner of the triangle, to know with absolute certainty that you are doing everything you can to net your seller the highest price for their home. If you have not mastered any portion of the Listing Triangle™, then I strongly advise you to align yourself with someone who has, before you take the listing. Don't take this lightly. You want to align yourself with the best people around to help you master the skills for the three corners of the Listing Triangle™. You may make less money because potentially you'll have to share your commission or pay a fee for the help— *but it's the right thing to do,* so don't be selfish or greedy. You will learn a lot by partnering with agents who have mastered aspects of the listing. You'll be able to up your game, and one day you'll be a master of all three corners of the triangle. If you're new or inexperienced and haven't mastered these techniques, you could be costing your seller (who might be your friend, a family member, or someone important to you) tens of thousands of dollars. I've seen this happen way too many times. Sellers are paying a lot for your services, so make sure you provide the A-team for them.

Let's talk about each corner of the Listing Triangle™.

Visibility

The main distribution channel for marketing visibility for real estate is the Multiple Listing Service (MLS). However, there's a problem with the MLS: *everyone uses it.* The home that you're listing may get lost in a sea of thousands of other homes with a similar look and features. Sure, the MLS syndicates your listing to hundreds if not thousands of real estate websites, but is that enough to get noticed? Is your listing just one of the masses, or is it best in its class? How do you rise above what everyone else is doing so you can provide higher visibility to your client's listing?

You need a visibility strategy. I can't tell you exactly what to do in this chapter, because every market and every home is different. Your strategies for visibility may change depending on the type and location of the home. But there are ways I can help you understand the importance of visibility and how to implement certain aspects that few other agents will be implementing in your marketplace.

First, let's break down what I mean by visibility. Visibility is not just how many people view your listing online or in person, but more importantly how many of the *right buyers* slow down enough to really consider it. The listing may look great and might be priced right, but if the targeted buyers are just skipping over it before they realize how great the home is, you haven't done a good job—the right buyer just sailed past you. You may feel you are doing everything you can to prevent this from happening, but chances are there's a lot more you can do.

How do you improve the visibility of your listing? There are a lot of strategies you can use to not only increase the volume of listing views but improve the quality of targeted buyers as well. There are strategies you can use to bring in new buyers who didn't even have your listing on their radar.

Here are some strategies that can help you improve a listing's visibility:

SYNDICATE - Syndicate means to broadcast the listings to more places and more websites. This is the first way most agents think of to increase visibility of their listings, but it still doesn't solve their inherent problem. You might get your listing to appear on more buyers' computer screens, but that doesn't mean it will hold their attention. If the people who see it aren't the right buyers, or if they skim over it, it doesn't matter.

A lot of agents will syndicate by putting their listings on websites like Zillow, Trulia, and other similar sites, which are big hubs where people search for homes. They can even pay for better placement on those sites. They can create listings on Craigslist or other local classified sites. This will get their listing seen by more people, but whether or not the listing is effective has to do with other aspects of the Listing Triangle™.

A more successful approach to syndicating would be to find unique websites no one else is using that might get your listings in front of the right audience, such as neighborhood clubs, organizations, job posting sites, local sports teams, churches— really any site that may already have the attention of your target audience. Alternative social media platforms are another way to syndicate your listing, and they allow you to target specific buyers. Think of the kind of targeted buyer you want to reach and research where those buyers are spending their time online and what they're doing there. If you can reach your targeted buyers where they already are, that will be a more effective way to syndicate your listing. For instance, you can find specific

Facebook groups, Pinterest boards, and Twitter and Instagram hashtags that are full of your targeted client. You can pay to get in front of very specific demographics on Facebook, Google, and other platforms. Your target audience could be using something that only exists locally, like specific publications, venues, or community organizations.

CREATE NEW DISTRIBUTION CHANNELS - Beyond websites, you can create all kinds of distribution channels to get your listings out there and increase visibility. Social media is one of the most common channels, but it's often underutilized. You can also use print media, audio podcasts, or YouTube videos—there are a lot of unique distribution channels you can use to increase the visibility of your listing.

Social media is a channel that people often don't leverage. You can put information about your listing on Facebook, but if you're just posting the generic details about a house, you're doing what everybody else is doing, and it's going to be ignored. Instead, do something unique and creative. Talk about the property in a unique way. Think about the headline you're using. People are on social media to be entertained, so entertain them. If the home has a swimming pool, why not have someone film you going down the slide into the water with your clothes on? Snap a picture of you standing in front of their giant garage full of antique cars, or a video of you touring their game room. A fun fifteen-second video posted on Instagram and Facebook with a link to the listing and more pictures will grab more attention than a plain picture of the front of the house.

Social media includes Facebook, of course, but also newer sites like Snapchat, Periscope, Meerkat, and Instagram. Use any or all of them to distribute unique and creative content that guides buyers back to your listing so they can investigate more closely.

You can also create your own publication or broadcast media to get out information to a target audience. For example, you could start a podcast for people interested in moving to your city—give good information and follow up with an update on a new listing you have and who would be a perfect fit for it. Or you could do a video broadcast on YouTube and talk about three new listings a day—sure, some of them will be yours, but you could mention other ones in the neighborhood. The fact that you're the one talking about them and sharing information leads people to believe that you're the go-to source for information about homes in the area. (Just don't make it sound as though each new listing is yours—give credit where credit is due. Or be on the safe side and just discuss listings from your office.)

You could create specific weekly emails that go out to all the real estate agents in your marketplace—share local market stats, tips you've learned from other real estate professionals, anything helpful for real estate agents so they appreciate the email. Below that you could showcase your listings and offer awards or fun gift options for the agent who closes that specific home. Have fun with it.

Rather than pay through the nose for ad space in your local newspaper or magazines, you could create your own publication. The amount you currently pay for advertising could be re-applied to paying a young graphic designer looking to get a start. Enlist them to help build your own print or online publication to share with your targeted demographic. Just make sure if you do this, the publication includes information that's unique, authentic, or hyper-focused on your target readers' interests. Otherwise it may go unnoticed (see chapter 19).

WAKE UP SLEEPING BUYERS - Another way to improve visibility is to wake up sleeping buyers. Imagine who the ideal buyer for your property would be. Maybe it's a high-end home in your community, and the ideal buyer is somebody in the medical profession with a good income. Your ideal buyer might be so busy that they don't have time to look for homes, but you know that if they saw this amazing and unique home, they would say, "I wasn't thinking about moving, but I have to have that house." That's how you wake up sleeping buyers—get your listing in front of your ideal buyers and pique their curiosity. You may need to think outside the box to find ways to get in front of them.

> **CASE IN POINT**: *I recently sold a million-dollar-plus home in my market that happened to be close to a local hospital. Many of the high-end homes I've sold in the past have been to doctors working at this hospital. So I acquired a list of medical professionals in my zip code from a marketing firm and mailed out a newsletter to them telling them the story of this new, unique home I had just listed. About a week later, I got a call from a doctor who received my mailing. He said he had always liked this home, and once he saw it was listed and learned some new things about the place from my newsletter, he decided he had to see it. He closed on the home a month later, and I helped him sell his other home. I helped my seller find the right buyer who wasn't even actively looking at the time, and I got an unexpected boost to my business.*

Agents can also use this strategy to reach out to people who are currently renting, to start them thinking about buying a home. Maybe your listing is the perfect opportunity for them to save money over their current rent, get more square footage and yard space, and improve their location. Suddenly those renters who weren't looking to buy realize they should. It's not hard to obtain a list of renters' addresses in a specific area of town. Send something that gets their attention, that makes them laugh or strikes a pain point they're feeling, or solves a problem they're facing.

Don't rule out traditional print media with classified ads or online classifieds like Craigslist. Remember, however, that the same rules apply: if you're not entertaining people or piquing their curiosity—if you're posting the same vanilla information as everyone else—then you won't increase visibility.

SLOW BUYERS DOWN - This is very important for visibility. Your listing might show up on people's screens, but they don't click through to read it. Even if they do, they might quickly move on to some other listing that grabs their attention. It's important that you get them to slow down enough to really give your listing a hard look. How do you do this?

It's important to have high-quality pictures on your listing, but there's so much more you can do. You can put text over your pictures, which gets buyers to read while they're browsing pictures. For example, if your first picture is the front of the house, but the best part of the home is the amazing city views out the back, you can mention this core feature of the home by writing text directly onto the first photo. Let's say the second picture is of views—you can overlay text describing some cool benefit of having views, such as how they're a great backdrop to the outdoor entertaining space, etc. You can also write something eye-catching in the listing remarks other than the bedroom count and the fact that the home has new siding. How about instead you write about what truly makes this home unique or special compared to all the other similarly priced homes in the area?

Another tactic to slow buyers down is, instead of using the front of the home as the first picture of the listing (especially if it's not the home's strength), show something unique inside the house. What is the home's most unique feature? You can even include pictures of community and neighborhood highlights like walking paths, playgrounds, even downtown and recreational attractions that show the lifestyle of people who live there. If you can get buyers to slow down, they'll spend time on your listing and explore the details, virtual tour, and all the rest of the pictures of the home. Your goal initially is to immediately grab their attention with the things that are special and unique about the property.

Slowing buyers down can have a huge impact. An agent in my

office was struggling to get a listing sold. She was sure the price was right, the home showed great, the location was awesome, but offers weren't coming in, and the seller didn't want to go any lower. The problem, she said, was that buyers were going to a trendy new development down the road that offered new construction. Buyers were paying more money and getting smaller lots in a development further from downtown than her listing was. She listed five or six of her listing's other benefits— parks, walking trails, etc. Despite those benefits, people were going straight to the trendy community and ignoring her listing. I asked to see her listing. It had very nice professional pictures, the house was staged and looked great, the price was good—the problem was with visibility. Buyers were skipping over it.

The property was in a golf course community. I pulled up an aerial view from Google Maps and created a screenshot image that we cropped to show the house and its proximity to the golf course and trail system. We used image-editing software to make the location of the house extra obvious on the map, and put arrows pointing out key features of the neighborhood. That was this listing's strongest selling point. We were able not only to illustrate where the key features were in proximity to the property but that this listing was better than the trendy community everybody was paying more money for. She changed that to the lead photo in her listing and got an offer the next day. Before she made the change, she was about to lose the listing. The buyer said the map and new information were exactly what drew him to that property. This is why it's so important to get buyers to slow down.

SPEED BUYERS UP - After you slow buyers down enough to really notice your listing, you want to speed them up to take action. They're intrigued by what they've seen online. Now you need to get them to schedule a showing. First, work with your seller and set a plan to make it as easy as possible for the buyer to schedule a showing. Make sure it's clear to the buyer how easy it is to see the house. Maybe you set designated hours on certain days of the week when the house will be open. If the house is occupied, try to remove all barriers to being able to show the house often.

What else can you do in your marketing and listing strategy to create urgency and speed up the likelihood of getting more showings? Think about the buyers' agent. You might offer agent bonuses to get agents to make showing your property a priority. You can also create an environment of urgency where buyers know that if they take too long to make a decision, the property might be gone. If a buyer feels the property is a great option but notices it's been on the market for 120 days for whatever reason, they will feel like they can take their time and keep looking and come back to your listing later. If you are getting a lot of interest, make sure you communicate that to the other agent. Is your listing the last of its type or the only one available in this neighborhood? You want to communicate with the buyer and their agent that the home could go under contract very soon, so you want to help them get in to see it as soon as possible. These tactics are all part of your visibility strategy.

DON'T LET THEM RULE IT OUT TOO SOON – Buyers often rule out the best home for them too soon when they first view properties online, based on how the agent is showcasing the home. When buyers search for homes, they have many homes to search through, so initially they're focused on ruling out homes to narrow down their list. Your listing could be ruled out too soon if you give the buyer ammunition to do so.

Let's say you get a listing. You take pictures, but online they don't do the house justice. They're too dark, and buyers viewing them online think, *It's a great location, but look how dark the house is.* Skip. Or you get nice photos, but you include every bathroom and bedroom. Buyers viewing them online see that one of the bathrooms hasn't been updated, or see a room that's dark because a teenager painted it black. You don't need to put in every picture just because your MLS gives you a slot to put in a bunch of photos. Only include pictures that promote the listing in a positive way.

If the home has some negative, I'll try to address and overcome those negatives in the remarks. But I don't feel the need to showcase an outdated bathroom in the photos. I don't want buyers to focus on things that might be very minor and inexpensive to change. They may not even give the home a chance or go look at it because they rule it out.

Think about that as you prepare the listing. Go through it again. Are there pictures or information that buyers might misinterpret? Maybe the ceilings look unnaturally low in a certain photo. Don't use that photo. Maybe a room looks abnormally dark in a photo. Don't use that photo, or brighten it up with editing software. If there's anything that doesn't move the listing forward, it's holding it back. So take it out of there. Same thing goes with the remarks you write. Ask yourself, "Is there anything I'm saying that will make people want to rule out this property before they should?"

At the very least, I want to make sure that buyers don't skip over my listings because of a picture that confuses or distracts them, or a remark that allows them to rule it out in general. I see this happen every day in our profession. Buyers skip right past a listing or rule it out quickly when, in fact, it might be a great option for them. So think about what is being conveyed with your listing so that doesn't happen to you.

In some cases, of course, buyers should rule it out. If they need four bedrooms and a home only has three, they should rule it out. But if it has three bedrooms and an office or den, then you want to make sure you highlight that. Think about the possible objections buyers might have, and if you have solutions to overcome those, make sure they see that in the listing so they don't rule it out prematurely.

Amplify the best features and reasons to buy - Sometimes agents don't fully highlight the best features of the house. It might have an amazing view and say that in the remarks, but the pictures don't show it. That's a huge mistake. Buyers will look at the pictures before they read the words. So make sure the pictures quickly illustrate and help them understand the best features of the house so they'll want to read further.

If a house has an amazing pool, show it. If the owner has put fire pits and cool stuff in a spacious backyard, show them. If the home has a view that's most spectacular at sunset, then find a way to get an amazing picture of this amazing selling feature. Use aerial photos if you need to show the size of a lot or proximity to important features, like the golf course in my earlier example. Make sure those features are clear as day in your listing so buyers understand how awesome that property is. If you hire a professional photographer (and you should every time), but they miss or don't quite capture the unique, awesome thing about this home, then pay more until you get it. It's just too critical. I'd rather pay another $100 to $200 to get the photos just right, to help reduce the time on market by a month or two. Wouldn't you? Yet this is rare in our industry.

LEVERAGE THE HOMEOWNER'S NETWORK - Once you have the pricing, presentation, and visibility looking good on your listing, you may want to ask your seller to share your social media posts about their home with their family, friends, and networks. Sometimes you'll find a homeowner has a huge network of friends and contacts. Make it easy for them to share. That creates a whole new distribution channel for your listing and your business. The seller may even have a distribution channel of coworkers and connections at their workplace they can leverage. Most sellers are eager to deploy this option if you make their home look amazing and your marketing is fun and professional.

LEVERAGE THE NEIGHBORHOOD - Most agents try to leverage the neighborhood by doing open houses, to get neighbors interested and spreading the word. Or they'll send out "Just Listed" postcards to the neighbors.

That's what everybody else does. So is it really going to get the job done for you?

What if, instead of a "Just Listed" card, you sent something really different, something beyond a postcard or real estate flyer? Something that made the neighbors say, "Huh, now *that's* interesting"—or made them laugh or slow down and look harder at that property. What if you wrote a story about that home and the people who live there? Maybe they have a unique backstory or the house has a special history. Spotlight the house's amazing features and what the owners have done to make it ready to sell, but tell it as a story with highs and lows, with drama and humor. Throw in some good pictures. Send that out to the neighborhood. Not only would the neighbors be more impressed with that house, they would also realize that is one heck of an agent listing it. They may remember your name or keep that marketing piece to refer to the next time they're ready to sell.

Go beyond what everybody else is doing. Stop, take notes, find a quiet place for twenty minutes, and think about different ways you can create more visibility for your listing (see chapter 16). Sure, some of it will be hard work, but visibility can't be ignored. If you do ignore it, some other agent is going to get it right and get more listings. It's a huge aspect of delivering the highest and best service for your clients.

Presentation

When I say presentation, I'm referring to how the home comes across to buyers when they browse online or walk through the home for the first time.

Every day I see agents screwing up this critical step. In some cases, it's because the agent is battling with an uncooperative seller. However, the vast majority of the time it's the agent who fails to emphasize the importance of presentation with their listing. Agents are failing their client if the presentation of the home is not above the other competing homes listed for sale.

If you become skilled at helping your clients present their homes in the best possible way for buyers, you will not only net way more money for your seller, but your time on the market will be a fraction of what it would have been otherwise—which means happier sellers and fewer hours invested into each listing. This is why you invest more time, money, and energy up front, before you list the home, so that you are virtually guaranteed a positive outcome and higher return on investment (in less time) for your clients.

Five Reasons Why Buyers Need the Presentation of Your Listing to Be Amazing:

1. **BUYERS BELIEVE THEY CAN SEE POTENTIAL,** but experience has proven they only see problems. Buyers think they have good vision for a home's potential. Then they'll look at a home that is dirty or dark, they'll get distracted by the owner's stuff piled in a closet, and they'll notice the funky pet smell. They will be significantly impacted by distractions that are easy to fix—the right buyer may dismiss the house because of it. Or if they do like the home, their offer will be far below asking price.

2. **BUYERS ARE VIEWING HUNDREDS OF HOMES ONLINE** before viewing one in person. Not only does the presentation need to be perfect when they tour the house, it needs to be perfect well before that. Buyers will view online listings, and the one that has dark photos and doesn't capture what's unique about the house will be dismissed. The online presentation has to be great enough to capture the buyer's attention, and in person the home needs to show immaculately. That will net the most money for the seller.

3. **BUYERS LIKE A VERY CLEAN HOUSE.** Sellers should give their house a deep clean or hire a professional to do a thorough

cleaning before listing. A buyer is going to walk through and see all the little things the sellers don't notice anymore. A professional cleaner can come through with fresh eyes and see everything that needs to be cleaned, like dust built up on the baseboards and cobwebs on the ceiling. The seller may do a good job keeping their house clean, so a professional cleaner may not be necessary. But definitely stress to sellers the importance of keeping the house clean. If they're worried because they have a family living there, then come up with a strategy so maybe they only show it at certain times when they know they can have it clean. If they don't have someone to help them clean the home, provide a referral. If they already have someone who comes once a week, double up that service while their home is on the market. When buyers see a home that's dirty, they don't get excited about the idea of living there. When it's dirty or messy, the buyers become uncomfortable as they look through the house, because they feel they're invading someone else's home. They are not seeing themselves in that home—they just want to move on. However, if the home looks and feels like a model/staged home ready for them, they'll start to picture themselves in that space.

4. **BUYERS WORRY ABOUT WEAR AND TEAR.** If buyers see initial maintenance issues when they first enter the house, guess what they're going to do next? They're going to start looking high and low for other issues. It may be a small thing, but once they see it, their entire opinion of the house is impacted. Instead of envisioning themselves living in the house, they'll think about what else needs to be repaired and worry about what else in the house has been neglected. That is not the feeling you want buyers to have when they tour a home. Therefore, you need to help your sellers address these issues before you list the house. Waiting to see if the buyers ask

for those items to be addressed always backfires and leads to lower-priced offers and more time on market.

5. **BUYERS FEEL LIKE THEY'RE IN SOMEONE ELSE'S HOME.** A seller might have unique decor and furnishings, and that's what makes it a nice home—for them. They might be proud of the time and money they spent decorating their home and want to show it off. The challenge is to scale back so that buyers don't feel like they're in somebody else's home. Buyers should be able to imagine themselves living in that home. Buyers might even be pleasantly distracted by a seller's knick-knacks and family pictures, but that keeps them from imagining themselves in the home. They may not fall in love with it because it's just not their style or because it clearly feels like someone else's house, not potentially theirs. They're going to wonder more about the lives of the people who live there than about how their own furniture is going to fit in a room. The home should be staged like a model home instead of a personal home, or buyers might not end up making an offer. A seller doesn't need to remove everything to the point where the home feels sterile. But the more the home is designed and decorated to make it feel like home for the sellers, the less it will feel like home to the buyers.

Seven Reasons Why Agents Fail at Presentation:

1. **THEY'RE BROKE OR AFRAID TO SPEND MONEY.** Agents work long periods of time without a paycheck. When they get a new listing, they need to get good photography and possibly help with staging—and it all costs money. Agents can try to do it on the cheap, taking pictures with their phone or camera and staging the home themselves, and that's when quality suffers and our industry gets a bad reputation. If you're going to list homes, invest in doing it right. If you're broke, you can partner with another agent who can help

you, or you can work with your seller on the commission fees if they pay for the photography, staging, and specific marketing campaigns you have planned. There are a lot of ways to solve this problem—don't let the fact that you don't have any room on your credit card keep you from providing the quality of service the sellers deserve on their listing.

2. **ARROGANCE OR IGNORANCE.** Agents might assume that the efforts they're making are good enough, or do things a certain way because that's how they've always done them. They don't change and learn. Agents should constantly evaluate how they're performing compared to the listings they're competing with. If they're being outmatched on presentation by other agents, it ultimately could be costing the sellers money and affecting their reputation.

3. **LACK OF IDEAS OR LACK OF RESEARCH.** A lot of times, agents don't really know what to do. They may not have any idea how to improve their presentation. They might hire a photographer and get pictures that aren't very good. And even if they are good, they may not know what else to do besides posting pictures on the MLS. A lack of ideas comes from a lack of research. If agents want to improve, they should study the best. They should identify other agents who are doing a great job. When they see a listing that catches their attention, they should research and find out if that agent is using a particular photographer. What else are they doing that makes their listings look amazing? Sometimes it's not what's there, it's what's *not* there. Sometimes it's a unique way that agent is delivering the message about that property. Agents can also look outside their market and see what techniques are working elsewhere and then be the first to bring those to their market. Innovation grabs attention.

4. **THEY'RE AFRAID TO SPEAK UP TO A CLIENT.** A client might be tough and opinionated. They might dismiss their agent's

suggestions. They refuse to make adjustments to minimize the impact of their home's shortcomings. An agent might be too afraid of losing the listing by standing firm on what needs to be done to improve the presentation of a property. Sellers can be tough and intimidating, but if you can stress that your only goal is to maximize what they net when they sell, and you can articulate the problems with not following your recommendations, then you'll find that most sellers will get behind your strategy. Not all sellers will, and that's when you have to decide if you'll continue to help the sellers or recommend they hire another agent. Many agents, however, are afraid of having this critical conversation with their clients.

5. **AGENTS BELIEVE THAT A PASSING GRADE IS GOOD ENOUGH.** Too many agents do the minimum work with their listings. They put them on the MLS and feel like they did their part. Now they just wait idly for a buyer. An agent needs to constantly reevaluate a listing. If the home looked great the first time you saw it, have you been back over there recently? Maybe since the sellers moved out, the yard looks horrible, and the house has a funky smell. Or the home might be clean and well maintained, but the furniture and décor could be old and worn out. Agents too often say it's good enough, but in reality they may need to hire a professional stager or a contractor to help resolve an issue. When a home shows "okay," that's *not* good enough. Buyers need to walk into the home and say, "Wow, this is nice," and not be distracted by the furniture. An example of this is a luxury home I was recently asked to list. The owners bought it at foreclosure, and they were only living there part-time. The home was amazing, but the furniture inside resembled something you would see in the home of first-time homebuyers. A couple of their items were a bit nicer, likely family heirlooms, but they belonged in a different style of home. They stuck out like a

sore thumb and did nothing to help illustrate how nice the home was. The house was very clean, but half the lightbulbs were burnt out. The sellers were trying to get more than a million dollars for their home and struggling. I gave them my list of recommendations we needed to do to get their target price for their home. The sellers didn't disagree with *all* my recommendations—just most of them. I offered them a couple other solutions, but ultimately they chose to list the home with an agent who said it was good enough just the way it was at the price the sellers wanted. I believe the agent was so excited about the idea of selling a million-dollar home that she would have done just about anything to get the listing. Last I checked, the home had been on the market for over a year. The agent got good photography on the home, but the presentation is seriously lacking. They are on their third price drop, and ultimately the seller is going to net at least $100,000 less than they should have to sell that home.

6. **THEY'RE TOO ANXIOUS TO GET THE HOME LISTED.** Instead of getting the details right and getting everything ready up front, either the seller or the agent is too anxious to get the listing online. They are convinced they need to get it on the market fast and make adjustments later. Listings shouldn't be rushed if they're not ready. An agent may need to take time to tweak photos even after they come back from a professional photographer, or add elements to the listing to make the property appear much more attractive. Getting the deferred maintenance issues resolved is really important, even if it means holding back the listing another week or two. The extra effort will make the home sell faster and encourage the best-looking offers from buyers. That's what the client is paying for.

7. **THEY HIRE THE WRONG TEAM MEMBERS.** Agents may take the right initiative to deliver a great service and presentation

but end up hiring the wrong people to work with. Meaning they hire the wrong people to help take pictures, stage, repair, or clean the home. I once co-listed a high-end property with an agent in the next county. The seller had heard about the reputation of my brokerage, and he wasn't getting any bites in his area, so he asked if I would co-list it with his current agent to see if that would help bring in buyers from my county. I decided I would help, and I met with the other agent about his listing. First, I looked at how he'd been marketing the property and knew right away we needed better photography. The agent was hesitant because he'd already paid for professional photography—but the results looked amateurish to me. I was surprised this photographer called himself professional, and even more surprised that the agent had hired him and used his photos. Then he hired someone else locally, and those pictures were a little better but still well below my expectations. So I paid my photographer to drive two hours both ways to get the photos I was looking for. It was money well spent but frustrating because the other agent didn't have better team members to resolve the matter. I call my photographer, videographer, cleaners, handymen, and stager "my team" because they are all a major part of how I deliver the top-level service my clients deserve and need to get the best price for their home.

Ways to Improve Presentation:

1. **HIRE THE RIGHT PEOPLE TO HELP YOU.** As I state above, you need to develop an awesome team of professionals who can help deliver the best experience and results for your clients. If your photographer is not delivering at the highest level and you can see that other photographers are better, talk to her about it. Show her the pictures. Show her the listings that are more impressive and tell her, "I want them to look

like that." A photographer might make excuses and tell you it will cost more because that process takes longer, etc. You might research the other photographer and see what he charges. Maybe the process is more expensive. But if the more expensive process offers the highest quality, it's worth it. Hiring the right people to help you, and using them even on the lower-priced homes, makes your presentation really stand out. You might sell a house in one day, and that's just good business.

2. **LEARN HOW TO EDIT PHOTOS, OR FIND SOMEONE WHO CAN HELP YOU INEXPENSIVELY.** Sometimes you'll need to illustrate or point out things on a photo. You might add an arrow and description to an aerial photo to highlight a feature that's next to a house. A photo might need its brightness or color adjusted to make it really pop. There are a lot of free apps and more expensive software to help you tweak photos. Learn to use them, or find someone in your office or someone you can hire inexpensively to help you. Humans are visual. It's so critical that you deliver astounding photos on your listings.

3. **THERE IS A LOT MORE TO STAGING THAN FURNITURE.** Maybe you already use a stager or hire one only under certain circumstances like vacant homes or new construction. Staging is becoming more popular because it's proven itself to work over and over again. Staging doesn't always mean spending big money. Sometimes it's a matter of consulting and hearing a professional designer say that a wall color has to be changed or some furnishings rearranged. Agents must become skilled at articulating the importance of staging, because sellers often don't budget the cost of staging the home to look its best. I will often cover the cost of the home consultation from the stager, to get their recommendations not only on how to rearrange the sellers' furniture but also whether the home needs new paint or flooring in some of

the rooms. She will also point out the wear and tear mainte-nance items that should be addressed, like heavily scratched wood floors. The report also gives an approximate cost to solve each issue if you hire the stager, or the sellers can do it themselves. Often the sellers elect to have the stager make the arrangements, in part because her pricing is good. But the fact still remains that many sellers don't budget or plan for this cost, so you may have to work with them to resolve how this work gets completed. Note that a lot of people call themselves stagers the way some people call themselves land-scapers, and they're not all good. So look in your marketplace and see who is doing staging well, and talk to them—find out what they charge and what all the variables are. Some agents bring their own fresh towels and attempt to do their own staging, and that works okay for them. I prefer to hire a professional so I can focus on other things. They're going to do a better job than I will anyway.

4. **BECOME MASTERFUL AT HELPING THE SELLER** get the neces-sary steps done before listing the home. There is so much to do before listing a home—de-clutter, clean, move things to storage, touch up paint, clean the garage, landscaping, and curb appeal. Those things all cost time and energy. Any agent could tell the seller not to worry about those things, because the house will sell just like it is. Yes, it will sell, but it will sell for a lot less. As a good agent, you should become masterful at communicating the importance of these tasks. Then become creative about how you help sellers tackle those problems. Maybe you help coordinate and get all those things done. If they can't afford to make repairs and move things to storage, maybe you help them pay for it in return for a higher commission at closing. Whether you arrange delayed payments with contractors, create partnerships with vendors, or whatever else you need to do to get the house

looking its best before listing, that is a skill you need to emphasize with your business.

Occasionally you'll have a seller who has their home looking amazing, de-cluttered, staged, and ready to show. They've watched HGTV and organized the rooms like their house is staged for TV. They've gotten the presentation right for you already. You know they'll keep it that way because that's the type of people they are. Those kinds of clients are a gift.

What you need to do is to get all your clients shooting for that level of professional presentation. It's your job to help them get there. Selling a home like that is a breeze because it shows well, you get great feedback, and you get a quick, good offer.

Price

As a broker, I see many agents make big mistakes when they price listings. I've made my share of them over the years. This advice comes from making those mistakes. Hopefully you can avoid the pain of learning this the hard way.

It's true that, ultimately, if you mess up the presentation and visibility of your listing, it will still eventually sell if you keep dropping the price. But hopefully you already realize that it's your job to help the client get the highest price the market will bear when they sell their home.

Many agents fall victim to letting the client make all the decisions on pricing. This happens in part because the agent may be unsure what the home will sell for, and therefore they let the seller dictate how the home will be priced. Sellers often base their pricing on the amount of work and money they've put into it.

Here is a secret that nobody tells you in real estate school: Unless you're selling carbon copies of homes on the same street, nobody knows for sure what the home will sell for. There are too many variables.

I have confidence in my ability to market a home to maximize its visibility. But until I know how cooperative the sellers will be with the tasks I suggest they take care of prior to putting the home on the market, I'm still uncertain about the list price. When I first do my research to see what the house might sell for, I come up with a range: high end to low. Until I know how much effort the seller is willing to contribute toward the presentation of the house, I don't know what price I'll be able to set within that range. I explain that to the seller. Experience has taught me the hard lesson that my ability to convey the importance of following my recommended steps to sellers is a critical skill. If I can't articulate to the seller a strong enough reason for them to jump through the hoops I'm asking them to, they will ultimately pay a huge price for my inability to convince them.

It's not the seller's fault. I blame myself. I need to show confidence in my recommendations, and I need to use stories, examples, and case studies to illustrate the importance of—and the dangers of not—following the recommended path.

To fully understand how to price a home, you need to fully understand the context of the situation. Meaning you need to understand your clients and any variables that could affect the pricing of the home.

Sellers in a Hurry

Often you have a seller who is cooperative but who is unable (due to being out of money, out of time, or out of patience) to do anything with the home to make it show better to potential buyers. In these cases, it's critical that you explain to the homeowner how that will affect the price they'll get for the home. They'll need to price it accordingly to avoid the home sitting on the market for an indefinite time.

For example, the homeowner needs to sell within thirty days; therefore, you've got to price the home aggressively to get offers in just a few days, likely at the bottom range of what you had previously thought you could sell it for. If they don't have time to do everything you recommend, hopefully they can do a few things like clean and stage the house a bit. Other clients may just want out, so they don't want to raise a finger or spend a dollar on the home to get it ready to sell.

If you take a listing with sellers who are unable or unwilling to take the recommended steps to get the best price for their home, here are the potential problems:

IT MIGHT IMPACT YOUR REPUTATION - If you can't sell it because they're not doing the things they need to do—either because they're out of money or out of options—and it sits on the market forever, that doesn't reflect well on you.

YOU MIGHT NEED TO WALK AWAY - If they won't agree to the price and the price schedule you're recommending, you might need to walk away. If you don't see a positive outcome—if the price they want and the timeline they need to sell it by aren't realistic for the level of improvements they're (not) willing to make—then why would you continue down a path to failure when it's clear that it's not going to work out?

YOU MIGHT NEED TO ASSIST THE SELLER FINANCIALLY - If they're out of money but have equity and they need to do repairs, you may need to give them options to help pay for the work up front. Maybe you arrange an extra-large commission and you pay for the repairs up front, so you get reimbursed at closing. You decide if that's something you want to do, or how you want to operate your business.

It will be tougher if they have no money and no equity. That limits your ability to drop the price, so you need to be more cautious or creative on how you help the sellers.

Sellers in No Hurry

Sometimes you'll encounter sellers who are in no hurry to sell. They have a price in mind that they want to achieve if they're going to sell. You, as a real estate professional, have to decide if you want to sign up for such a situation. This happens most often with very high-end homes. The owners have put a lot into the house, and they want to get that money out, but the market may not be there. If it's a unique house, there's a shot in the dark that it could sell, but the evidence says the chances are extremely low. Agents are often thrilled to have such a listing in their portfolio, but they often underestimate the challenge they're walking into. In these types of situations, it's best to take those listings on a case-by-case basis and always have the following talk with the client:

HOW MUCH YOU'RE SPENDING UP FRONT - On every listing, you're making an investment of time and money in hopes that you will not only get reimbursed but that those efforts will be rewarded with a commission. When you have a seller who has little motivation to sell their home, you might be spending a lot of time and money up front on something that's going to be unrealistic for your marketplace.

As an alternative to turning down the listing, you can protect yourself by altering your listing agreement. Start this conversation with your client by saying, "I'm taking on a lot of risk and expense, and these types of listings can take a very long time to sell." You might have the seller pay for some of the marketing up front. If it's a big house, maybe there's room to cut off some of the commission in exchange for the sellers paying costs up front.

THE SELLER WILL BEGIN TO DOUBT YOU AFTER SIX MONTHS - You want to talk to the client about what's going to happen long term. Tell the seller, "I'll take this listing, but here's what's going to happen. After six months or maybe a year, you're going to get pretty sick of having your house on the market because I'll call to schedule a showing at what seems like always the worst time. You're going to have to clean the house; occasionally the buyer isn't going to show; it's going to be a big, continual frustration so long as the house is listed for sale." It's going to get annoying, and at some point the seller is going to think: *I wish this thing would sell already. Why can't my agent sell this? It's the agent's fault. I maybe need to find a new one.* I guarantee they will start to feel that way if the home remains on the market for a year or more. So I have this conversation with them before I take the listing: "Here's what happens in these situations. The seller starts to get frustrated and begins to doubt their agent's abilities. Then they get a new agent. The new agent comes along and says, 'The problem is you're overpriced.' By this time, the seller is so discouraged that they're then open to a lower price. So the new agent lists the home at a lower price, and then it sells and he looks like the hero and gets all the credit—and the commission. Meanwhile, the agent who listed it the whole first year is left with nothing." I have that exact conversation with the sellers. I tell them, "I'll ride this wave with you, and we can go down this path, but you have to agree that if you ever consider dropping the price, you do it with me, because it's not fair for me to put all this time, work, and energy in, and then you dump me and hire somebody else and list at a lower price. That's messed up." I even get a verbal agreement and a handshake on that.

Divorce

This happens a lot. Divorce is common, and it does impact price. You've got to decide if you even want these listings. The first meetings are always great. It seems to be amicable in the beginning. The couple says, "Yeah, this is the plan we both agree to." But it eventually gets nasty, and it's only a matter of time before you, as their agent, have crosshairs on your back. One or both parties will blame you for taking sides or being unfair. You're going to try to keep the deal together, but emotions run so high in these things that it can be an extremely difficult situation. You almost need an agent per spouse. That helps minimize some of the back and forth, being put in the middle of the mess.

You need to make sure before you take these listings that there's a clear understanding of expectations and likelihood of pricing. You want to avoid the whole rigmarole of getting an offer to the table and then having one party say, "No, I want more." And they'll do this, not because they don't want to sell but because they want to be spiteful to the other spouse. They want to cause pain, hurt, and frustration because that's what they feel. So you've got to be extremely careful when you get in these situations. You want to be very clear on your listing agreement about pricing and what's an acceptable offer to each party. Then you go into far more detail in your listing agreement on divorce situations, because if you get into that situation and suddenly someone refuses to sign something, you have a listing agreement—a contract—that says they agreed to do this. Usually in a divorce, each side has their own attorney, so you can show that to their attorney, which will help them help their client understand that they need to sign the offer. Even with that, there are still so many potential nightmares.

Knowing all that, here's what I do when I have clients who come to me and say, "Hey, Mike, we need to sell. We're getting a divorce." I'll go to the appointment and tell them some of the stories of what has happened to me in the past with divorce situations. I don't go into great detail, but I do have a tough talk with them. I say, "I'm happy to do this, and I'll work my butt off and make sure you guys get the best price for this house, but here's what I don't want to happen. I don't want to be considered an enemy a month down the road if things get tough or emotional." I have the talk with them right then, because trying to have it later would be next to impossible. Even if they're in the same room at the beginning, there's a chance they may not be in the same room before the thing is over. So it's really important to make sure everyone has a clear understanding before you jump in. A lot of times the house is not going to be able to show to the best of its ability in these situations because of all the dynamics going on. That impacts pricing significantly. The person remaining in the house might potentially need a lot more help getting the house cleaned or tackling chores that need to be handled before the house is listed. These situations need a lot more handholding. And if you can't do it, it's going to impact pricing. All of these things should be discussed before you take the listing.

Funky Floor Plans

I see agents screw up the pricing all the time on a house that has a funky floor plan. People underestimate how impactful that is on pricing. Sometimes when you're looking at comps in the area, and you look at properties with a similar size, same bedroom count, same vicinity and neighborhood, etc., you think yours should list at a similar price. But if the home you're listing has a really funky floor plan, it's going to sell for a heck of a lot less. Unless it's in a highly desired neighborhood and that is the only house on the market, a funky floor plan is going to have a drastic effect on the sales price. Nobody talks about that in real estate school, or at least not enough. Appraisers don't account for it when they're doing their appraisals. They might mention some sort of functional issue with the house, but that's about it.

So you can be impacted positively or negatively by knowing if a house has a funky floor plan. If the comp down the street had a funky floor plan, then understanding that could help you get more for your listing than the other house sold for. But if your listing has a funky floor plan, then it's going to be difficult to determine how much that will impact pricing. In that case, you say to the sellers, "You know what? This floor plan is not ideal for most buyers." And most of the time the sellers will agree. That might be half the reason why they're moving. Because they're sick of the layout of the house and they want a better setup. You say, "I'm looking at comparable properties, and this floor plan is going to impact your asking price." Share stories about listings that were greatly impacted by undesirable floor plans. Because sometimes it's not five or ten grand less that a house might sell for, it's twenty-five or fifty grand less in some cases. So sellers really need to understand this. Hopefully when they bought the house they got a deal on it because it was a funky floor plan. If they built the house and it was a funky floor plan, they kind of created a bad situation they may not have seen coming. So be careful. That's my warning on this one. Be careful with funky floor plans because you might walk into a listing thinking, *I can get what these other homes are selling for in this neighborhood.* But don't bank on it if that floor plan is really odd or less desirable.

Basements

Agents, you can't attribute the same weight to the square footage of a home that doesn't have a basement to one that does. Let's say you're talking about two 2,000-square-foot homes. One has 1,000 square feet above grade and 1,000 square feet below grade; the other one has it all above grade. Those houses are not similar at all. They look similar on paper, but they're not similar in the price you can ask for each house. Yes, in some cases, basements are desirable. In most cases, people prefer to have the square footage above grade. Usually it's more expensive to build a house above grade than it is to include a basement. Basement square footage is often less expensive per square foot to put in. So they shouldn't hold the same amount of weight.

Many basements have low ceilings, tiny windows, and undesirable living spaces. You need to understand that when you're pricing houses. I see this mistake too often, and agents over-price a house. Yes, some are daylight basements, and that's good. When I work out values on those two different 2,000-square-foot houses, I would treat the one with the basement like a house that is all above grade but only 1,500 square feet. I cut the basement square footage in half as far as usable square footage. And I'm just doing that so I can understand how that square footage is going to hold weight compared to other homes in the neighborhood.

Price per Foot

Many agents were taught in school, or by their brokers and trainers, to get a list of homes and comps and compare their price per foot to help determine what a home in that area should sell for. They're told to present those figures to their client: "Houses in the neighborhood are selling for about $125 per foot," or whatever the number is. I've seen that burn agents and sellers so many times where they could have gotten a lot more for their house, but that was the method the agent used to determine the price. Even more common, the home is over-priced using this method, and the sellers eventually replace the agent because she failed to sell the home. Or they just cancel their listing, assuming the timing is not right to sell.

So let me be as blunt as I can be: just don't do it. Price per foot doesn't account for the quality or condition of the house, the appeal of the floor plan, the bedroom count, ceiling height, or amount of windows. Is it light or is it dark in that house? Does it need a lot of maintenance, or is it in pristine condition? Most of the time, you're not including garage size with the price-per-foot calculation, or the size and condition of the yard. Square footage doesn't account for anything outside the house that adds value to the property for potential buyers. So price per foot is such a bad method to determine pricing unless you're in a neighborhood of homes that are exact carbon copies up and down the street, on the same size lots, the same distance from the neighbors. Of course, that still could throw you off, because maybe the last three that sold were all trashed or outdated inside, and the one you're about to list has been remodeled and is immaculate. But if you're going for the same price per foot, you're potentially leaving money on the table for the seller. You could underprice the home. So keep that in mind, or just don't do it. I have agents in my office who are still tempted to use that method, and it drives me a little batty.

Garage Size

Garage size is something that impacts a lot of buyers. Can they park their car in there or not? Even though it has a one- or two-car garage, how practical and functional that garage is means a lot to potential buyers. Two similar houses might have three-car garages, which seem like nice features, but one of them is extra deep and has a lot of space for parking bigger trucks and bikes or allows room for a shop. The other one is very shallow, so they could maybe park the car in there and not the truck. Those kinds of things make a big difference when it comes time to sell. The buyer's going to pick the one with a bigger garage, or pay more for it because he's going to value that feature more. It's something to keep in mind when you're pricing a house.

Curb Appeal

First impressions are so important. This goes back to the presentation of the house, because curb appeal is something that is going to have huge implications. When you first pull up and look at that house, pay attention to see if there's anything you can do to improve the first impression.

Sometimes there's nothing you can do, because sometimes the first impression of the house is not the house at all, it's the house next door. If the neighbors have a junkyard, that is going to have huge implications for the pricing of your house. Buyers are going to pay less for the house because it's in less desirable surroundings. What do you do about it? Maybe you can talk to the sellers about having a work party and offering to clean the neighbors' yard—do something nice for them rather than demanding they do it themselves. Maybe help the neighbors paint their house or repair their fence. Curb appeal and first impressions can hugely impact pricing, so you're going to want to pay attention to that when you determine the right pricing for the house.

Improvements Don't Always Mean Improvements

You'll have sellers who want to talk to you about the improvements they've made to the house in recent years. When you go see it, you might say, "Yeah, that was definitely money well spent." But if it's not work that was either well done or added value, it might have been $5,000 spent on the house that no buyer is going to appreciate. Improvements don't necessarily add value to the price of the home. A lot of times when sellers put in a $15,000 new roof they think they're going to get $15,000 more for their house, so you're going to have to have a delicate conversation with them. "Actually, you're not going to get any more for the house," you tell them, "you're just not going to get less." Some improvements are just that. They won't help you necessarily get more for the house—they help you get what the house should sell for in that neighborhood and help the sellers avoid getting something less than market value for their home.

The improvements that tend to hold the most weight for buyers are the ones most visible: the updated kitchen and baths, the new flooring and paint, the front door, or high-end garage doors. These will all have impact on buyers. Adding new insulation to make the home more comfortable is something buyers should pay more attention to, but often they don't focus on those types of upgrades on the first walkthrough. It's more about appearance, layout, and functionality.

Deferred Maintenance

When you first walk through a house with the sellers, you need to really pay attention to deferred maintenance and wear and tear, because they will have gigantic implications on what the house will sell for. I'm not talking about once the home inspection happens and then negotiating the costs for repairs that need to be made. That's too late in the process. When buyers walk through and they start seeing issues with the house, they're going to start thinking, *cha-ching, cha-ching*—dollar signs to fix all those maintenance items. It might be in the perfect area and have the perfect floor plan, but they see issues that are going to take time and money to fix. The offer is going to be far lower than it would be if the house was in great condition.

With an immaculate house, buyers will be worried that the house is going to fly off the market because it's so nice and shows so well, and they'll get excited about it and make a good offer. That's what you want. They can tell the home has been well cared for—and that means fewer headaches for them once they move in. But if a house has a lot of deferred maintenance, you've got to price it accordingly if the seller is unwilling or unable to address those issues.

Comps

When trying to determine pricing for houses, most agents will look at sold comps, pending comps, and active comps.

When you look at **sold comps,** you want to do a couple of things. First, you want to mirror what an appraiser is going to do. They're going to be under very strict guidelines of how and what they look for. They often can only be within 20 percent difference in square footage from comp to comp. Usually they're required to use a comp that sold within the past six months. Ideally they want to compare within a mile radius, but they'll sometimes make exceptions. They also try to match the levels a home has—if a house has a basement, for example, they try to find comps that have partial below-grade square footage. They can't compare a two-story house to a house with a single level with basement. You want to try to mimic what appraisers are going to do so you have an idea of the comps they're going to use. If the house isn't unique—if there are a lot of similar comps in the area—pricing can be very clear. But pricing gets tricky when you have a high-end or custom-built home that is extremely unique, which makes it nearly impossible to find a comparable property.

When I look at comps, I try to understand the appraiser's process, but I also follow my own personal instincts. I evaluate how buyers are likely to react to each home based on what I've learned about those buyers' specific wants and needs. Details like which direction a house faces can impact buyers' preferences, how long a home stays on the market, and the pricing it gets. Comps can be skewed by features that might not be obvious on the sold comp because the agent didn't list all of its unique features—or maybe adequate pictures of the sold comp aren't available for the appraiser to evaluate. So looking at sold comps, I might look back further to try to find a comp that was very close in style and size for what would mimic buyer behavior on my current listing, because that might give me a clue to how my listing is going to perform in the market. Many times I can't necessarily use it as a true comp or what an appraiser is going to use, but it might help me understand what will happen once I put that property on the market.

I recommend you take extra time with sold comps and really try to evaluate something other than a small radius of homes that have sold in the last six months. Otherwise, you might be missing some clues that will help you understand what you might be getting out of the sold comps.

Pending comps are great because they show you what buyers are actually taking action on now. Sometimes I'll look at pending comps on homes that are in a similar area but are maybe smaller or bigger than the house I'm listing, because I want to see what buyers are reacting to. What are they trending toward? Why did they pick that house over other homes listed for sale? That house will give clues to what buyers are taking action on, so I can leverage that knowledge to help me understand the pricing of my upcoming listing.

Active comps are a really valuable tool. Again, they're not typically used in a traditional appraisal sense, but active comps are what you're actually going to be competing against. I see many agents not even look at active comps and just focus on sold and pending comps when they're trying to figure out their valuations. Yes, the sold comps and pending comps are going to be more accurate because they show what houses are actually selling for. Active comps are just examples of what price people hope their homes will sell for. So you don't want to spend too much time discussing them, because you don't want to inflate your sellers' hopes. They'll see a house down the street and say, "Well, they're asking $350,000, and our house is nicer than theirs." Well that $350,000 for the neighbors' house may be way off. Maybe it will actually sell closer to $300,000. So it's throwing everything off. But it's important to realize what your competition is.

What I try to do is put myself in the place of the potential buyer. I ask myself, *If they look at my listing, what homes will they be asking to see?* If I can predict what homes they will be comparing my listing to, I can see how we stack up to the competition and share those findings with my sellers. This process helps me have the conversation with sellers about finding the right price. For example, I might say "There are only so many homes that sell in this area in this price range in a given period of time. Yet there are X number of homes listed for sale. So your home could either take one month to sell or ten months to sell. Here is how we stack up to the competition; therefore, we should list your home at X price." I talk to them about what happens if they start too high and why we don't need to list it as low as some of the competition. When I have that conversation using active comps, it often helps me make the case I want to make about pricing their home.

Another area you can compare that's often underutilized is expired or cancelled listings. Look for homes in the immediate area that were listed for sale within the past six months to a year but didn't sell. In almost every listing appointment, there is usually some home that was listed in the neighborhood that the sellers know about. They compare their home to that one because it has similar square footage and features. But it didn't sell. The neighbors took their home off the market, yet your clients are still comparing their home to that listing. So I'll research that and try to understand why it didn't sell—was it because of the price, the presentation, or the visibility? All of those things could have played a role. Those can be really good examples of what's happening in the market, or at least help you understand what to expect once you list the home.

What do you do if you have no comps? You can't identify a single home similar to the house you're listing that sold recently. Maybe your listing has a great view, but all of the homes surrounding it that sold in the last year don't have that view. You know a spectacular view can greatly increase your asking price, but you don't have the comps to calculate by how much. This happens all the time when you have a unique house, and if you don't have the comps to support what you think it's worth, you struggle to figure out the right price for the home.

With all listings—and unique ones especially—you need to go a little bit on gut. With experience, you might see that your gut hunch about what a home might sell for is often right on target. With training and by learning to listen to that gut instinct, you'll gain confidence when dealing with unique homes.

Sometimes all you can do if there are no comps available is try to weigh similar features on different houses. You can make certain adjustments to them—find a house that is slightly smaller or larger, calculate what a recent sale might have sold for if it had your house's spectacular view, etc.—and try to equate what the house would sell for based on the evidence you can gather. You might even get a number of agents from your office to look at the house and give you their feedback on valuation.

Case in Point: *I always have a number in my head that I think a home is going to sell for, and I'm shocked how often it's correct. Every once in a while, that number's off, but it's spot-on most of the time. Sometimes I don't listen to my gut because evidence says something totally different. When I've done that, I've wished I had listened to my gut more. Without comps, you definitely have to rely on instinct and experience and judge how your home stacks up to the competition.*

Occasionally, the best move is to get an appraisal—especially if you're convinced the house should list at one price, and the seller wants a totally different price. An appraisal costs $300–$500. That might be worth the investment, since we're talking a price difference of tens of thousands of dollars (hundreds of thousands of dollars in a higher-end home). Every once in a while, the appraisal comes in close to what I'm thinking, but the sellers still say, "The appraisal is really low. That's ridiculous. Look at these comps they used." So it doesn't settle all your problems, but it does give you more backup to make your case.

I often have a conversation with the appraiser before he goes out to the house. I don't try to influence him; I just let him know what I see in the property and what my concerns are, and what the sellers see and what they're thinking. I just let the appraiser know the situation and let him make his own determination. Sometimes it comes in higher than I think, and sometimes it's lower than I think. It's always nice to have another viewpoint on what the house might sell for.

Sometimes the appraisal comes in way higher than I feel it should, so then I need to understand why. I'll point out my concerns about the appraisal to the sellers before we list the house, and I'll say, "We'll still go in at this price, but here are my concerns." So later on when it's not selling, at least I know I brought up the possibility it might not sell, and then we can talk about lowering the price.

How do you know when your price is too high?

Don't make the mistake many agents make of assuming when a house hasn't sold within a month or two that it's overpriced. It might be overpriced, but make sure you're spot-on with your presentation and your visibility before you make that determination.

Ask yourself the following questions:

1. Is the visibility of your listing exceeding other competing homes on the market?

2. Are you getting a healthy amount of showings for what is expected for a home in that price range for your market?

3. Have you successfully communicated or illustrated the best features of the home in the listing?

4. Is the home being shown when it is looking the best it can look?

5. Is the feedback you get from buyers and agents all positive, but you still have no offers after weeks or months on the market?

If you answered YES to these five questions, then the price of the home is most likely too high for the market at that time. That doesn't automatically mean the solution is to drop the price. It might mean that depending on the seller's goals, you need to wait for the right buyer or for there to be less inventory. You may need to try selling it at another time of year or when the market is stronger. The point is, lowering the price is not the only solution. However, if you've been able to communicate to the sellers what you've done to be able to say YES to the questions above, you'll be in a much better position to have a productive conversation with them about the pricing of the home.

Can you underprice a home, or will the market self-correct?

If a market is healthy with a fair amount of demand from buyers, and you do a good job with visibility and presentation, and you unexpectedly underprice a home—maybe it's tricky to price, and the house is superior in some ways to other listings—you may get multiple offers in the first day. Most agents experience that in some form or fashion. The question always becomes, "Did I underprice it? Could I have gotten more?" Much of the time, a healthy market will self-correct. If you underprice a listing, the likelihood is that you'll get multiple offers on the property, and it will push the pricing up—so long as you have good visibility so everyone knows about it in time. If you don't have good visibility, the first person along is going to get a heck of a deal. You're leaving money on the table for the seller. You've got to be careful. Don't underprice it if your marketing skills and visibility are just mediocre. And if you drastically underprice it, then yeah, you're definitely leaving money on the table for your client. I've seen that happen. I've seen it happen where a home that should have been priced at $500,000 got priced by the agent at $400,000, and it sold at $450,000 in a day. The sellers really lost out by hiring that agent, unfortunately. If they had listed that home at $480,000, buyers might have still pushed it up to $500,000. The market doesn't always self-correct to where it should. It depends on how far you're off and on your visibility and marketing skills.

The biggest thing is that you're always going to have sellers who want to overprice the listing. If you give them a range, they're always going to want to be at the top of the range. It's okay to list at the top of the range, so long as they're going out of their way to maximize the presentation of their listing. But it's important to illustrate that there is risk by pushing up too far. You might have a range, but they have their own range. You think it's $300,000–$320,000, and the sellers think $340,000–$350,000. There's always this issue of the sellers wanting to get the most for their house. It's just human nature. They want to price it high. Some agents use charts and different things in their listing presentation to show the dangers of overpricing a home, and that's okay.

I like to use stories. I recommend you use stories because each time someone argues for overpricing, you just need to tell a story. If you don't have a story of your own, talk to agents in your office. They've likely had a client overprice their house and therefore chased the price down until they finally got an offer that was likely far below what they would have gotten normally. I've seen this happen numerous times. The sellers are overconfident in their house and what it should sell for, and maybe ignore the first offer that comes in because they're insulted by it. But they'll end up selling for far lower than that in the end, because the market can be brutal to homes that are on the market too long. After days of market exposure, people start wanting to know what's wrong with it. When a new buyer comes along, they don't care that the seller has done two, three, or even five price drops. They're going to look at it and say, "Oh, it's been on the market for 180 days." They don't care if you just dropped your price yesterday; they're going to offer an even lower number that is meant for a property that's been on the market for 180 days. So that's the conversation you need to have with your sellers and give examples and stories so that they don't make that mistake. You have to be really confident in your ability to get them the best price with your strategy.

I've made that mistake too many times, so this is something you really want to understand and get good at. The implications for your sellers are just too high otherwise.

Understanding, respecting, and implementing the principles of the Listing Triangle™ will have profound effects on your real estate career and your legacy as a real estate agent. It will change how you handle your listing appointments to where you don't end up needing a fancy presentation. You just need to be able to articulate the importance of these three important foundations to your clients and give them the information they need so they can get the most out of their house when they go to sell it.

You don't have to complicate it. Using the principles of the

Listing Triangle™, I typically walk into the first visit with my notepad and take notes about the house. I don't bring a fancy presentation. Occasionally I'll bring something that helps me articulate the importance of visibility and presentation for a listing or examples of how we maximize those efforts. I might scribble a couple things to the clients on my notepad to help illustrate something. But mostly I just tell stories and I listen. And then when they have questions, I'll use principles of the Listing Triangle™ to help explain the importance of certain elements. Mastering the principles of setting price, ensuring the greatest visibility, and procuring the best presentation for the home is the foundation of getting the best outcome for your clients.

PART V:

The End Game:
Happiness, Balance, Success

Have you put much thought into what you want to do down the road, possibly when you retire? Can you retire? What do your later years in real estate look like? Five, ten, fifteen years from now, will you still be selling real estate in some capacity? If you're not planning and thinking ahead about how you want things to be down the road, there's a good chance it won't happen.

This section is dedicated to those of you who are committed to this profession. You know you're in it for the long haul, so why not make it as pleasurable and fulfilling as possible? The term "lifestyle design" is a bit overused these days, but I still like it because of the word "design." You have to plan. Take steps and implement great discipline in order to earn your freedom and the ability to choose how and when you retire, take time off, spend more time with your family, travel, pursue other passions and hobbies, etc. Part V could have been titled "Lifestyle Design for Agents" or "Earn Your Freedom." It means the same thing. Invest time and energy to gain more freedom now and in the future.

CHAPTER 28
More Closings = More Happiness
... Right?

Do more closings mean a real estate agent will earn more money and find happiness? The answer, quite simply, is no.

This doesn't apply to new agents who are trying to build a business while keeping food on the table. This is more a question for experienced agents who have already found some level of success but want to push it to new levels. On one hand, that's great—agents should have drive and ambition and goals. But they need to be cautious about how they push themselves to achieve higher levels of success.

I've seen agents make serious mistakes when they try to expand their business, whether it's based on bad advice from someone in their brokerage, a coach, or an agent they admire. They hire a buyers' agent too soon. They hire somebody to help them grow their business by working more prospects or leads before their business can support that. They don't realize how expensive that particular hire is and how much time management is needed for that hire. I've seen agents who are already pushing themselves pretty hard try to push themselves to even higher levels, and they burn out. They start hating the profession and eventually lose their drive and ambition. Or they exhaust themselves physically and emotionally. Agents lose marriages because they're so absorbed in their business, and then they look back bitterly and think, *I wish I wouldn't have been so driven and missed my kids growing up.*

These are risks you should consider when you ask yourself, "Are more closings really what I want?" Maybe ask yourself a different question: "What if I could make the same amount of money while working half the time? Or even a quarter of the time?"

That idea might appeal to you for different reasons, depending on what stage your career is in. If you're in the latter half of your career, the idea of working fewer hours probably makes you think of more leisure time, while others will need to focus on how to make more without increasing how many hours they work. If you try to take on more business before you figure out how to get more done in fewer hours, something's going to snap. You're already working full days, and then you try to push your business to new levels by doubling your volume, and something is bound to fall through the cracks—maybe customer service or following up with past and current clients. To be successful at growing, you need to be more efficient and streamline your business. So why not make that a goal to begin with?

When you think about it, is it really more money you want? Or is it more predictability of money? People who aren't real estate agents might not understand that question. Agents might earn well over $100,000 one year and have no idea what they'll earn the next. There is so much unpredictability in real estate. Is that what's causing you stress and pushing you to work so many hours—not knowing what you're going to earn next year? Are you trying to compensate by making sure you have more and more closings each year?

More money is not necessarily the answer—but maybe consistency is. The secret to happiness in your business might not be to push your business to new heights but to guide it to a place of predictable and consistent income, so that you can plan accordingly and not stress as much about money.

Work Less, Earn the Same

How do you work half the hours and make the same amount of money? How do you establish more predictability for your business? Many of the answers are in this book. Before you push your business to new heights, make sure you use the techniques in this book to fix the current systems within your business and make sure you're leading it down the path to more predictability.

Let's review the techniques, looking at them from this perspective, with the goal of working less and earning the same:

1. Hand off more tasks to other people while you stay focused on offering a high level of service. See chapter 3 for examples and how to do this.

2. Hone in on when to sprint in your business and in your personal life. See chapter 10.

3. Reengineer your business using the 80/20 principle. See chapter 12 for strategies to accomplish this.

4. Keep your business relevant to your sphere of influence. See chapters 13 and 19 for more information about this.

5. Never stop learning and infusing new ideas into your business. See chapters 6 and 16 for guidance.

6. Become more efficient by "batching." If you normally answer emails fifteen times each day, consider cutting that number to three or five. It disrupts your workflow to constantly come back to your computer, re-read the messages in your inbox, and decide which ones you're going to respond to this hour. You'll be more efficient knowing that you won't deal with email again for another three hours, so you better slam through all the messages you need to answer right now. When you start to batch and attack tasks in this way, you'll find many more efficiencies in your business. When you batch, you tend to get less distracted because you give yourself only so much time to complete a batch of tasks. You may

discover that you get through your to-do list a heck of a lot faster than you expected.

CASE IN POINT: *I learned about the concept of batching from many business and time-management books, and once I started practicing it, I was shocked by how hard it was not to check my email every hour (or every fifteen minutes) like I was used to, but also how much time was freed up in my day by batching when I worked on emails and many other tasks. My wife and I travel a lot with our kids, typically two to four months each year, which is fun if I'm not working all day. I still work most days, but by batching my work activities without interruptions, I can accomplish a lot in a short amount of time. Instead of working all day, I can work just a fraction of the day and accomplish a surprising amount of work, which makes me feel good about spending the rest of the day with my family.*

You don't need to create a bunch of complicated systems in order to make a comfortable, steady income and enjoy running your business the way you want to. You don't need to grow your business into a gigantic moneymaking monster that takes up all of your time, just to assure you'll have income next year. Just make sure in your current business that you're doing the right tasks, the right kinds of marketing and follow-up, and the right solid business practices that are going to help ensure you have consistent earnings, year after year. Keep getting those referrals long after you plan to work them. You need to spend the majority of your time on the high-dollar activities. (See chapter 12.)

Let's return to the question: do more closings equal more money or happiness? The answer is a resounding no. A lot of agents never realize that. They focus only on getting more and more closings, and the advice they often get is to build a team and/or to buy more Internet leads. The agent now has to invest time and money into managing those leads. He will have to spend more time coaching other agents to work those leads—and all that time invested is taking away from other tasks that are critical to the business.

If you revisit the 80/20 principle for real estate agents explained earlier in this book, you may find that a lot of the tasks you create to make money with your business are not the right tasks to focus on. They're $10-per-hour tasks that should be handled by others instead of slowing down your workflow. Maybe you create $100-per-hour tasks, but they're keeping you from creating the $1,000-per-hour tasks you should be focused on instead. Sometimes following up with clients is a $1,000-per-hour activity, and agents don't realize its importance.

When More Closings Doesn't Mean More Money

Before the bubble burst in the real estate market, there were a lot of investors buying homes. After the market crashed, those homes they were buying became a heck of a lot cheaper. If you were an agent working with those investors, suddenly those properties cost 50 percent less than they did the previous year, and your commission income was suddenly cut in half. You might have been doing more closings but earning less income.

Some agents try to make more money by selling higher-end homes. That's a good goal, because it focuses on closing fewer homes but making more money. However, a lot of agents don't realize that luxury homes tend to stay on the market longer. Instead of selling in a month, a luxury home may not sell for six months or a year. It can be a good career move as long as the agent understands what to expect and sets the right career goals so the slower sales don't cause undue stress and take away his enjoyment of the business.

When setting goals and making plans, rather than picking arbitrary sales or income-level goals, think deeper. Think about what you want your business to look like. And if you want it to make more money than it's making right now, *how* does it make more money? Does it require you to invest more time? Or will you achieve your goal by working smarter and investing in the right systems to streamline your business? The right goals are the ones that will ultimately deliver you the most enjoyable business with less stress. The goals that should be avoided (or removed) are the ones that will cause you sleepless nights and anxiety.

> **CASE IN POINT:** *When I had buyers' agents, I had to close far more homes to make the same amount of money. I didn't mind this at first, but once the market changed and sales slowed, this grew into a large problem for me. Because I cared about the livelihood of the agents on my team, I didn't remove their position, which of course only created more anxiety and pressure to make things work. Looking back, it would have been smarter to offer the agents involved other opportunities and even administrative roles—to have paid them hourly, having them cover specific tasks with which I needed help, which would have allowed me to focus on the highest dollar-producing activities. Offering them alternative ways to make some money during the slow times would have drastically lowered my stress levels during that time.*

Think about what you enjoy most about your business. By delegating, partnering, and outsourcing, you can find ways to make more or even the same amount while spending your time doing the things you enjoy and less time doing the things you don't.

CHAPTER 29
Industry Threats: Should We Be Scared?

Many real estate agents get freaked out by how quickly our industry is changing. They see threats from new types of apps that resemble Uber but for real estate and giant companies like Zillow that are basically taking over the online world of real estate. They've positioned themselves in a powerful place where they control the way that millions of consumers look at and shop for homes.

The concern among agents is, what if Zillow suddenly decides to bypass real estate agents and sell directly to the consumer? The truth is they're already close to being able to do that. With the reach of modern technology, the for-sale-by-owner model is more viable than it was in the past. Technology has created more distribution channels for sellers to use and take the risk of bypassing real estate agents altogether.

Agents see a huge threat from these new entities. And they shouldn't ignore them with dismissive thoughts like *we're too valuable to be replaced* and continue doing business as usual. Instead, agents need to be proactive in addressing changes within the industry and implement new practices, procedures, and ways of doing business that keep them in front of the changes.

If your eyes are open and you're paying attention to your industry, you'll see that change doesn't happen as quickly as some people say. Changes occur over time, and clues are apparent months or years in advance. This gives you time to change or adapt if you are paying attention. Even when the bubble burst in real estate, there were so many clues that a crash was imminent. It became more and more obvious over time. It didn't happen overnight.

What to Do Instead of Worrying

As threatening as it may feel, technology cannot replace the real estate agent's expertise. It can't duplicate the agent's consultative knowledge. This component of an agent's role is undervalued and underappreciated—until the consumer has concerns and needs expert assistance. If you truly have that expertise and wisdom to share with them and you have put in the time to become something more than merely a commodity or a facilitator for real estate—if you have developed into a go-to counselor and a bank of knowledge and resources—then you don't need to worry. The problem is that 70 percent or more of licensed real estate agents fall into the commodity group. They just facilitate real estate; they don't actually bring irreplaceable value to the process.

New technology, industry changes, and threats like Zillow will continue to come and go. Some will be fads, and some things will alter the face of the real estate industry. If you're watching it all and paying attention, you'll be on the front lines of understanding how each new change will impact consumers. You'll know what questions and concerns are most important to your clients, and you'll be able to solve problems for them just as effectively as you always have. You won't need to worry about your business imploding.

If you maintain focus on solving problems for buyers and sellers—not the same problems that every other agent knows how to solve (that is a commodity that can be replaced by technology) but really difficult problems, such as putting out fires (see chapter 23) or how you counsel your sellers for their listing, or how you're able to help and connect people outside of your real estate business (see chapter 22)—then you'll be solving problems that few others are solving. If you're solving problems that clients can't find solutions to anywhere else, you're always going to have business. You won't have to stress about changes in your industry—you just have to stay focused on being positioned uniquely with consumers as a solver of difficult problems. Always stay focused on what you bring to the table for your clients and strive to be the best at solving the most difficult real estate challenges.

CHAPTER 30

Keep the Spark

The best days are the ones when the alarm goes off in the morning and you jump out of bed going "Woo-hoo!"—excited to start your day. Or you work late into the evening, not because you have to but because something is driving you to. You're excited about accomplishing something. Going to work is so much more fun if you enjoy it.

You've probably also experienced those days when you dread going into work. It's like pulling teeth to get yourself out of bed, because you're not excited about anything on your to-do list, and you've lost your ambition and your drive to push your business forward.

Sometimes you have that spark, and sometimes you don't. Sometimes it burns bright and then you lose it. Keeping the spark alive in your business is important—not just for you to find success as a real estate agent but for your internal happiness as well.

A lot of people start a career in real estate not because they love real estate but because it was something they thought they could do as a job. Many agents don't have a burning love of real estate—they may like helping people and touring homes, but it's the day-to-day grind and uncertain drama that burns them out. So how can agents create and keep alive that spark that drives them to perform their jobs passionately for years to come?

Ignite Your Spark

It's important to identify what ignites your spark. What causes you to enjoy the work you're doing, and why? Why do you enjoy certain aspects of the job or certain clients? Is it because you're working with friends, and that interaction makes it more enjoyable? Do certain types of properties or clients challenge and motivate you?

If you consider yourself merely a real estate agent, you'd better really love homes and properties and the day-to-day work you're expected to do as an agent. If that's not what ignites your spark, you can create a mission for yourself that makes your job so much more meaningful. Maybe you're on a mission to help people—not only with real estate but helping them with their business or helping people connect within their communities. Think about what you want your business to look like in five or ten years. Is it different than it is right now? What do you want to change, add, remove, create, do, or give with your business? Thinking about these questions is a simplified way of identifying untapped fuel to drive your business.

Five Ways to Ignite Your Spark

1. **WHAT TYPE OF LEGACY DO YOU WANT TO LEAVE?** Not only for your family but within your local community? If you make it a part of your business to do amazing charitable work in your community or help out a struggling demographic of people in your community, you're going to feel good when you look back on that. You want to be able to look back twenty, thirty, forty years later and feel good about the time you invested in your community. If you build your career around the identity of a business that does amazing things for its community, that's going to warm your heart, inspire others, and give you spark to keep going. Leaving a legacy like that is not only a good business decision, it's a good life decision.

As real estate agents, we don't put enough emphasis on that point. We occasionally do things to help out in our community if somebody asks us to, or we have a charity we donate to annually. Those are good things, but I'm talking about something much bigger. It's worth investing a lot of thought into the legacy you'll leave, because if you can engineer your career and business around helping more people in your community or leveraging your success in real estate to help others outside of real estate, then you're going to leave a legacy that really impacts people. People will think of you as something more than just a real estate agent. You'll look back at the time you spent in this profession and feel good about everything you achieved.

2. **WHAT IS YOUR WHY?** Think about the root cause that drives you. There is no judging in this exercise. There are no wrong answers. Just take the answer that comes to your head and then dig deeper. For example, if making money is what excites you about your real estate business, then take a moment to consider why that excites you. What do you hope to do with the money? What need or desire will it hopefully satisfy in you? If you can remove a few layers of the onion, you may be able to identify your "why." Whatever is the most meaningful motivator for you, remind yourself of it often. Write down your why and put it some place(s) where you will see it often. I know it helps me to actually read it rather than to just think about it. When I read it, it seems to trigger the drive in me, as if I'm just going through the motions until I read my "why." It wakes me up inside.

3. **CHANGE THINGS UP.** A great way to ignite your spark is to be honest with yourself about things that aren't working or have gotten dull. Make a change. That could be a new brokerage, a new office, maybe even a new town. Remove or redirect your efforts on a new system, a different plan—one that is more fun and exciting.

4. **GET INSPIRED.** Stimulate yourself with thoughts that electrify and encourage you. Read something every week about someone who inspires you. Attend a conference or lecture where you can hear from others who have accomplished great things. Talk to or watch videos of people who love what they do. Make it a habit to seek out and absorb inspiration.

> **CASE IN POINT:** *I make a point to get in front of inspiring people at least a couple of times a year. I'll go to a conference or meet with a mastermind group of agents from around the country to share ideas, setbacks, and accomplishments. To see others working hard and finding success fuels me like nothing else. Of course, I don't have to travel to get inspired. If I see someone in my marketplace doing something really cool, or if I see someone is consistently working their butt off at the gym, it inspires me. It helps me up my game, to push harder for my goals. I have always set big goals for myself that are very hard to obtain, which is why I'm so grateful that there are others in this world who inspire me. Be strategic about with whom you spend time; find time to be around those who inspire you.*

5. **USE YOUR IDEA MUSCLE.** In chapter 16, I detail the concept of exercising your idea muscle. Use your idea muscle and write down ten to twenty ideas that may ignite your spark. Remember when you're warming up your idea muscle to give yourself permission to write down bad ideas. This will help you get your juices flowing. These can be big ideas or simple, easy ideas. The process of this exercise will help you identify missing links or new ways to alter your business. Pick one or two from your list and then drill them down further to see how and when you can incorporate the idea into your life or business. This is a great exercise to do regularly.

If you've lost your spark—either because you burned out or you're working with the wrong clients, brokerage, or whatever—it's time to reengineer your business. Whether it's small adjustments each week or a large change in direction, the process will keep you moving and dreaming and planning for the future instead of walking away from the profession. Ultimately, I encourage you to look beyond the present, beyond your day job, to dream of who or what you want to positively impact with the remaining time you have. I hope this doesn't come across as overdramatic or clichéd. It's just a concept I like to suggest to all real estate agents. It's about igniting a spark, not just in their business but lighting a fire that will last long after they stop selling real estate.

CHAPTER 31

The Unhurried Retirement

As a real estate agent, have you thought about what your end game looks like? Will you work forever, or do you have another plan?

Some of the brokerages try to convince you that you can build a team and eventually sell your business off. In their mind, that's your retirement. And part of your retirement starts early because you'll hire these agents who will do all the work for you.

Let me dispel that myth right now. First of all, even though you are an independent business owner, don't bank on ever selling your real estate business. It's not likely to happen. That's not something that really happens anymore in our industry. People do occasionally buy brokerages but never for big money, because the industry is too risky and subject to change. A very large brokerage may be purchased because it is easier to evaluate—the brokerage has X number of agents working there, here's the annual volume, these are the expenses, etc. But selling your team business or your small brokerage is not really an option you can bank on when you're ready to retire or scale back your workload. So what are your options?

Start Now

Start planning an unhurried retirement. You can decide to start working less at any point in your business. Once you reach a certain level of success and decide you don't want to work so hard, you can engineer your career so that you hand out referrals instead of handling those clients yourself. Or hire the right personnel to assist you so you don't have to do many tasks each day. You may love showing homes and having client meetings, but if you dread all the other hassles, you can find part-time help for that. If you don't want to give up your clients but don't have time to show homes all day, then pay an agent $25 per hour to show homes to your buyer clients and have them report back to you at the end of the day with details.

If you start off early with the knowledge that there is little to no chance that someone will buy your business when you retire, then your alternative is to create a business that will feed you for life. Establish practices early on that make it likely you'll keep getting referrals long after you stop working full-time. (The principles of doing this successfully are laid out in this book.) Having an unhurried retirement—and starting it sooner than later—is a more realistic retirement option than hoping to be bought out some day.

Rather than working your tail off for years and not planning your retirement until it's upon you (like most agents do), why not start your retirement now? It doesn't matter if you're thirty-five or seventy-five—if you are the trusted advisor for not just real estate matters but also make an impact and solve problems outside of real estate, those practices will pay dividends for many years to come. It's as good as investing in a retirement plan.

Business owners typically reinvest their earnings back into their business. They don't have much left over to invest in their retirement. If you're not investing in your retirement, make sure you're implementing the strategies in this book so your business will pay you dividends well into your later years. However, another piece of advice I wish I had been given when I started my career as a real estate agent was to establish a retirement fund of some kind. This is easier said than done for newer agents—and even for experienced agents, as so much of what you earn is reinvested or saved for the next dry spell in business.

However, if you take a percentage or fixed dollar amount from every closing, just like your broker does from your commission, and put it in some sort of investment account, you'll thank yourself immensely later in life.

> **CASE IN POINT:** *I'm not a fan of the stock market myself. I learned enough about it to not trust it earlier in life when I was studying to be a securities broker, and I didn't want to invest the time to get more comfortable with it once I was busy with my real estate business. I also didn't want to stick my money in an IRA, as I wanted access to it if I fell on hard times. With traditional retirement accounts, if you pull the funds out early, you are heavily penalized. Ultimately, through my financial planner, I found that a life insurance policy investment was the perfect fit for me. I put money into it each month after tax, and therefore, the money that grows in that account is tax free, and I can access the majority of cash from it anytime without penalty. I can also direct those funds into other investments, such as real estate. It works great for me. Find something that works for you. Set it up so you feed money to it automatically without feeling it or seeing it.*

Start Enjoying Periods of Early Retirement

Don't wait until you're ready to retire to start doing amazing things. If your goal is to travel the world, or spend more time with your family, or get in shape and live healthier, don't put it all off because you're too busy selling real estate. It's time for you to start your retirement plan.

If you start implementing your plans rather than putting them off until retirement, you can enjoy those experiences as you continue to work your business. If you want to travel, put practices in place that will allow you to travel for a month during your slow season. That may seem impossible for you right now, and it did for me too until after I did for the first time.

CASE IN POINT: *My wife and I have always enjoyed traveling, but once I entered into a career in real estate, travel just seemed like a luxury we couldn't afford. Then we had kids, and the idea of travel appeared to be near impossible.*

But I've always been a bit of a dreamer. When my two daughters were still toddlers, I was getting my butt kicked by the real estate market. I was working fifteen- and sixteen-hour days doing everything I could think of to keep my business going. I was scared of losing everything, and I felt guilty because I wasn't seeing much of my kids.

That guilt got me thinking.

When I dream, I often dream big. I was confident that I could eventually turn my business around, and when I did, I would take my family on an extended adventure in a foreign land. I liked this dream so much that when writing out my long-term goals that year, I put down that I wanted to be doing so well from my business that we would be able to travel one to three months every year. I couldn't think of a better gift I could give my family. I didn't know how much money I needed to make in order to accomplish such a feat; I just knew it was more than what I was making at the time.

A couple of years went by, and the housing market was even worse than it was before. I wasn't making any more money and still working ridiculous hours. I was frustrated, and I felt stuck, as if there was some glass ceiling in my business holding me back.

When my youngest daughter turned three, I realized that if I waited until I had more money or more time to travel with my family, that could be decades away. So I decided it was time to change the rules, to take a risk, to get creative. I told my wife we were going to figure out a way to travel two months over the next winter, even it if meant my business imploded and we had to start over. We set the dates. I was near a breaking point emotionally and physically with my business, but the excitement of this upcoming trip was like pouring gasoline on embers. I was able to buy the tickets with mileage points from my credit card. I put our home up as a vacation rental on Craigslist and found a family relocating to our town who wanted to rent our home the entire time we were on our trip. Through family connections, we decided to go to Mexico because we had a place to stay that wouldn't cost much. I hadn't taken a day off in years, so I didn't expect to just take a vacation from my business. I knew I'd have to work during my trip, but the thought of leaving during the cold winter months for a warm, sunny location by the ocean with my family was intoxicating, so I didn't care if I had to work every day during my trip.

Once we got there, we didn't act like we were on vacation. We spent our money conservatively, and we just lived. I would wake up before dawn and begin working, then about 1 or 2 P.M. I would stop, and we would go on an adventure or do something fun, something I rarely made time for back at home. The whole trip was an amazing success.

My business didn't implode. I was able to put out fires from afar. In fact, it was very much like working from a home office. It just so happened my home office was in Mexico that winter. I had a couple of great agents back home helping out with my clients and listings. I realized that my dream of traveling with my family every year was possible and one of the best ideas I'd ever had. Four years later, we still travel for two to four months every year. Every time we go on an extended trip, there are obstacles we have to overcome, with money, business, and the kids' school. However, we have confidence that we can indeed overcome those obstacles, and all that effort is so worth it. I feel wealthy when I go on foreign adventures with my family, even if we are on a very low budget and I work almost every day of the trip. It just feels like we are really living when we travel. Even when it's hard, it's good.

Most of us who got into real estate envisioned that this career would allow us to take more vacations or at least allow us flexibility to decide our schedules. When you go from being a salaried employee with a boss who tells you when and where you have to work, the freedom for you to set your own hours and not have to ask for permission to take a day off is supposed to be one of the many perks of being a business owner. But for most agents, taking full days off from work seems out of reach.

Something time sensitive pops up every day, and if you're not available to solve it, it could blow up into a huge problem that could negatively impact your clients. Which is why I often suggest to agents who are in this trap to try taking some working vacations. It is very difficult to remove all responsibilities so that you can totally go off the grid, so instead have the goal of working a set amount of time every day of your trip. If you go in with that plan, you don't get so frustrated when you have to spend time working on something. Your family and friends know your plan from the start, so they plan their day accordingly so you don't have to feel guilty by working while traveling. You may find you enjoy the time you have so much more while on vacation because you're not worrying about what is going on back at your office. You are fully aware of everything that is going on, and you have managed and delegated all necessary tasks for the day.

When you go on working vacations from your business, you find that you can be away much longer than a typical vacation. If you are just going on a trip for a few days, then by all means try not working while on your trip. I find that I enjoy working when I'm on an extended trip, but I do work on being as productive and as focused as I can with my time so that I'm not stuck working all day if I don't want to. I actively work on principles discussed in chapter 12, using the 80/20 principle and other time-management strategies so that I don't burn up time I could spend hanging out with my family.

If you want to travel abroad, spend your winters in warmer climates—whatever you're putting off until retirement—find a way to do it now. The cliché is true: you have only one life to live. So start living it now.

Whatever you are dreaming to "do more of" when you retire, start making goals and plans to implement that more in your life now. You might have to start by being creative to overcome obstacles, or you may have to squeeze in time at night or early each morning to do something on your bucket list that you were waiting to do in retirement, such as writing a book or working on your favorite hobby. If the goal is that important to you, why wait until retirement to start experiencing it?

If you're waiting until you have more money, that day may not come. Even if does, there may be other things keeping you from enjoying whatever the money was designed to help you "do more of" anyway.

You can engineer your business any way that suits you. It may take some time, but if you don't start now, it may never happen. Invest in this process so that you can start your unhurried retirement and continue to enjoy the parts you love about your real estate business for years to come.

I wish you nothing but success in your real estate career. If you have questions or would like to share your stories, comments, advice, etc., you can reach me directly at: Mike@AgentEntrepreneurs.com.

PRIVATE FACEBOOK GROUP: I've created a private Facebook group for readers of this book to share additional ideas and advice for your business. It's a place for you to ask questions, share your stories, and collaborate with other like-minded agents. Go to http://AgentEntrepreneurs.com to gain access.

WRITE A REVIEW: It would mean so much to me if you could take two minutes to write a review of this book online and help spread the word about it to other agents.

NEWSLETTER: Subscribe to the Agent Entrepreneur Letter where I will be sharing more stories and advice I've learned in my own business and from other agent entrepreneurs. Go to http://AgentEntrepreneurs.com.

Media Contacts

BULK ORDERS: If you are interested in purchasing a bulk order of books, send a request to: Publisher@FeverStreakPress.com.

SPEAKING: If your company or organization is interested in having Mike Turner speak at your upcoming event, send inquires to: Speaking@AgentEntrepreneurs.com.

Acknowledgments

Without the support and encouragement of my amazing wife, this book would have never been written. Without the help of Greg Likins, Sarah Tregay, and Elizabeth Day, this book may have never been finished. Without the awesome group of agents I have in my office, I may never have been inspired to start this book. Without the many mentors who have been so willing to share their knowledge with me over the years, I may never have learned the lessons that now fill the pages of this book. Thank you all so much.

Made in the USA
Columbia, SC
29 June 2017